The

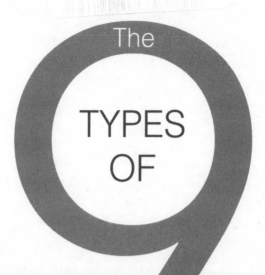

TYPES
OF

LEADERSHIP

MASTERING THE ART OF PEOPLE
IN THE 21ST-CENTURY WORKPLACE

BEATRICE CHESTNUT, PhD

A POST HILL PRESS BOOK

The 9 Types of Leadership:
Mastering the Art of People in the 21st-Century Workplace
© 2017 by Beatrice Chestnut
All Rights Reserved

First Post Hill Hardcover Edition: January 2017

ISBN: 978-1-68261-638-3

Cover Art by Quincy Alivio
Interior Design and Composition by Greg Johnson/Textbook Perfect

Post Hill Press
New York • Nashville
posthillpress.com

Published in the United States of America

Dedication

This book is dedicated to the leaders who share their stories
of personal and professional development in this book,
and to leaders everywhere doing the work of becoming more conscious.
They are our greatest hope for positive change and a brighter future.

Table of Contents

Acknowledgments

I would like to thank all the people who helped to make this book a reality. I'm especially grateful to my agent, Peter Steinberg, for his role in initiating this project and for all he did to help me create this book and guide it toward publication. Big thanks also go to Lisa Lipson Canfield for being my personal editor and dedicated sounding board and for helping me at every step in the writing process to make the book happen (in a timely way). I also want to thank Anthony Ziccardi and Post Hill Press for taking a chance on me and this book and Billie Brownell at Post Hill Press for her work in shepherding the book through the publication process. And I'm grateful to Claudio Naranjo for being the seminal author of the substance of the Enneagram personality types and subtypes as they are presented in this book.

Many people have supported the work that created the foundation for this book. Ginger Lapid-Bogda has been a great teacher and friend, and I'm grateful to her for the enormous contribution she has made to integrating the Enneagram with business through her books and trainings. My good friend and colleague Uranio Paes has helped me in ways both tangible and intangible to bring my work out into the world. I want to thank my organization development friends and associates who work with the Enneagram for the many ways they helped with the creation of this book: Valerie Atkin, Deborah Egerton, Julie Jackle, Joni Minault, Diane Ring, and Jane Tight. And I'm also very grateful to Matt Ahrens, Claire Barnum, Elizabeth Cotton, Kyle Corsiglia, Marianne Dray, Helen English, Kathleen Gallagher, Linda Pino, Stacy Price, Lynn Roulo, Vicky Rybka, Roxanne Strauss, and Barbara Whiteside for being friends in the Enneagram work, listening to me talk through ideas, reading early chapter drafts, and much more. My heartfelt thanks also go to Jennifer Joss and Dave Warner for being both dear friends and valued OD colleagues who have supported me and the development of this book.

Finally, I want to thank the leaders who shared their stories with me for providing practical, relatable, real-world examples of the impact of the Enneagram in leadership development and business practices—and also for the incredible work they are doing to bring more empathy and consciousness to the working world. Their success proves that leaders who invest in "people skills" are also the most effective leaders.

CHAPTER 1

Leading in the 21st Century
The Power of Understanding Your Personality

"Becoming a leader is synonymous with becoming yourself. It is precisely that simple and it is also that difficult."
> Warren Bennis—Author, scholar, leadership expert

"To develop leadership is less about learning new skills and more about unlearning habits and breaking free from limiting mindsets we have already acquired."
> Peter Hawkins, in *The Wise Fool's Guide to Leadership*—
> Author, leadership professor, management consultant

Have you ever had a manager that you just couldn't get along with, no matter how hard you tried? Have you ever suffered through a team meeting feeling bothered by a coworker for reasons you couldn't quite put into words, much less do anything about?

While I was finishing graduate school, I worked in a large restaurant owned by a woman who created more problems than she solved as she attempted to direct the day-to-day workings of the business. Whether she was planning menus with the kitchen staff or interacting with the managers, waiters, and bartenders, she wreaked havoc everywhere she went. She criticized people unfairly, leveled accusations at innocent bystanders, and caused unnecessary stress for everyone through excessive micromanaging and nit-picking. Whenever she left the building, all of her capable employees heaved a collective sigh of relief, and the business of the restaurant ran more smoothly and peacefully. The worst part, of course, was that she had no idea she was having such a negative impact on the people around her, and her employees who suffered under her "leadership" believed it would be hopeless to even try talking to her about it.

Coincidentally, during this period, I was also studying the approach to improving self-awareness and communication that this book is all about. By

1

using this model of personality, I was able to recognize why my boss was likely doing the things she was doing and figure out what I could do to get along with her. I knew I couldn't change her, but by identifying specific patterns in her behavior, I could understand her personality and shift the way I interacted with her in a way that ultimately transformed our working relationship.

Nearly everyone has experienced some kind of "people problem" at some point in their work lives—a manager they had trouble with, a direct report they didn't know how to get through to or a client they couldn't fully understand. In every area of life, this kind of relationship confusion can be frustrating and problematic, but in the workplace, it causes extra stress because your livelihood and your everyday happiness are often at stake.

This is compounded by the fact that, in the 21st-century organization, every employee is rightly encouraged to think of themselves as a leader—a designation that comes with seemingly endless challenges beyond just "doing your job." Being a leader in this new work world means dealing with the fast pace of change, the need to improve communication to foster better collaboration, and the need to relate to an increasingly diverse workforce. More than ever, leaders need reliable tools to help them decode and resolve the misunderstandings and relationship problems that happen all the time in businesses large and small.

This book, and the remarkable personality framework it presents, is one such tool. It provides an amazingly useful method for understanding yourself and others so you can master the art of relating to the people you work with in a way that will impact both the "bottom line" and your quality of life.

The Problem: The Need for Effective Leadership that Can Rise Above Ego

In our current era, leaders face more tests of their capacities and resilience than ever. Business is becoming more global, new technologies are changing the way work happens at a continually accelerating rate, and existential threats like terrorism, political gridlock, and the health of the planet hang over everything we do, charging our lives with anxiety and fear and the pressure to "keep up."

In the face of these challenges, we desperately need leaders who can rise above the narrow focus of their own ego concerns, create bold visions to get results, and mobilize people to take action in service of ambitious agendas. But what, exactly, does it mean to "rise above your ego concerns?" And how do we define "ego?"

Both psychological theory and age-old "wisdom" traditions tell us that we humans exist in a kind of waking sleep, or limited consciousness. As we grow up, we "go to sleep to" certain aspects of our lived experience as a way of protecting ourselves from the inevitable hurts that happen to us from the outside world. It's a natural human reflex to protect ourselves, and so, starting in childhood, we automatically avoid becoming aware of experiences that cause us to feel difficult emotions like pain, shame, anger, or fear. If we were punished for getting angry, we may lose touch with our anger. If we felt insecure about whether people liked us, we might excessively care-take others or overcompensate by adopting a superior attitude.

As we continually adapt to our environment, we gradually lose touch with certain aspects of our experience that threaten us or make us uncomfortable. At the same time, we develop a persona that emphasizes "what works"—the ways we think we can control ourselves and the world around us so that we can get what we need and avoid what feels bad. That persona, mask, or false self we develop is the ego or personality—the "Executive Director" of our "waking-sleep self." Its purpose is to help us to feel okay enough to get around in the world. The downside is, it eventually builds a wall around us that serves as a kind of defensive buffer against being aware of parts of ourselves or our experience.

Through this process of "going unconscious," we develop blind spots, or parts of ourselves that we "go asleep to" as a way of getting through life and not getting hurt. As Carl Jung observed, we all have our "shadows," or parts of ourselves that we remain unconscious to or don't want to see. And because, without knowing it, we become unaware of some things that are true about ourselves, we often don't know ourselves as well as we think we do.

Instead, when it comes to who we really are and why we do the things we do, we often only see ourselves as our personality (or ego or self-image)—the person we want others to see. So we become limited by the fact that we don't know all of who we are, and don't know that we don't know. And when we don't understand who we really are, both in terms of what we defensively hide from ourselves and our higher potentials, it's hard for us to grow and develop the people skills we need to be as successful as we can be in our personal and professional lives.

Luckily for us, we are living at a very exciting moment in history. More and more, visionary business leaders understand that the ancient maxim "know thyself" is the secret formula for positive outcomes at work as well as in life. Individuals in all walks of life are realizing that success in any kind of work occurs when the individuals working together are self-aware and "emotionally intelligent"—when they can acknowledge their blind spots and more consciously manage their feelings and reactions, empathize with others, and navigate social situations with skill and sensitivity.

Many people are increasingly open to the idea that becoming aware of our unconscious habits and motives is the first step to growing far beyond our self-imposed limitations. While as humans we fall asleep to all of who we are, we also have the inborn capacity to wake up and live from a more enlivened (and contented) sense of all of who we can be, in our personal and professional lives.

This book is about this type of conscious leadership: what it is, how it can help us, and how to develop it. It is written for people who are open to the idea that the first and main challenge involved in being a good or great leader (or person) is waking up to what's happening in the present moment and coming to know yourself in a deeper and more mindful way.

On a worldwide level, we need leaders who can be self-aware and conscious enough to understand how to meet the enormous challenges we face and to overcome the blocks—especially the human ones—to developing greater awareness so that we can solve big problems and find innovative solutions together. Most of all, leaders (and all of us) need effective ways to learn to be kinder and more compassionate with ourselves and with others, and less defensive, reactive, and inflexible in the ways we respond to the people and events around us.

The Solution: Knowing What Makes a Leader Successful

So, if good leadership is more important than ever, how do we get it? What exactly makes a good leader? *Emotional Intelligence* author Daniel Goleman has famously addressed this question at length in his books and popular *Harvard Business Review* articles. [1] It turns out, according to research as well as the testimony of people who have studied and worked with leaders extensively, the key factors in high-quality leadership are *self-awareness*—the ability to be mindful, or "conscious," about what you do, how you do it, and why you do it—and *emotional intelligence*—the ability to recognize, understand, and manage your own emotions and the capacity to recognize, understand, and empathize with the emotions of others.

Increasingly, it's becoming clear that 21st-century leaders must have excellent "people skills" to be successful. They need to have ways to understand themselves and listen to others not only at the surface level, but at a deeper, less visible, more emotional level. In becoming more aware and mindful of more of what is happening within themselves and others, leaders need to purposefully apply themselves to developing more flexibility and skill in managing the ways people with different worldviews interact. Most importantly, and undergirding all of this, they must be able to develop a kind of moment-to-moment awareness of themselves—and be able to maintain the inner space to reflect on and understand their own assumptions, reactions, emotions, and behavior.

Why Are Self-Awareness and Emotional Intelligence the Most Vital Factors in Excellent Leadership?

Interestingly, it turns out that if you are unkind to people, if you regularly engender negative feelings in others, you tend not to be an effective leader. Being disrespectful, controlling and insensitive tends to be correlated with being bad at managing people. Of course, throughout history, there have undoubtedly been many examples of successful jerks, but more and more, leaders who are self-centered, ego-driven, unaware of their own reactions, unskilled in managing their emotions, and unsympathetic with those of others, don't have success over the long haul.

After all, the work of doing business happens through people interacting with people. Even in our technological age, the ability of people to understand each other so they can communicate clearly and work together seamlessly—without the personality conflicts and interpersonal tensions that can impede progress—still underlies much of what makes leaders and their businesses successful.

In the book *Good to Great: Why Some Companies Make the Leap... and Others Don't*, author Jim Collins explains that "the type of leadership required for turning a good company into a great one... [was] self-effacing, quiet, reserved...a paradoxical blend of personal humility and professional will...more like Lincoln and Socrates than Patton or Caesar."[2] More and more, it is becoming clear that the ability to achieve and maintain harmonious and productive working relationships depends on one thing: *how well the people involved have the humility and the will to understand and manage themselves and understand and relate well to others.*

Just like the rest of us, leaders can operate in one of two ways: 1) they can do the things they do in an unconscious, automatic, and habitual way; or, 2) they can do the things they do in a conscious, self-aware, more open and creative way.

Unconscious leaders operate from a narrow focus on doing what feels safe, what has "worked" before or what protects their identity or self-image. Protecting your sense of who you are (and who you imagine others see you as) is only natural, given that we all want to feel good about ourselves. But when defending a positive sense of your image is your top priority, all of your attention and energy gets focused on protecting your self-image or ego. This is why unconscious leaders wind up stuck in a kind of defensive mode, in which they run on fear, insecurity, and a narrow sense of self-interest, like my boss at that restaurant I worked at when I was in graduate school.

Conversely, conscious leaders operate from a place of practiced, mindful awareness. They are able to observe the things they think, feel, and do, and act not just to protect their ego needs, but in the service of finding the most effective strategy to get optimal results and create positive relationships.

When a leader becomes more aware of their assumptions, their emotions, their motivations, and the impact of their behavior, they can not only manage themselves more skillfully, they can also talk about points of vulnerability from a position of strength, which makes them more approachable and accessible to others. When I worked at Stanford's Graduate School of Business as a group facilitator, the leadership experts there often noted that one of the key traits of a successful leader is the ability to "selectively self-disclose vulnerability." Paradoxically, it takes a great deal of inner strength to discuss your own weak points, and this practice usually attracts, rather than repels, others. When leaders are honest about both their strengths and their weaknesses, they demonstrate the capacity to be open and authentic and model what real self-awareness looks like. And this capacity gives them great power in achieving stronger working relationships.

Conscious Leadership Equals Successful Leadership: What It Means to Be a Conscious (vs. Unconscious) Leader

In their book *The 15 Commitments of Conscious Leadership*, leadership consultants Dethmer, Chapman, and Klemp use a simple model to highlight these two ways of leading. They draw a horizontal line across the page and say, when leaders are "below the line" they are "closed and defensive" and less conscious, and when they are "above the line" they are "open and curious" and more self-aware.[3] They go on to say, "It matters far more that leaders can accurately determine whether they are above or below the line in any moment than where they actually are."[4] In other words, the most vital element in good leadership is whether a given leader has the ability to observe and be honest about whether they are acting from a closed-minded, defensive position—not whether they can sustain super-human levels of conscious awareness all the time.

People who study what makes a good leader thus increasingly point to traits that might be called "good people skills," "soft power" or emotional intelligence ("EQ" or emotional intelligence quotient) as the secret sauce. And the key skill is the ability to reflect on what you are doing enough to be able to tell the difference between operating from a knee-jerk, habitual posture designed to defend your ego and being open to seeing how your ego might be impacting the situation in the moment. Again, defending your ego is only natural, since your ego, or personality, reflects your everyday sense of who you are in the world. And importantly, part of the good news of developing more self-awareness is the realization that we are much more than our egos, or personas. But before we make conscious efforts to become more aware of ourselves, it's just part of being human to act from ego and not realize that there is another, more effective option.

Unfortunately, a low level of awareness in a leader can make work painful, tedious, and unpleasant for everyone. Conversely, a good leader inspires people to do their best work and creates an environment where people enjoy what they do. An unconscious leader thinks he is always right and has a hard time listening to anything but the sound of his own voice, while a conscious leader actively listens to others and takes the time to fully consider others' points of view. Both the "bottom line," reflecting the productivity and profitability of an enterprise, and the health and happiness of the people within a workplace are directly impacted by the level of consciousness and self-awareness of the leader.

Dave Aitken, CEO of FNB Tanzania, generously allowed me to interview him for this book. Here, he talks about his own transformation from unconscious to conscious leadership:

"Before I learned more about myself and my reactions, I had to at all costs dominate situations, to be in control. If I didn't have all the facts, there was definitely a conspiracy against me and something to be worried about—that's been my whole life.

"Now I react differently, and I can see where my corporate career could have been—I could have gone further in life—if I had been a more pleasant person or less aggressive when I was young. Now I have more respect for humans. Before, I occupied a life devoid of human beings. I was very left-brained, very task-oriented. Now I see people as humans and I understand that there is no single story. There are multiple stories that are as valid as your story. And to actually acknowledge that yours is not the only story, it puts a completely different perspective on how you deal with situations, especially people. I'm also more receptive to constructive criticism now. I ask my staff how I can be a more effective leader. And I listen more."

So if being aware and emotionally intelligent makes you a better leader and a healthier person, what does a "conscious leader" look like, and how does a leader—or anyone—go from being "unconscious" to "conscious"? How did Dave Aitken go from being conscious to unconscious? How can leaders become more self-aware and raise their EQ? What exactly does this mean and how do we go about it?

At a very basic level, becoming more conscious means developing the ability to be "present," or "mindful"—to build the internal "muscle" of noticing where your attention goes and to be able to regularly observe yourself from a slight distance within your own mind. It's developing the ability to catch yourself in the act of getting lost in what you are doing, going on autopilot, or just unquestioningly doing things by rote or according to what is familiar and comfortable. And when you catch yourself going to sleep in this way, it's being able to wake yourself up and make the conscious choice to do something on purpose, through an act of will.

This ability to witness our own minds at work and have the space to note what we think, feel, and do without judgment echoes what psychiatry professor and interpersonal neurobiologist Dan Siegel calls "Mindsight":

> [Mindsight is] a kind of focused attention that allows us to see the internal workings of our own minds. It helps us to be aware of our mental processes without being swept away by them, enables us to get ourselves off the auto-pilot of ingrained behaviors and habitual responses, and moves us beyond the reactive emotional loops we all have a tendency to get trapped in. It helps us 'name and tame' the emotions we are experiencing, rather than being overwhelmed by them…. A uniquely human ability, mindsight allows us to examine closely, in detail and in depth, the processes by which we think, feel, and behave. And it allows us to reshape and redirect our inner experiences so that we have more freedom of choice in our everyday actions, more power to create the future, to become author of our own story.[5]

When leaders have this capacity to observe themselves, study their inner experience, and reflect on what they are doing and why, they become more "conscious" and more able to solve people problems on the job in a more efficient and satisfying way. To do this, they must build up their "attentional muscles"—the inner ability to remind themselves to wake up and pay attention to what they are thinking, feeling, and doing—so they become more adept at observing what is happening inside themselves in an ongoing, mindful, nonjudgmental way.

We don't always choose the people we have to get along with to do the work we need to do. So it's only natural that we will experience tensions, problems, and conflicts as we work with others. But if we can learn to be more consciously aware of our own habitual patterns of thinking, feeling, and behaving, we take a huge first step toward being more mindfully aware of what is happening between ourselves and others, and being able to talk about it with more confidence and openness. In particular, by developing a greater level of conscious awareness of your own personality style—that part of you that developed to help you interact with the outside world when you were young, but now runs the show in everyday life—and the personality styles of others, you have the key to improving your experience with the people you live and work with every day.

How Leaders Can Become More Conscious and Emotionally Intelligent Using "The Enneagram Model of Personality"

Understanding your personality, or "ego," in real-time is one of the best ways to work on being conscious more of the time.

More and more, mindfulness and other approaches to increasing consciousness and self-awareness have begun to transform the American workplace. Many large companies, such as General Mills, Ford, Aetna, and Target, have built extensive programs to foster mindful practices among their workers as a way of helping people be more conscious as they manage their health, do their work, and interact with others. Google now offers meditation classes and in-house therapists. Genentech offers its employees a structured, yearlong coaching program and a range of leadership development interventions. Stanford's Graduate School of Business also offers a class in mindfulness, and the most popular elective in their entire MBA program is a course on "interpersonal dynamics" that everyone refers to affectionately as "Touchy Feely."

But while the idea that adopting practices that actively promote leaders' self-awareness, social skill, and "emotional intelligence" is the key to success is increasingly accepted, the most direct route to achieving that success often remains unclear. The Western business world has lacked an effective and efficient tool to help busy leaders find ways to raise their level of consciousness in a long-term and sustainable way amidst the challenges of day-to-day life. Too often, the work of increasing emotional intelligence gets relegated to semiannual off sites, in which a consultant brings in the Myers-Briggs Type Indicator (MBTI) or another such inventory, and the work team gains a few new insights that don't last much longer than a couple of days. The ways leaders have sincerely sought to increase awareness many times just doesn't stick.

The Enneagram of personality provides the missing piece—a pathway to greater self-awareness and social skillfulness that lasts. It is a growth tool rooted in ancient philosophy that maps the habitual patterns of thinking, feeling, and behaving of nine personality "types" or styles with surprising accuracy. As a holistic framework for understanding personality, the Enneagram serves as a roadmap you can consult any time you find yourself lost or confused by what is happening between you and the people around you. As a coach I know once told a corporate vice president who needed an effective tool to use with his team, unlike many more superficial approaches to understanding "what makes people tick," the Enneagram "has legs." You can do more with it and take it further because it provides you with so much more information.

Completely aligned with the latest research in neuroscience and cognitive psychology, the Enneagram operates as a tool leaders can use to help focus "mindful awareness" on their key pre-programmed patterns and habits. As laid out in the following chapters, it provides a guidebook to look to when you don't understand why you keep having the same conflict with your business partner about how to invest your company's resources. It can aid you in figuring out what is going on when your coworker never seems to respond in a timely fashion, even when you're on a deadline. And it can help you to see what function may be missing in your team when you fail to win that big contract you worked for months to get.

The Enneagram is similar to the MBTI, a tool widely used in business to make sense of differences among people, in that it also provides information about the varied ways we humans operate in the world. However, the Enneagram can be a more effective tool than the MBTI in some situations because it offers more thorough descriptions of well-defined sets of distinct, yet interconnected personality patterns at three levels of functioning—thought, emotion, and behavior. For this reason, it allows people to quickly and efficiently gain a large amount of information about their own inner workings—and the internal programming of others. In short, the Enneagram system of personality types is like the MBTI of the 21st century. It provides more and more specific and actionable data about leadership and work styles at exactly the moment when a new generation of innovative leaders is recognizing the power of this kind of depth of insight.

And far from being a "one-size-fits-all" approach, the Enneagram zeroes in on the most important aspect of comprehending people problems: acknowledging that all people are not alike and explaining how basic differences in style, perspective, and focus can lead to problems. To see why two people are having a conflict and fix it in an efficient way, you have to be able to rapidly assess how they differ and what kind of disconnect is causing the dispute. The Enneagram offers a means of doing exactly this kind of assessment.

By providing extremely detailed descriptions of nine readily recognizable personalities, the Enneagram is an unmatched method for decoding the mysteries of why people do what they do, why we have conflicts with some people but not others, and how we can become aware of our blind spots.

Most importantly, it can help leaders to know themselves in a deeper way so they can more effectively lead others and more powerfully model conscious behaviors for their direct reports.

I once worked with a vice president (Bill) in charge of the information technology division of a big biotech firm. Bill loved using the Enneagram to improve his own self-awareness and to clarify communication within his executive team. It worked so well with his team and the managers below them, he eventually had us teach the Enneagram as a development tool to all 400 people in his part of the company to help them improve productivity and manage change.

Whenever Bill would explain to a new group of managers or employees why he was having them learn about their personality types to clarify inter-actions and improve teamwork, he used himself as an example. As a "Type Seven," he would say, he often created confusion and stress within his team without meaning to and without knowing he was doing it. People who lead with a Type Seven style love new ideas and can be very enthusiastic in the early stages of a project. Frequently, he would actually cause problems for his team by excitedly coming up with ten or twelve new initiatives in one meeting and seeming excessively thrilled about every one of them. Bill's people would leave meetings with him feeling overwhelmed and demoralized, believing they had been tasked with following up on every one of his fully elaborated ideas and wondering how they were ever going to do all that work.

After Bill learned the Enneagram and shared it with his team, however, they were able to talk about this dynamic openly. Bill saw that some of his personality characteristics, including displaying intense interest and rapturous delight in the brainstorming and planning process, were stressing out his team members, which was the opposite of what he had intended. By understanding himself through the Enneagram system, Bill was able to clarify that his love of envisioning positive possibilities didn't mean that his team had to execute all of his ideas—that he was just having fun playing with potential plans. Going forward, he was able to be much clearer that while he enjoyed generating ideas, he did not expect his team to take action on all of them.

Many times, people in work situations lack the information they need to understand what is happening among people so that they can diagnose what is really going on and address it in straightforward and efficient ways. The information provided through the Enneagram serves as a powerful guide for raising awareness about our own underlying patterns and biases as well as those of others, so we can learn how to more effectively—and consciously—manage our relationships with the people we work with. For instance, if someone you work with continually expresses frustration with the pace at which you accomplish tasks, it can help enormously to know what (exactly) motivates their speediness and your (relative) sluggishness—and that neither one is "right" or "wrong."

All Kinds of Leaders—and People—Can Benefit from This Kind of "Personality Decoder" Tool

The material in this book can help anyone who needs to find effective ways to get along with others so that they can work together productively and harmoniously. It is especially for leaders who want to understand their own strengths and blind spots, so that they can be more powerful and effective. It is for managers who need to understand the individual needs and tendencies of their team members and employees, so they can better motivate and inspire them. It is for people in every industry who want to know how to influence, develop, and relate to the various people they work with.

The Enneagram framework for understanding personality speaks to anyone who would like to be more satisfied in their jobs, happier in everyday life, and more successful in their careers. It is for people in all industries who want to know how to have richer, more enjoyable, and more trouble-free relationships with the people they work with. It's for anyone with an interest in knowing what "makes people tick," so they can better decode and comprehend other people's behavior. And it is for every person who wants to have more success, more fun, and less stress in working with others to get things done.

Business as Usual: We Are More Unconscious than We Think We Are

Without knowing it, we all tend to get stuck in a "default mode" set up by our early "programming."

Whether we know it or not, we all rely on a few basic strategies for moving through the social world—strategies that develop as part of the defensive "ego" or personality structure discussed earlier. Different people adopt different core strategies: some people try to be helpful and friendly, others try to be perfect, some try to be productive or attractive to have value, and others endeavor to be knowledgeable. The problem is, we've been using these strategies for so long (usually because they worked at some point) that we forget we perceive the world through a particular lens that forms the basis for our strengths as well as our limitations. These adaptive strategies-turned core strengths and patterns become a kind of "programming" or "operating system" that we repeat over and over again, even when it doesn't fit the situation we are in.

The Enneagram system of personality enables us to gain a much deeper understanding of this programming—and the nine kinds of programming we find in people generally. By reading about the traits and habits of the nine personality styles, we can learn how our unconscious adherence to our inner program—in the form of our personality patterns—both helps us get ahead and gets us into trouble. And once we see how that happens, we can use that same insight to learn how to solve the problems caused by getting stuck in the "default" mode dictated by our programming.

To do this, we will need to learn more about personality. But what exactly is "personality?" Personality is the "ego" part of ourselves I referred to earlier—the part that develops to interface with the outside world as a kind of inner defensive structure. Personality is the sum total of strategies we develop to help us find ways to calm our anxieties, locate an inner sense of well-being, and have some feeling of control in the world. And personality is a set of interrelated adaptive patterns of thinking, feeling and behaving—the way we usually think, the emotions we tend to feel and avoid, and the behavior we act out in the world. In short, it's our "default mode"—the unquestioned patterns of thought, emotion, and action we revert back to when we go on autopilot in everyday life.

Becoming a Better Leader Through Understanding Personality

We've probably all heard someone describe somebody else (often somebody they don't like) as having a "big ego." And we all know what this means—this person displays an outsized sense of themselves and their own importance.

But the ego—or personality—is not the "bad guy" in this story. Being an "unconscious" person or an "unconscious" leader is actually a fairly normal way of functioning: it simply means your personality or ego, or the automatic, habitual programming that you developed to survive in the world ends up driving most of the things you do. The core strategies that initially shaped our programming become "the way we do things" or "just the way we are." And we often don't question it precisely because our programming is our operating system—it forms the basis of how we view the world and our assumptions about how things go and the choices we automatically make.

So, by the time we reach adulthood, our programming—the strategies and patterned responses that make up our personality—is running the show. And often, when this is the case, we are operating mostly unconsciously to protect ourselves from threats. This is what it means to be "defensive." Complicating this defensive process is the fact that our physical brains also get involved. The design of our brains motivates us to react according to biological, wired-in programming we often don't have conscious control over (unless and until we learn our way out of it). As neuropsychologist and meditation teacher Rick Hanson states in his book *Buddha's Brain: the practical neuroscience of happiness, love & wisdom,* our brains have a built-in "negativity bias" that primes us to avoid certain experiences, but ends up making us suffer in a variety of ways. This bias originally helped us to survive by enabling us to recognize threats—like lions chasing us or the dangerous possibility of falling off a nearby cliff—but even when we aren't really in danger, it "generates an unpleasant background of anxiety," which can "make it harder to bring attention inward for self-awareness."[6]

Since negative experiences have the most impact on survival, we get locked into response patterns that helped us avoid painful situations early on. This negativity bias also "fosters or intensifies other unpleasant emotions, such as anger, sorrow, depression, guilt, and shame. It highlights past losses and failures, it downplays present abilities, and it exaggerates future obstacles."[7] So, it's part of being human to get defensive, respond impulsively from a negative filter designed to detect threats to our well-being, and get emotionally triggered by things that make us anxious or fearful. When you feel anxious about paying your mortgage or terrified before the big speech you have to give or you throw a fit when someone cuts you off in traffic, you can relax in the knowledge that you are a normal member of the human race.

However, while it's just a natural part of being human to respond in automatic, preprogrammed ways, these automatic defensive responses to perceived threats are often ineffective strategies for addressing situations successfully. Because they were created out of an early event (that may have felt like an emergency) our reactions can be rigid and fixed and hard to change. So, we can overuse a specific strategy or strength, simply because it worked in the original setting.

In light of the omnipresence of these preprogrammed strategies and reactions, the most important thing we must do to more consciously manage our behavior (and have the ability to rise above our defensiveness) is to develop the ability to notice, observe, and reflect on our automatic, defensive, habitual responses in a nonjudgmental and compassionate way.

According to the Enneagram model, there are a finite number of personality styles or "types" corresponding to a finite number of key adaptive strategies. And when I say there are a "finite number" of identifiable coping strategies, there are exactly... nine. The Enneagram map of these nine personality styles provides a clarifying framework for understanding why you (and others) do the things you do, because it highlights the specific patterns of reactions associated with the nine styles and what motivates them. And when you can study your habits and patterns with more clarity and objectivity—which the Enneagram personality descriptions provide—you can use your increased self-awareness to decide what behaviors you want to continue to engage in, and what behaviors you may want to change, if any. You can also come to know yourself better and share yourself more authentically with others, to build stronger working relationships.

Andrew Greenberg, Founder and CEO of Greenberg Strategy, a brand strategy and market research company based in the San Francisco Bay Area, has worked extensively with the Enneagram model to develop his leadership, his team, and his organization:

> "There can be a dearth of authenticity in an organization. It's like high school; everybody is trying to fit in to the guiding culture. The Enneagram offers an opportunity to be real. If you are a Type Two, I know something about you that's personal. When people can be vulnerable enough to say, 'I'm a this,' to share something about themselves, it creates opportunities to like them more, to know them more.
>
> "The Enneagram is the great organizer, unifier, tenderizer. It nails you on your shit. Because there are nine types—and not 16 or four—you get a nice balance. Each type is deep enough, but not too hard to understand. It's like a meat tenderizer or a field plower, it takes the hard chunks of earth that are our habitual patterns and unexamined assumptions and makes them something you can plant on. It makes people more mindful and aware and open."

To be a conscious leader—or person—you need to have a clear sense of your programming and be able to recognize when you get stuck on your personal autopilot. The solution to unknowingly operating in this default mode thus lies in your ability to see and own what you are really doing, thinking, and feeling. This allows you (eventually) to expand the repertoire of strategies you use to cope and function in the world—and to deploy the best strategy in each situation instead of always employing the narrow set you are most accustomed to using. Having a clear window into your personality and the motivations that drive you—how your programming operates as it does and why it operates that way—through the Enneagram system thus gives you a way to wake up out of your "sleep mode" in a lasting way.

The Human Personality as OS: How Knowing the Nine Kinds of Operating Systems Can Help You Be More Conscious

This book provides uniquely useful insights into the basic "operating systems" or "programming" of the nine different personality styles that exist in the world—and in business environments. It provides practical and actionable answers to questions like, "Why does that person always seem overly concerned about following the rules in a way that strikes me as annoyingly rigid?" "Why does this other person seem to want to dominate every conversation and overpower everyone?" "Why does that person always seem to have to look on the bright side or lighten things up such that we can never tackle tough issues?" and "What is going on when this other person never seems to be able to make a decision?"

The uniquely effective framework presented in this book helps you decode what these behaviors mean, what motivates them, and what to do about them. Equipped with such clarifying insights, you can navigate the bumps in the road that understandably occur when you work with others. When you can more easily identify exactly what is happening in troubled or strained relationships, you can more readily fix these human problems and enjoy your coworkers rather than resent them.

Once we have access to the basic strategies and motivations of the people around us—*accurate information about what they are doing and why*—we have already made progress toward understanding and accepting them, and knowing how to work with them. And, even more important, once we discover our own personality biases, we can have more compassion for ourselves, and more insight into what *we* bring to the table in our work relationships.

When we learn about the underlying "programming" of different types of people—the automatic patterns that make up the nine kinds of personalities—we instantly have a lot more clarity about why different people think, feel, and react in the ways they do. When we recognize that these varied personality styles exist in the world—and that not everyone sees the world the way we do—we can be more open to seeing what habits and worldviews others bring to interactions. And when we have more insight into both our own and others' personality-based points of view, we can more readily see how to tease apart "what I am doing" and "what you are doing" without defensiveness so we can resolve conflicts.

For example, I once had repeated conflicts with a woman I worked with on a board of directors for a large professional organization. We were able to untangle what was happening and work well together after we communicated about how the interaction of our different styles was causing the tension between us. I was the president of the board and she was the vice president. She was a Type Eight and I am a Type Two. Conflicts arose when she continually made significant decisions unilaterally without consulting me (or anyone else), especially when bad things happened as a result of those decisions.

After a particularly unpleasant conflict, we talked through what we were each doing that contributed to our problems with each other. I let her know that my Type Two style led me to be upset when I thought that my needs and feelings—and those of the people and relationships involved—weren't respected and considered in her decision-making. She was able to own that her Type Eight style meant that she felt impatient when it came to waiting to hear from people when she wanted to move things forward and assert herself quickly and independently. Through discussing the intersection of our different personalities, and taking responsibility for our own biases, we created a basis for mutual understanding and trust that allowed us to work things out and work well together.

Both an "owner's manual" for your "self" and a roadmap to interacting with others, I've intended this book to be a user-friendly introduction to "The Enneagram of Personality." In what follows, I will introduce you to its personality types and subtypes, share stories of real-life leaders who have used the Enneagram model to create enormous changes in their organizations, and provide a step-by-step guide to using the Enneagram to increase self-awareness and emotional intelligence—both to learn much more about yourself than you thought was possible, and to gain a greater ability to understand coworkers, team dynamics, and organizational culture.

It is my hope that you will find the Enneagram not only a useful source of solutions for the people problems you might encounter at the office (and at home), but also a fun and enlightening way to get to know yourself and others in a deeper, richer, and more satisfying way.

What's in This Book and How to Use It

The next two chapters provide some introductory information about the Enneagram system of personality types and how it can be used to guide and support leadership development and establish improved relationships in the workplace. The subsequent nine chapters present descriptions of the nine Enneagram personality styles—in general and how they typically get expressed at work. The final chapter helps you understand how to apply the Enneagram as a tool in your organization by providing examples of how different leaders have used it to be more successful and offering practical suggestions for how to put it to work in your own business. You can read the book cover-to-cover, use it as a reference—looking up specific types as needed to access information about how to deal with specific challenges (or challenging people)—or use it just to know more about yourself and your own patterns.

Most of all, the Enneagram is about growth. At the end of each chapter, I propose some ideas for each type, about what they can observe in themselves, explore, and adjust, so they can create positive change and be easier to work with. However, space permits only a limited amount of information about this all-important topic of how to work with your type patterns to be happier, calmer, and more effective. But you can access much more material about how to use the Enneagram to be your best self and access your higher potential on my website: www.beatricechestnut.com.

CHAPTER 2

Getting to Know the Enneagram System of Personality Types

"'[Director] David [Fincher]'s really, really into it,' Mara reports,... 'and he got me really into it, so I read a lot about the Enneagram.... It's this personality typing where there are these nine different types—nine different categories that people can fall into. So I had him tell me what number every character was [in the film], and I did a lot of reading on that. I sort of became obsessed with it.'"

Rooney Mara, actress—discussing her preparation for the role of Lisbeth Salander in Fincher's movie *The Girl with the Dragon Tattoo*

"The last thing I wanted to do was sit through four hours of a personality assessment I had never heard of... I'm glad I did, because the four hours that followed changed my life and the way I communicate with others and understand myself forever.

"'This is the Enneagram,' our psychologist instructor informed the eight of us. 'While much less famous than the Myers-Briggs or DISC assessment, it's actually far more reliable than those two or any other personality assessment... and its wisdom has been used and passed on over centuries.'

"Over the next four hours that followed, I picked up a wealth of information about myself and how people can best communicate with me... I was blown away by how accurate it was. It was like he was reading my mind!"

Dave Kerpen, entrepreneur, speaker, and author—from his book *The Art of People: 11 Simple People Skills That Will Get You Everything You Want*

Unlike some personality "typologies," the Enneagram provides a great deal of very accurate information that helps us understand why we do what we do. Instead of addressing just the mental or surface level of human interaction, it reveals the archetypal patterns—or the prototypical habits—of nine ways of operating in the world in terms of thinking, (emotional) feeling, and behaving.

As discussed in the last chapter, personality is that part of us that develops, starting in childhood, as an interface with the outside world. It reflects both "who we really are" at a deep level, and a kind of "false self" or persona that we present to the external world as a defensive armor to protect our "real self." When we can compassionately and nonjudgmentally study how our personality operates in everyday life, as a way to know ourselves more completely, we naturally free ourselves from the limitations our personality patterns impose on us when they remain unconscious and automatic.

How does this happen exactly? By understanding personality, we gain access to both our default programming—the motives, preferences, super powers, gifts, weak points, and blind spots we walk through daily life with—and an avenue toward seeing, owning, and expressing our deeper or more essential selves, and our highest potentials.

In my first book, *The Complete Enneagram*, I used the acorn as a metaphor for this process of learning about our personalities as a way to grow and develop. The acorn provides a relatable example of what I mean by personality being both a protective covering and the seed of what we may become if we work to manifest all of our latent talents.

Every acorn holds a potential oak tree, but to actually grow into an oak tree, the acorn must drop into the ground and lose its outer shell. In much the same way, all of us can grow to reach our full potential of success and happiness by exploring our "underground territory"—our unconscious patterns and blind spots—in order to break out of our own protective coverings.

Leaders—and all of us—can most effectively grow to their full potential if they are willing to let go of their limiting shell through understanding it—and the vulnerabilities and hard-to-face feelings it's designed to protect. Our personas help us get around in life. But if we don't get to know them and learn to let them go, to release the old habits that don't serve us and do the work of growing beyond the need for our defenses, we will remain limited and constricted, instead of liberated and free to express all of who we really are.

While the Enneagram is intended to help people achieve exactly this kind of freedom and growth, when some people first meet the Enneagram, they fear that it will "put them in a box." And while stereotyping is a real danger in using the Enneagram, for the most part, when used well, the system actually shows you the dimensions of the box you are already in—but don't know you are in—so that you can find your way out.

This is really what the Enneagram is all about. It teaches us about our personality so that our personality can teach us about what lies beyond the personality—the strengths and abilities and capacities that express who we really are and all we may become when we move beyond old fears and habitual reactions.

I hope you will enjoy getting to know the Enneagram and that it can help you get to know yourself (and others) in a way that allows you to develop your individual leadership gifts, and excel and find meaning and happiness in whatever you do every day.

What Is the Enneagram?

The "Enneagram of Personality" details nine personality descriptions or categories and the interconnections among them. Each of the nine personality "types," or "styles," represents a distinct way of operating in the world based on a specific "focus of attention": what you pay attention to and what you don't pay attention to.

For instance, what do you typically pay attention to when you first wake up in the morning? Different people with different personality types tend to start the day with different moods and different thoughts. Some types wake up angry, some immediately start thinking about their mental list of "things to do," and others feel happy and excited at the possibilities of the new day.

This idea that different people pay attention to different things in different ways plays a central role in defining the distinct Enneagram styles. The nine styles or types can be differentiated in terms of their focus of attention or "perceptual bias"—what occupies the central place in what they think about, see, and prioritize in their experience.

To determine a person's Enneagram style, we ask the question: What's on their "view screen" and what isn't? This is both the method for figuring out what your main Enneagram type is and a key strength of the Enneagram as a personality model: it highlights how individuals differ in specific ways and it shows how the nine types differ on several levels. It shows what they think about (and don't think about), what emotions they tend to feel (and not feel), what behaviors are typical of their style, and what actions they rarely take.

For example, a group of people could enter into the same situation—say, a birthday party—and they might all focus on different aspects of the gathering, depending on what their personality programming directs them to pay attention to. One person might focus on finding particular people they know, another person might be drawn to the food table, someone else might worry that they forgot to bring the host a gift, and yet another person might gravitate toward whomever seems to be having the most fun. The Enneagram thus reveals a basic truth that often surprises people: other people don't all view the world the way we do; different people can look at the same situation and see completely different things.

Each of the Enneagram's nine types of specific focus of attention grows out of a central "coping strategy"—the go-to method for getting around, adapting to the environment, and surviving in the world. This primary coping strategy and attentional bias gives rise to a matching worldview and corresponding habitual patterns of thought, emotion, and behavior. At its core, each of these nine personality styles is basically a "defensive" structure—an inner program that operates automatically to protect us from being hurt or feeling uncomfortable. In addition, the patterns that make up the personality also represent our particular strengths, specialties, and super powers.

Oriented around a nine-pointed figure ("ennea" meaning nine and "gram" meaning something drawn) that serves as a graphic framework for these nine personalities, the Enneagram helps solve much of the mystery behind why different people see the world in totally different ways. (And no, this isn't some sort of sinister sign or cultish emblem!—it's a perfectly innocent nine-pointed star inscribed in a circle that has deep symbolic meaning about the way natural processes get created and unfold in particular patterns or sequences.) Each of the nine personalities can be identified by its distinct adaptive strategy, and matching strengths, habits, challenges, and blind spots that grow out of whatever strategic way they have adopted to get what they need in life.

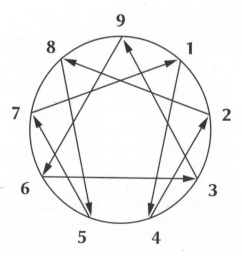

The exact history of the Enneagram—where it comes from and who "invented" it—is largely unknown, but it is thought to be hundreds or perhaps thousands of years old. We can trace it back to root teachings from very old spiritual traditions (that also functioned as psychological lessons), and it is thought to have informed ancient Greek philosophical ideas that addressed some of the big questions about being human, like, "What is the purpose of life?" and "What gets in the way of humans developing their higher potentials?" and "What stands between me and living a better life?" Evidence of the key features of the types can be found in early esoteric (meaning hidden or secret and aimed at understanding inner experience) Christian teachings, as well as The Kabbalah, or Tree of Life, in mystical Judaism, Sufism (the mystical branch of Islam), and Hindu teachings. We also see parallels in Pythagoras's study of "sacred arithmetic."

Most startling and significant of all, however, is that we also find evidence of the Enneagram personalities in Homer's epic poem *The Odyssey*. One of the first written texts in western literature, *The Odyssey* tells the story of the metaphoric journey "home" to the "true self." In the story, the hero, Odysseus (the guy who thought up the "Trojan Horse"), returning home from the Trojan war, travels to nine "lands" populated with mythic creatures whose characters match the nine Enneagram types exactly—in the same order as the modern teaching![8] This direct parallel can hardly be a coincidence. It is this kind of historical clue that suggests why the Enneagram's nine character descriptions are so accurate and powerful. Like the mythic story elements in *The Odyssey*, they are universal, timeless, deeply instructive, and enduring.

We Are "Three-Brained" Beings: The Enneagram's Three "Centers of Intelligence"

The nine types, or styles, come grouped in three sets of three, according to three "centers of intelligence"—the idea that we humans process information from the outside through three modes, or forms, of intelligence. The easiest way to begin to understand the content of the Enneagram system's nine personality types is to see how (and why) these nine types are grouped into three buckets of three types each.

According to the Enneagram map, every person has not one, but three "brains" or "centers of intelligence": the head, the heart, and the body. The *head* is the center of thinking and analyzing, the *heart* is the center of feeling emotions and relating to others through empathy, and the *body* is the center of sensing things physically, through "gut knowing" and instinctive responses. The body also houses the "movement" center, which directs action or inaction.

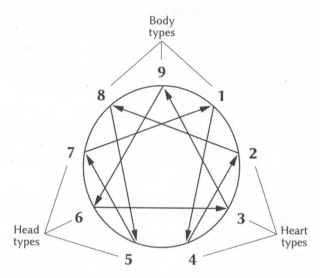

Although we all use all three of these centers all the time, three of the nine Enneagram styles (8, 9, and 1) "live in" or "overuse" the body center, three of the styles (2, 3, and 4) operate primarily from the heart center, and three of the styles (5, 6, and 7) are based in or biased toward the head center. These three "centers of intelligence" also have a direct relationship to the three parts of the human brain: the brain stem and amygdala (the reptilian or instinctual brain), the limbic (or emotional) brain, and the neo-cortex (the mental brain). We all call upon all three brain functions all the time, but one of these centers plays a dominant role in the expression of our personality.

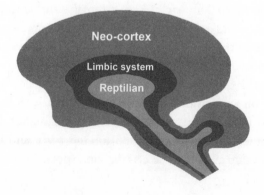

In this way, the Enneagram model embodies the idea that while we all have the potential for "wholeness," that is, we all potentially have access to all nine strategies for making our way in the world, we tend to get "out of balance" by learning to rely on one mode of relating to the world more than others. Working with the Enneagram involves noticing how we tend to be biased toward one center of intelligence over the others and intentionally trying to achieve a more conscious balance among the three modes of functioning.

In fact, the whole point of the Enneagram is about growth and balance—by seeing how we resort to one point of focus among nine possibilities, we can begin to see how we fixate on a narrow slice of 360 degrees of reality and learn to expand our perspective.

Each of the nine types describes a set of habitual ways of thinking, feeling, and acting, based on a specific view of what strategy works best for getting what you need. For instance, there's one type (Type Five) that automatically assumes it's best to focus on gaining knowledge and protecting boundaries to find the sense of safety they need. So they prioritize thinking above feeling and maintaining a strong sense of privacy. Fives have the most introverted style of relating, which underscores their view that to feel safe they need to guard their inner resources. Another type (Type Nine) believes that the best strategy to gain the sense of well-being they need is to be in harmony with other people. So, Nines tend to be preoccupied with maintaining peaceful relations with others, "going along to get along," and mediating among different points of view to create harmony and consensus. Still another kind of personality (Type Three) focuses like a laser beam on goals and tasks as a way of achieving success and looking good in the eyes of others to get the approval and admiration they need.

All of these personality styles have strengths and corresponding challenges—an upside and a downside. As the different Enneagram styles show, when we approach the world through a specific lens or filter, it allows us to develop particular areas of clarity and strength based on becoming a specialist at what that lens brings most into focus. However, on the downside, each style can over-focus on a relatively narrow set of strengths, such that they overdo those strengths to the point where they become liabilities. Unconsciously focusing too much of your attention on too narrow a set of strengths can cause you to develop and maintain certain blind spots.

This is where the Enneagram is invaluable—it shows us how, in leaning into our most developed capacities, we develop blind spots when it comes to other abilities. The Enneagram highlights our strengths, so we can appreciate and mobilize our assets, and it helps us see our weak points, so we can work to grow aspects of ourselves that we have neglected or overlooked or avoided.

For instance, when I learned my Enneagram type (Type Two), I realized that while I was good at making friends, being generally likable, and supporting others, I continually avoided conflicts (fearing that such problems would cause people to dislike me) and often focused on other people's needs and feelings (as a strategy for being liked) at the expense of my own. This caused problems in my relationships when the needs and feelings I avoided being aware of caused me to be resentful when people didn't give me what I needed. The Enneagram helped me see the problem in my basic life strategy: by trying to get along with people by not burdening them with my needs, and then getting mad when they didn't read my mind and respond to the needs I hadn't expressed, I ended up driving people away and ensuring the rejection I was trying to avoid in the first place!

Every person can benefit through learning the strengths and blind spots associated with their personality style. For instance, Type Eights are very good at asserting themselves in a strong way, confronting people with hard truths, and holding their ground in a conflict. But they have a blind spot when it comes to the value of being vulnerable or understanding their weak points: they tend to be out of touch with their more vulnerable feelings, which can lead them to overcompensate for the unconscious fear of being weak through expressing too much strength. Seeing this blind spot around vulnerability and consciously getting in touch with their softer feelings balances Eights out, so they can be both strong and approachable, powerful and empathetic.

As another example, Type Sixes make excellent troubleshooters, as they are great at seeing what can go wrong ahead of time and preparing to fix it, but they have a blind spot around the impact and consequences of always looking for trouble. Type Sixes often don't see that they can become overly "problem-seeking" instead of constructively solution-focused, can appear paranoid, and can get caught in "analysis-paralysis," when their fear of potential threats causes them to avoid taking action. Sixes can be more effective and easier to work with when they consciously take account of the blind spot around their fear and its effects and blend their talent for careful analysis with bold action.

What Number Are You? A Brief Sketch of the Enneagram's Nine Personality Styles

I first became fascinated with the Enneagram when I learned that I was a Type Two, about 26 years ago. Most people want to know more about why they do the things they do, and when I read a description of my type, it was a profound revelation. I felt shocked and surprised that *any* personality typology could paint such a clear, straightforward, and accurate picture of how I operate in the world: both in terms of what I knew to be true about myself and (embarrassing) aspects of myself I didn't really want to admit to.

Learning about my personality style as mapped out by the Enneagram changed my life. It helped me see things about myself I hadn't wanted to see before—things that created obstacles in my life because I didn't want to acknowledge them. For example, as a Type Two, I would (ironically) get mad when people would tell me I was "oversensitive" or "too emotional." But when I came to see why I, as a Type Two, became emotional, and understood the reasons behind my sensitivity, I could more easily value my emotional nature, recognize the strength in it, have compassion for myself, and learn to be less sensitive in certain situations. The Enneagram helped me see—in a gentle way—that sometimes I *was* oversensitive and overly emotional. But it also helped me see that I could both value my emotional capacity and empathic ability and consciously rein in some related tendencies to be more effective and happy in my life and work. Learning about myself through the Enneagram has made me much happier, much easier to be around, and much easier to work with.

Here is a brief sketch of the Enneagram's nine types. It may take a bit of study to find your correct type, because some of the types can look alike, and we sometimes don't know ourselves as well as we think we do. However, many people immediately recognize their own style—or the style of people they know—in even the shortest descriptions.

Individuals with a Type One style tend to view the world in terms of how it matches (or doesn't match) what they view as perfect or ideal. They focus attention on whether things are "right or wrong" or "good or bad." Their central concerns include doing the right thing and/or making sure others do the right thing, noticing and correcting errors, and working hard to improve things. They can be very self-critical and usually conform to the rules. *Type One leaders are idealistic reformers of high integrity who focus on ethics and meeting high standards of quality.*

Individuals with a Type Two style tend to be friendly, upbeat, emotional, and generous (to a fault). They focus their attention on relationships and what other people think and feel about them. A central concern is making other people like them, and they may be giving, helpful, or self-sacrificing to strategically gain others' approval. They "shape-shift" to present themselves in whatever ways they think will help them create positive rapport with others. They empathize (or overempathize) with others, and they automatically sense the moods, needs, and preferences of the people around them, but may be out of touch with their own feelings and needs. *Type Two leaders focus on how to support people so they can perform at their best, and how to create positive, productive connections with the people around them.*

Individuals with a Type Three style view the world in terms of tasks, goals, image, achievement, and success. They focus their attention on being perceived as successful and getting a lot done. They excel at matching the ideal model of material success and cultural signs of achievement (having a nice car, attaining high status, having impressive credentials). They usually focus on doing at the expense of feeling (emotions) and being. They can be workaholics who have difficulty slowing down and knowing what they are feeling, but they accomplish a great deal in the most efficient way. *Type Three leaders focus on results, working hard, and managing perceptions so that they can assure success for their team and their organization.*

Individuals with a Type Four style value authenticity and tend to be comfortable with a wide range of emotions, including pain. They focus their attention on their own internal world, connection and disconnection with others, what's missing in a given situation, and the aesthetic aspects of their environment. Because they live more in their feelings than other types, they can at times over-identify with their emotions. They value depth and the genuine expression of feeling in relationships. Idealistic and creative, they regularly experience longing and melancholy and may at times be preoccupied with the past. *Type Four leaders promote the value of authentic expression and communication and support creativity and mutual understanding.*

Individuals with a Type Five style tend to be introverted, shy and less emotionally expressive than other types. They focus their attention on thinking, gaining knowledge, interesting intellectual pursuits, and creating boundaries to maintain privacy. They often have the sense that they have a limited amount of energy and so are sensitive to others potentially draining them of their finite stores of time or resources. Because they value personal

space, they may have a hard time sharing themselves with others in relationships. *Type Five leaders focus on the importance of gaining knowledge and
generating and relying on the best information available, and they highly value
technical expertise.*

Individuals with a Type Six style focus attention on detecting threats
to their safety and preparing to meet danger or trouble. Naturally vigilant,
they can be either actively fearful (phobic) or strong and intimidating as a
proactive move against fear (counterphobic). They tend to be loyal, analytical, contrarian, and suspicious of authority. Their natural tendency to assess
threats and risks makes them good troubleshooters, but they can also struggle
with paranoia, indecision, and catastrophic or "worst-case scenario" thinking.
Most Sixes have authority issues—they both want a good authority and may
test or rebel against authority figures. *Type Six leaders are sensitive to power
dynamics and issues of safety and security. They focus on preparation and risk-as-
sessment and support their workers at every level of an organization.*

Individuals with a Type Seven style tend to be energetic, fast-paced,
and optimistic. They focus their attention on fun and stimulating things to
think about and do, on creating many options, and planning. They are usually
enthusiastic, future-oriented, fun-loving people who dislike feeling uncomfortable feelings including sadness, anxiety, boredom, or pain. They are good
at reframing negatives into positives, have quick minds, and usually have
many interests and enjoy engaging socially with others. *Type Seven leaders are
optimistic visionaries who like to play with ideas and innovate as a way to move
things forward.*

Individuals with a Type Eight style tend to be attuned to strength and
power—who has it and how they wield it. They usually have more access to
their anger and a higher tolerance for conflict and confrontation than other
types. Eights focus their attention on creating order, seeing the big picture,
and noticing whether things are fair and just. They are assertive, direct, and
strong. They have a large energetic presence, can be intimidating, and may
underestimate their impact on others. They can be excessive, impulsive,
generous, and protective of others. *Type Eight leaders enjoy exercising power,
establishing order, and moving work forward in direct ways. They are fearless in
dealing head-on with challenges and make strong mentors to subordinates.*

Individuals with a Type Nine style make good mediators because they
can naturally see all sides of an issue and feel motivated to reduce conflict
and create harmony. Affable and easy-going, they "go with the flow," focusing

attention on blending with and over-adapting to others as a way of staying comfortable and avoiding separation and conflict. Because they value harmony and dislike conflict, they tend to be distractible and out of touch with their own anger and personal agenda. The lack of a connection with their own priorities makes it difficult to make decisions, so they often remain on the fence or procrastinate. *Type Nine leaders value inclusion, usually don't have big egos, are easy-going and approachable, and lead by creating consensus.*

Breaking It Down Again: The Additional Information Provided by the 27 Subtypes

At the risk of overwhelming you completely, I now need to tell you that there is another level to the Enneagram types beyond the nine personality styles. Just as the three centers of intelligence (head, heart, and body) "house" three types each, each of the nine types breaks down into three versions again. So, there are actually 27 types, or "sub-types." This additional level of "sub-types" adds yet another degree of specificity to the personalities we find in the world that the Enneagram describes.[9] While adding another layer of types may seem like too much information, the 27 subtypes are crucially important to understand, because the additional, more nuanced information they provide helps with finding your correct type and understanding the nine types with greater clarity.

The three subtypes of the nine main types are defined by which of three "instincts" or "instinctual biases" is dominant. We all have all three animal instincts—for *self-preservation*, establishing *social* relationships and positioning in relation to groups, and the instinct for *one-to-one* bonding—that help us function in the world and keep us safe. And just as each person favors one center and one type within that center, we each favor one of these three instincts as kind of a "first line of defense."

Type Ones

Type Ones focus on making things more perfect, but they do it in three ways:

▶ *Self-Preservation Ones* focus on making everything they do more perfect. They are the true perfectionists of the Enneagram. They see themselves as highly flawed and try to improve themselves and make every detail of what they do right. These people are the most anxious and worried Ones, but also the most friendly and warm.

▶ *Social Ones* focus on doing things perfectly in a larger sense—knowing the right way to do things—and modeling how to do things right for others. An intellectual type of person, these Ones have a teacher mentality in that they see their role as helping others see what they already know: how to be perfect.

▶ *One-to-One Ones* focus on making other people—and society as a whole—more perfect. More reformers than perfectionists, they tend to display more anger and zeal than the other Ones. These Ones focus less attention on perfecting their own behavior and pay more attention to whether others are doing things right.

Type Twos

Type Twos focus on gaining approval and creating positive rapport with others, but they do it in three ways:

▶ *Self-Preservation Twos* seek to gain approval through being charming and youthful. Less oriented to giving and more burdened by helping, they charm others into liking them as a way of getting people to take care of them. More self-indulgent, playful, and irresponsible than the other two Twos, they are more fearful and ambivalent about connecting with others.

▶ *Social Twos* seek to gain approval from others through being powerful, competent, and influential. More of a powerful, leader type of person, they take charge of things and play to a larger audience as a way of proving their value.

▶ *One-to-One Twos* gain approval through being generous and attractive. They emphasize their personal appeal and promises of support to make others like them and do things for them—this is a more emotional, passionate Two.

Type Threes

Type Threes focus on looking good and working hard to get things done and do this in three ways:

▶ *Self-Preservation Threes* work hard to assure material security for themselves and the people around them. Oriented to being good (as well as looking good) according to social consensus, they want to appear successful to others, but they don't want to brag or self-promote in an obvious way (because that wouldn't be good). SP Threes are self-sufficient, extremely hardworking, results-oriented, and modest.

▶ *Social Threes* work hard to look flawless in the eyes of others. Oriented to competing to win and attaining the material and status symbols of success, they focus on getting things done and always having the right image for every social context. Social Threes enjoy being onstage, have a corporate mentality, and know how to climb the social ladder.

▶ *One-to-One Threes* focus on creating an image that is appealing to others and supporting and pleasing the people around them—especially partners, coworkers, and family members. They have a relationship or team mentality and can work very hard to support the success of others (rather than their own).

Type Fours

Type Fours focus on expressing themselves creatively and authentically to build meaningful connections, and make themselves understood in three ways:

▶ *Self-Preservation Fours* are stoic and strong—emotionally sensitive by nature, they hold their feelings in to prove themselves and connect with others. While they feel things deeply, they often have a sunny, upbeat exterior. They may feel anxious inside, but they tough things out and have a high tolerance for frustration.

▶ *Social Fours* focus on their own emotions and the underlying emotional tone of whatever situation they are in. They compare themselves to others and tend to see themselves as less worthy or lacking in some way. They are more emotionally sensitive than most other types and connect to themselves through the authenticity of their emotional truth.

▶ *One-to-One Fours* are more assertive and competitive. These Fours are not afraid to ask for what they need or complain when they don't get it. They can appear aggressive to others, and strive to be the best.

Type Fives

Type Fives focus on attaining knowledge and maintaining boundaries with others to protect their private space and avoid having their energy and inner resources depleted by others. They do this in three ways:

▶ *Self-Preservation Fives* focus mainly on maintaining good boundaries with others. Friendly and warm, SP Fives like to have a private space they can withdraw to if they want to be alone.

▶ *Social Fives* enjoy becoming experts in the specific subject areas that interest them. They like acquiring knowledge and connecting with others with common intellectual interests and causes.

▶ *One-to-One Fives* have more of a need for connecting with other individuals under the right conditions. These Fives are more in touch with their emotions inside, though they may not show it on the outside.

Type Sixes

Type Sixes focus on detecting threats and preparing to meet them. They seek safety and certainty, are slow to trust, try to manage risk, and are sensitive to power dynamics. These traits manifest in three ways:

▶ *Self-Preservation Sixes* are the more actively fearful (the phobic or "flight") Six. They doubt and question things in an effort to find a sense of certainty and safety (that often eludes them). They seek to be warm and friendly to attract allies as a form of outside support or protection in a dangerous world.

▶ *Social Sixes* are more intellectual types who find a sense of safety in following the guidelines of a system or way of thinking to feel protected by a kind of impersonal outside authority. They tend to be logical, rational, and concerned with reference points and benchmarks.

▶ *One-to-One Sixes* cope with underlying fear (that they may not be aware of) by appearing strong and intimidating to others. Of the "fight" or "flight" reactions to fear, they choose "fight," and tend to be risk-takers, contrarians, or rebels. They have an inner program that tells them that the best defense is a good offense.

Type Sevens

Type Sevens focus on whatever feels pleasurable and like to think about stimulating ideas and positive visions of the future as a way of unconsciously moving away from whatever might feel uncomfortable or painful. They do this in three ways:

▶ *Self-Preservation Sevens* are very practical. Good at getting what they want, they readily recognize opportunities and know how to make things happen, whether through pragmatic planning or a network of allies. They tend to have a talkative, amiable, hedonistic style.

▶ *Social Sevens* want to avoid being seen as excessively opportunistic and self-interested, so they focus on sacrificing their immediate desires to pursue an ideal of being of service to others. They take responsibility for the group or family and want to be seen as good by easing others' suffering.

▶ *One-to-One Sevens* are idealistic dreamers, who have a need to imagine something better than what might be true in their everyday reality. Extremely enthusiastic and optimistic, they have a passion for seeing things as they could be or as they imagine them to be (as opposed to how they really are).

Type Eights

Type Eights focus on power, control, justice, and fairness—who has the power, and will they be competent and fair. Assertive and direct, they are good at seeing the big picture and like to exert strength to make things happen. These traits manifest in three ways:

▶ *Self-Preservation Eights* focus on getting what they need to survive in a direct, no-nonsense way. They have a low tolerance for frustration and a strong desire for the timely satisfaction of their material needs. They know how to do business and get things done and don't need to talk about it very much.

▶ *Social Eights* focus on protecting and mentoring others they are connected to or anyone they view as needing their support. While they can be rebellious and assertive, they appear less aggressive as they have a softer side when it comes to taking care of others.

▶ *One-to-One Eights* have a strong rebellious tendency and like to be the center of things. More provocative and passionate than the other Eights, they like to have power over people and situations.

Type Nines

Type Nines focus on creating harmony and mediating potential conflicts when they arise to maintain a sense of peacefulness and get to consensus. Often out of touch with their own desires or opinions, they like to go with the flow and adapt to others as a way of maintaining positive feelings and avoiding conflict. This happens in three ways:

▶ *Self-Preservation Nines* focus on finding comfort in familiar routines and the satisfaction of their physical needs. Whether through eating, sleeping, reading, or doing crossword puzzles, SP Nines tend to lose themselves in whatever activities help them feel grounded and comfortable.

▶ *Social Nines* focus on working hard to support the groups they are a part of as a way of seeking a sense of comfort in belonging. Congenial people who like to feel a part of things, Social Nines tend to be light-hearted and fun, and expend a lot of effort in doing what it takes to be admitted to and supportive of the group or community.

▶ *One-to-One Nines* tend to merge with the agenda and attitudes of important others in their lives. Sweet, gentle, and less assertive than other types, this relationship-oriented Nine may take on the feelings and opinions of the people they are close to without realizing it.

Now that we've outlined the main "type" aspects of the Enneagram model as a framework for understanding both the complexity and the unifying patterns of the human personality, we can look at how we can put the Enneagram to work in helping people to grow on both a personal and a professional level.

In the next chapter, we will focus on how—exactly—the Enneagram functions as a tool to enhance self-understanding, leadership, and working relationships. Then we will take a deep dive into how each of the nine types—and 27 subtypes—can be understood in terms of a variety of features of the human personality, and what you might want to know about how those features show up at work.

CHAPTER 3

Becoming a Better Leader—and Leading More Effective Organizations

How to Use the Enneagram for Personal and Professional Growth

"In the workplace, we rarely share what's going on beneath the surface. At most companies, the unspoken expectation is that you park your emotional life at the door, put on your game face, and keep things light and professional. In short, you bring a part of yourself to work and try to suppress the rest.

"But at what cost—including to productivity? The more preoccupied we are with emotions we can't express, the less focus we bring to our work."

Tony Schwartz, author and CEO—from his *Harvard Business Review* article, "Seeing Through Your Blind Spots"

Historically, it has been a widely accepted idea that when you go to work, you check your emotions and your personal issues at the door. And while this still makes sense to a degree, in a world where people need to collaborate more and more, and the pace of change is getting faster and faster, it's becoming increasingly obvious that people who work together need to have efficient ways of knowing and understanding each other. Very often, this means sharing more about who they are and how they feel—so that the energy that might get wasted in holding ourselves back, hiding our emotional reactions, and dealing with subterranean personality conflicts can be used in service of furthering the work and creating a more positive work environment.

The Enneagram facilitates exactly the kind of sharing and open communication at work that helps people know themselves better, understand their colleagues at a deeper level, develop their leadership capacities, and build stronger relationships, teams, and organizations. How does it do this? Through giving people accurate and in-depth descriptions of their personality programming, including their blind spots, it acts as a guide for the development of greater self-awareness. By highlighting the motives and habitual patterns of all of the nine personality styles, it offers an interesting and efficient way to learn about the people you interact with. And it then provides a neutral language for communicating about yourself and hearing about your colleagues in a way that discourages judgment and minimizes defensiveness.

Tony Schwartz, a journalist, business book author, leadership expert, and now CEO of The Energy Project, which helps companies fuel sustainable high performance by better meeting the needs of their employees, has written about the Enneagram and how it helps people work better and smarter. Here is what he says about the importance of colleagues learning about each other as a way to improve working relationships—and how he has used the Enneagram himself to make that happen:

> *"As the CEO of a small but fast-growing company, I'm spending more and more of my time focused on… how people are feeling and how we're interacting with one another…. When strong feelings can't be acknowledged, they fester and get acted out, often in passive-aggressive ways. Over time, they drain energy, individually and organizationally.*
>
> *"With all that in mind, we decided to focus a recent company off-site on giving our people an opportunity simply to talk openly about themselves. The goal was to improve communication, decrease misunderstanding and free up positive energy.*
>
> *"…To facilitate this discussion, we used a tool called the Enneagram—a personality typing system akin to the Myers-Briggs, but for my money, much richer, more penetrating and more practically useful."*[10]

In this chapter, we will look at the specific elements involved in using the Enneagram at work for self-development and the development of greater leadership and team cohesion.

The Most Basic Element of Working with the Enneagram: Self-Observation

When using the Enneagram as a tool for self-development, the first and main task is self-observation. This may sound simple, and in some ways, it is, but in some ways, it isn't. It's simple in that it only requires you to practice remembering to nonjudgmentally watch and note all the things you think, feel, and do. But it can also be very hard, because it requires you to practice remembering to nonjudgmentally watch and note all the things you think, feel, and do.

The Enneagram supports and aids efforts at self-observation by giving you a map of the territory—by describing and highlighting specific habits to watch out for and track. "Mindfulness" has become a popular concept in the business world in recent years. Being "mindful" of ourselves helps us to be more present and more in tune with what we are feeling, thinking, and doing so we become more conscious. While simple meditation teachings can help with this task enormously, the practice of mindfulness can still be a bit amorphous: How do we do it? The Enneagram provides a structure that can help guide mindful awareness because it tells you what (exactly) to be mindful of—your specific personality patterns.

While self-observation may seem straightforward, the process of becoming more aware of what really happens in your experience can be eye-opening. Offering a map or guide for this self-study, the Enneagram shows you in clear detail what to watch out for—your job is to remember to tune in and really notice the patterns it maps out for you. The work of self-awareness gets done by learning to "catch yourself in the act" of engaging in the personality traits the Enneagram highlights. You will likely be surprised by what you find out.

Often, self-observation is enough to increase your self-awareness in certain areas. And it can be important to just do that for a while—just watch and notice and observe and note what you do without judgment. Keep an eye out especially for self-judgment and self-criticism. If you judge yourself for the things you observe yourself doing, you defeat the whole purpose, because now you have to defend yourself against your own inner attacks as well as all the usual stuff you habitually protect yourself from.

Developing the ability to create some space inside your own mind to see and reflect on the things you think, feel, and do lays the groundwork for making different choices—more conscious choices based on what works in each situation as opposed to your automatic, preprogrammed tendencies.

Leveraging Self-Awareness to Develop Self-Understanding and Improve Relationships

After self-observation, the next steps involve 1) further self-reflection and self-exploration into the things you are noticing that you do, and 2) leveraging your self-awareness to improve your relationships. This includes talking with others about what you observe in yourself, and learning to feel more comfortable communicating about what you do and hearing feedback from others.

These next steps allow you to deepen your self-understanding through reflecting on what you are noticing and asking yourself questions to probe more deeply into what you observe. First, you might ask yourself: Why am I doing this? And why do I keep doing this, even when it's not working for me? And why am I avoiding what I'm avoiding? What am I afraid of? What do I imagine the consequences to be? Am I right about what will happen or is it just my fear of "talking"?

Secondly, by sharing your observations with others who know you— or people you want to know you—you experience your new insights from another angle. Putting your observations into words and taking the risk of talking about your thoughts, feelings, and actions helps you expand your interpretation and understanding of what you notice in yourself by hearing feedback from someone else. This both allows you to explore yourself from another angle and potentially strengthens your relationships. In addition, if you can be open to hearing feedback from others, you can gain additional insight through seeing yourself through someone else's eyes, which can allow you to learn more about what you might not be seeing: your blind spots.

This is reinforced by Tony Schwartz's observations about his team's off-site in which people use the Enneagram as a tool to discuss the personality patterns they observed in themselves:

> *"[The company off-site] was an extraordinary day for several reasons. First, awareness by itself opens doors. In understanding the predictable patterns of each type, we each had multiple 'ah-ha' moments, such as recognizing a Six's acute sensitivity to danger, or the Seven's need to keep everything light and positive."*[11]

By observing what you think, feel, and do nonjudgmentally, you can be more objective about what you experience in the world, and not just be driven by unconscious biases and automatic habits. This results in an improved ability to make conscious choices and to respond creatively in each situation rather than being passively subject to knee-jerk, preprogrammed defensive reactions. And when you can discuss this with the people you work with—whether you are a leader or an individual contributor—you both gain important insights into yourself and learn about how you can understand each other at a deeper level.

Mapping the Growth Trajectory of Your Personality Style

Observing Your "Low Side"–What Happens When You're Stressed– and Aiming for the "High Side"–When You're at Your Best

One of the best things about the Enneagram is the way the personality types reveal that most of the things we observe in ourselves are double-edged: most all of our traits have an upside and a downside. We have specialized gifts and talents, but if we rely on a narrow set of strengths or preferences too much, they become liabilities. When we do something because it gets us something we want, often there is also an associated unintended consequence that brings us something we don't want.

Each of the nine personality types can be seen to have a "low side" and a "high side," associated behaviors and patterns that can be more "fixed" and rigid and less healthy and mature, and aspects that are more flexible, creative, healthy, and mature. The beauty of this developmental spectrum is that it helps us identify and reflect on our behaviors in terms of whether they are hurting us or helping us, whether we are remaining stuck in unconscious habits or learning to consciously stretch ourselves and grow.

With the help of the Enneagram map, you can envision the possible growth trajectory of your personality style and readily see when you are engaging in "low side" behaviors or "high side" behaviors. This provides you with a way to observe and study what you are doing in terms of how conscious, healthy, and effective it is, (or how unconscious, unhealthy, and ineffective it is).

For instance, one of my personality type patterns is avoiding asking for help, even when I really need it. When I observe myself actively turning down offers of help when I know I could really use it (like the time I couldn't figure out how to buy a train ticket in Germany and someone offered to help me, but I almost said "no" even though I was struggling and panicky because I was about to miss my train) I know I'm being limited by my personality pattern. When I actively seek out help, even though it feels vulnerable, embarrassing, and risky, I know I am doing something that's good for me, even if it feels uncomfortable. The Enneagram map shows us that when we stretch ourselves outside of our comfort zones in specific ways, we are making progress in our growth and becoming freer.

In this way, the Enneagram descriptions highlight very clearly where we are on a kind of "growth map." In the chapters that follow, for each of the nine types, I will provide information about what the type looks like when an individual is at his or her best, or most healthy and mature, as well as when stressed and pushed to the low side. This will allow you to chart your developmental progress up and down a kind of vertical spectrum of "self-mastery" or conscious self-awareness.

So, in addition to observing and studying yourself to develop your ability to know yourself and be aware of what you really do in the moment, you can also use the Enneagram to assess whether you are living from a lower or a higher level of awareness and conscious choice.

Using the Enneagram as a Tool for Professional Growth

The Key to Everything: Knowing Yourself

To use the Enneagram well as a leader in a work setting, the first step is necessarily to employ it to understand yourself. Reflecting the ancient Greek idea that the key to life is to "know thyself," the bedrock idea behind the Enneagram is that if we each come to know ourselves more completely, that shift in awareness in itself has an effect on the things we do and the ways we interact with others. When we are more mindful and conscious of our unconscious tendencies, not only will that naturally diminish our level of reactivity and defensiveness, but often others will be inspired to examine their own inner workings.

In seeking to understand yourself in a deeper way, the Enneagram helps you to:

- ▶ Recognize your strengths, automatic habits, motives, and blind spots more consciously within yourself.

- ▶ Think about your habits, motives, reactions, and automatic tendencies with more conscious awareness.

- ▶ Communicate about your habitual tendencies to clarify interactions with others—when you understand more about what you do and why you do it you can share this awareness with others as a way of being more known and creating mutual compassion.

- ▶ Have more flexibility to choose to make adjustments in the way you interact (if you choose to).

In short, the Enneagram supports you in the crucial process of learning to know yourself by aiding you in self-observation, self-reflection, self-acceptance, self-aware communication, and making more conscious choices. And this work forms the basis for any kind of positive change you might want to make in your life and your work.

Also Key: Knowing the People Around You

As you engage in a deeper effort to become more aware of your own internal world with the help of the Enneagram model, you also come to the important realization that other people don't all see the world the way you do. Usually this is a huge shift in awareness in itself. Before we learn about the Enneagram, we tend to believe that everyone views the world the same way we do. It's a natural assumption given that we are all in our own heads and most of us don't read minds. We simply don't have access to others' inner thoughts and subjective perspectives.

But when we come to know all nine types through the Enneagram, we suddenly get a great deal of insight into how the people around us see the world—and how their worldviews can be radically different from our own. When we use the Enneagram map to glimpse the world through their lenses, it becomes clear to us why we have conflicts with some people and not others, why people don't always act in the ways we expect them to, and how the people in our lives can hold completely different views of the same world.

The Enneagram model thus helps us to know ourselves more and accept that others' perspectives can differ greatly from our own. And in addition to this, it gives us a window into how the other eight kinds of people in the world think, feel, and behave. When we can see these different lenses on the world, and how the varied individuals we know view life from a whole different angle, and that no point of view is better or worse than any other—that they are all normal and natural—this immediately allows us to have much greater understanding and compassion for other people. And when we have more insight into and empathy for the worldviews of the people we live and work with, we can more easily accept them as they are and manage our expectations and responses to them.

Understanding Your Interactions

Through providing this map to understand ourselves and others in a deeper way, the Enneagram allows us to improve our working relationships. It helps us to communicate more effectively, understand other people's styles and preferences, and make adjustments in our presentation to more flexibly adapt to different individuals and situations. It provides the larger framework for learning to relate more effectively to the range of people—and personality styles—we meet in our everyday lives so we can more consciously employ a wider range of strategies for interacting with a diverse array of people.

Most of all, the Enneagram type descriptions provide a neutral language for talking about points of conflict that arise from the fact that different people see the same issue in different ways, through different lenses. Tony Schwartz illustrates this when he describes how the Enneagram allowed his team to have an open discussion in which they learned about each other's style in a way that was safe, yet revealing:

> *"Using the Enneagram made it possible to operate on a level playing field, without judgment. No type is superior to any other, and that helped each of us feel more comfortable exploring our blind spots and limitations, along with our gifts and strengths. We did our learning as a community, and everyone participated, to one degree or another.*
>
> *"Truly understanding the struggles of the world views of others makes it easier to feel empathy for them, and to hold their value, even when they interpret the world very differently than we do. For me, recognizing that one colleague—a Three—gets a sense of safety from feeling successful at each step of any process was very helpful. So was understanding why another colleague—an Eight—has such a high need to feel on top of every detail where most details make my eyes gloss over."[12]*

Once we understand the diverse lenses, or filters, or perceptual biases, we can talk about them openly, without blame or defensiveness. Once we understand more about why other people think, feel, and act the way they do—what their basic strategies and patterns of behavior are and where they come from—we have more information from which to more actively and effectively create mutual understanding.

Understanding your respective Enneagram styles makes it so much easier to communicate about what is going on: you and your boss don't disagree because you are always right and she is always wrong, or vice versa, or because you are sincere and she is underhanded—it's because you are a One and she is a Three, so you will look at the essential elements of the same situation and interpret them differently. It's only natural if you perceive reality through different lenses. And the Enneagram gives you this understanding and the language in which to discuss the divergence in your approaches in a way that honors your unique perspectives and clarifies the matter at hand.

"Enneagram Ethics"

It's a Powerful Tool: Don't Use It as an Accusation or an Excuse

When I tell the leaders I work with that I am writing a book about using the Enneagram in leadership development and the workplace, many of them ask me to make sure to talk about "Enneagram ethics." This is because it often happens that after the people on a team or in an organization learn the Enneagram, they begin to slip into some bad habits. The Enneagram's great descriptive power can be fun to play with and can inspire the desire to evangelize. Once you've seen the amazing accuracy with which the Enneagram styles reflect us to ourselves, it can be hard to remember that it's not a toy.

Anything that has power for good can also be used in a powerful way to cause harm. And this is definitely true of the Enneagram. If we aren't careful, we can start to use it as a "parlor game," or as a way to stereotype people, or as a way to justify any resistances we might have to being more aware and making active efforts to work against our bad habits. So, it is important, at this point, to talk about the need to use the Enneagram in an ethical way, because it is a tool of great depth, and when used without the proper sensitivity it can create more problems than it solves. (Plus, when we use it ethically, we also use it more effectively.)

The Enneagram can very easily be used as *a weapon* or *an excuse*, both of which are very bad. While it can be fun to tell people what type they are after we see how clear and clarifying the types are, this can have a very negative impact. Under the "a little knowledge is a dangerous thing" category, we can think we are experts when in reality we know very little about the types. We can tell people what type they are—and insist we are right—and be completely wrong. At best, this can confuse people and at worst, it can turn them off to the Enneagram and the whole idea of making efforts to be more self-aware.

I have also seen people use the Enneagram to negative effect when they hurl it at someone as an insult. Or they act as if they know the person totally, instead of just their personality, after finding out what type they are. Saying things like, "You can't do this because you are a Five," or, "You always do this because you are a Four" are examples of how the Enneagram can be used as a way of stereotyping people. This is just wrong—and a total misuse of the system.

Finally, the Enneagram and its types can also be used as an excuse for bad (or unconscious) behavior. In exactly the opposite way from the way it is intended to be used, people can use it to rationalize or justify their fixated, unhealthy behavior: "This is just what I do because I'm a Seven," or "I can't do that because I'm a Nine." The Enneagram is about growth, development and change—it's never about justifying unconscious habits as a way of avoiding the work you need to do on yourself to grow.

So, a few ethical rules to always, always, remember when using the Enneagram:

▶ Never tell someone what type they are and insist you know better than they do. (Especially don't do this with anger, arrogance or insensitivity.) No matter how well you think you know them, they are the experts on their own inner experience. And besides, even if you are right, they need to come to the realization themselves in their own way (if it's right for them)—it's not your job to force them to do their work or push them in any way.

▶ Never use your Enneagram style as an excuse to justify your unwillingness to grow beyond your personality. It's not "just who you are," and certainly isn't all of who you are—it's only your personality. There's much more of "you" to be discovered with the help of that personality.

▶ Never reference the Enneagram in anger, use it against someone as an insult, or to box them in to a stereotype of what you think a specific type is all about. Even people of the same Enneagram type can look different, and we are all unique despite the unifying characteristics of our types, so don't assume you know the system and types better than you do.

▶ Stay humble. Don't be an "instant expert" and act like you know more than you possibly could. Only teach or talk about the Enneagram system with authority if you have the requisite experience to do so (formal Enneagram training plus expertise in something like psychology or organization development). The Enneagram has been rediscovered fairly recently and it inspires a great deal of excitement in people who understand the insights it has to offer, so there is a problem in the larger Enneagram world with the overabundance of "instant experts."

Instead, hold the Enneagram and its insights with respect and care. Realize you can't push it on people—they must be able to decide on their own whether they feel motivated to grow and whether it's the tool they want to use for their self-development. If you are enthusiastic about the Enneagram because it's helped you, feel free to share it with others, but do so in a thoughtful way, realizing that ultimately, every individual is the best expert when it comes to his or her own inner territory.

While we may want to tell people what type they are because it seems so clear to us on the outside, that often backfires by turning them off to the whole enterprise. Instead, share what you have learned through your own experience and invite them to engage in their own exploration through pointing them toward high-quality Enneagram resources (like this book!) so they can choose for themselves.

The "Box" Issue: As in Getting Put in One or Already Being in One and Not Knowing It (and Getting Out!)

When I talk with people about the Enneagram, some react with skepticism or doubt. As I noted at the beginning of the last chapter, a common initial misperception of the Enneagram is that learning you have a specific personality type boxes you in or "pigeonholes" you, or makes you less unique or authentically you in the eyes of the people around you. This is a valid, understandable concern. No one wants to be misunderstood, viewed in a narrow or negative way, or subjected to a limited definition of who they are—especially at work, when being seen accurately and in a positive light can be so important.

Fortunately, while the Enneagram isn't necessarily for everybody—you have to be motivated to grow, see your blind spots, and increase your level of self-awareness—when used well, it does the opposite of "putting you in a box." Instead, the Enneagram shows us the invisible box we are already in in the form of familiar, automatic, self-limiting habits, and helps us see how we inadvertently keep ourselves in there! It reveals the exact dimensions of this box we are already in (but don't know we are in) so we can break out of the constraints that accompany the unconscious patterns that make up our personality.

As I mentioned previously, our automatic habits and patterns—our focus of attention and the self-restrictive way we see the world—fixate us in certain ways of seeing and reacting. We become limited by our habitual patterns and even more limited by not seeing the ways we unconsciously hold ourselves back. We become trapped in patterns that may not always serve us, which we have become so accustomed to and comfortable in that we don't know what we don't know.

The Enneagram describes the ways we put ourselves in a box (in great detail) so we can find the way out. When we are able to identify our blind spots, talk about them with colleagues, and learn to make those parts of us conscious, we create many new possibilities both for our own growth and our ability to enjoy the people we work with.

In his article "Seeing Through Your Blind Spots," Tony Schwartz describes the power of the Enneagram to aid self-discovery, facilitate open conversations that lead to greater understanding, and create greater empathy in the workplace. He notes that the process of sharing ourselves in the work setting can be challenging, but emphasizes the rewards of creating safety to learn more about our colleagues as a team:

> *"This isn't easy work. We had the advantage of a team that includes many people who have already done considerable self-exploration. Even so, acknowledging any level of vulnerability is challenging. By the end of the day, we all felt drained—but also exhilarated that we had gotten to know each other so much better, and we could more easily accept and even appreciate our differences. Even the most skeptical among us felt it was a rewarding use of our time.*
>
> *"The goal of getting people to talk about what makes them feel safe—or unsafe—is not to push them to share feelings they're not comfortable sharing. Rather it's to invite them to learn more about themselves, and to develop emotional skills that are critical to performance—among them self-awareness, empathy, and resilience. Since we're all fighting a difficult battle, why not take it on together?"[13]*

As Schwartz wisely points out, the Enneagram introduces an egalitarian method for talking about our strengths and our challenges, and our similarities and our differences. When we can maintain this kind of open dialogue with colleagues, we greatly enhance both our self-acceptance and our collaboration and sense of community. We allow ourselves to more intentionally manifest our higher potentials and grow in concert with the people around us. When we can do this, everybody wins, and we create the foundation for what we most need in the world today—more effective leadership.

In What Follows...

Now that I've introduced you to the Enneagram and its component parts, and reviewed some of the ethics to keep in mind when using it, we are ready to more deeply and thoroughly explore the nine personality types. In each of the next nine chapters I will describe the characteristics of a single personality style, including the type's main strategy, strengths, challenges, blind spots, low side and high side, communication style and typical workplace behaviors. I'll explain how to determine if you are a specific type, and what leaders with particular types may look like to us on the outside. I'll talk about the three versions of each type, and show how knowing these "sub-types" can provide you with more nuanced information that can help you to recognize the types more accurately.

I'll also share tips on getting along with people once you know their type and offer some insights about how people of a given type act when they are the leaders and when they are not the leader. I'll provide excerpts from interviews with real-life leaders who have used the Enneagram for their own growth and in their teams and organizations, to illustrate how you can use the Enneagram to grow personally and professionally. And finally, for each type, I'll offer tasks and suggestions to support you in becoming more self-aware and emotionally intelligent in the 21st-century workplace.

As you can probably already see, entering into the Enneagram approach to self-development does require a certain investment of time and energy at the outset. However, I can pretty much guarantee you that if you put some effort into understanding the Enneagram map, you will be richly rewarded with many new insights into yourself and others. As one leader I interviewed for this book said, "The useful lessons the Enneagram can give you that can help you improve your life experience are broad, deep, and unending." When you understand the personalities and their interconnections, when you come to see how the pieces fit together, it will help you to make sense of the variations in the personalities of the people around you in a way you could never imagine.

The concluding chapter tells some compelling stories of real-world leaders and business that achieved profound growth through the Enneagram—and shows you how you can do it too.

CHAPTER 4

The Type One Leadership Style
Doing the Right Thing Is the Right Thing

"The quality of a leader is reflected in the standards they set for themselves."

Ray Kroc, American businessman

"Be a yardstick of quality. Some people aren't used to an environment where excellence is expected."

Steve Jobs, entrepreneur and Apple Inc. founder

Isobel Crawley to Violet Crawley, Dowager Countess of Grantham: *"How you hate to be wrong."*

The Dowager Countess: *"I wouldn't know. I'm not familiar with the sensation."*

Downton Abbey (PBS television show), Season 4

The Type One archetype is that prototypical person who values structure, ethical conduct and high standards of quality above all else. Sometimes called "the Perfectionist" or "the Reformer," Type Ones have an internal sense—a kinesthetic feeling, or "knowing"—that tells them how "good" or "right" something feels, and what that thing would look like if it matched their inner ideal of perfection. A One's attention automatically goes to this gap between how something is and how it could be, as well as what is required to bridge that gap.

Ones' primary goal in every situation is to achieve a high-quality result. Their programming tells them that the best way to do this is to put the "right" processes and the "right" people in place—and then work hard, in an ethical way, to produce a product that reflects the highest standards. Type Ones tend to be logical and results-oriented, usually rational and methodical, respectful of the rules outlining appropriate behavior, and worried about making mistakes.

Ones strive to communicate in an effective and appropriate way, with a speaking style that tends to be precise, detail-oriented, logical, and task- or fact-based. They typically get to the point quickly, and will avoid including their personal feelings, which they may consider inappropriate or unproductive.[14] Either directly or by implication, they tend to speak in terms of imperatives— "shoulds," "musts," and "ought tos"—which may add an air of urgency to the things they say, and may also convey an underlying assertion that they know the right (or best) way to do things. And while Ones often communicate with the conscious intention of helping or supporting whatever is happening in the most direct way possible, others may hear what they say as containing implicit criticisms or judgments. Their tendency to over control their impulses and feelings, especially feelings of anger or resentment, may cause others to detect a hint of evaluation or impatience in their messages.

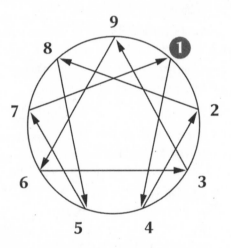

Leaders who have a Type One style tend to be responsible, honest, reliable, diligent, and ethical. Some lead by example, while others seek to reform society actively, lead others to make things better, and correct large social problems. In the workplace, Type One leaders naturally focus on the "process level," as structure, rules, and routine help them feel grounded in the basic processes required to create a quality product. Naturally detail-oriented and responsible, their central motivation is to strive for excellence and virtue in everything they do.

How to Tell if You Are a Type One: The View from the Inside

If most or all of the following characteristics apply to you, you may be a Type One:

▶ *You have an inner-critic or "coach" that operates most of the time.* This inner voice (or sense) continually monitors what you do and provides ongoing feedback about how well you did or how you missed the mark and could have done better.

▶ *You are sensitive to criticism.* While you welcome honest feedback (because you place a high value on constant attention to improvement), you feel sensitive to criticism from the outside because you are already your own harshest critic.

▶ *You naturally think in terms of "good and bad" and "right and wrong."* You try hard to be "good" and place a high value on doing the right thing. You often can't help seeing things in black and white, though you may have learned through time and experience to see more shades of grey.

▶ *You notice errors and want to correct them.* You easily spot typos and spelling errors and crooked pictures and other such misalignments and feel driven to fix them.

▶ *You follow the rules all or most of the time.* You believe rules support the well-ordered functioning of social and work life and therefore should be respected.

▶ *You live your life with a lot of "shoulds" and "musts" in mind.* This provides you with a clear set of principles and ideals to guide your choices and actions (and avoid mistakes).

▶ *You place a high value on being ethical, honest, and reliable.* Integrity is very important to you, and you strive to always do your best in everything you do. You may secretly judge others who do not aspire to the same level of quality or good behavior, even though you may also judge yourself for judging them.

▶ *You over-control your emotions and impulses.* Perhaps out of a desire to be responsible and appropriate, you control yourself a lot. You strive to engage in "good" behavior and (perhaps unconsciously) fear spontaneously unleashing your emotions and impulses would lead you to engage in bad behavior.

▶ *You can sometimes appear opinionated or self-righteous.* When you feel strongly about something, you tend to express yourself in ways that others may view as inflexible or dogmatic, but you can't help thinking that you are just telling the truth or voicing what you know is right.

▶ *Work has to come before play.* It feels hard to relax and allow yourself to have fun if you haven't fulfilled all your duties and responsibilities.

▶ *You believe in self-improvement.* You consider it important to always try to do your best and make things (and potentially yourself) more perfect.

▶ *You often believe there is one right way to do something, which is your way.* You enjoy the challenge of finding the best way to do something. Once you find the right way, you want to do it your way, since it is the best way, and you may become irritated if others don't agree.

▶ *It feels amazing when it's perfect.* You feel the loveliest sense of peace and well-being inside—more viscerally than emotionally—on those rare occasions when something you do or see feels absolutely perfect.

The Central Adaptive Strategy of the Type One Personality Style

Early in life, many Ones experience pressure to be good or responsible or to do things the "right way" according to an outside authority, followed by criticism when they aren't "good enough" or don't do it "right." In response, they unconsciously adopt a coping strategy that internalizes that external critical voice, and then monitor and criticize themselves to enforce good behavior. People with a Type One style are people who tried to be "good" boys and girls, who mostly follow the rules, who want things to be perfect, and who always make an effort to "do the right thing."

Ones adapt to their environment by making sure that they are working hard to do things "the right way," being good (in a moral sense), and trying to be perfect (to reduce the possibility of further criticism). They preemptively defuse potential critics on the outside by proactively criticizing themselves on the inside. By "beating others to the punch" when it comes to finding fault in their own behavior, Ones can relax a little, because they believe their proactive self-control will protect them from the (potentially painful) surprise attack of criticism from others.

Ones report experiencing a deep sensation of well-being when something they do meets their high standards of quality or perfection. Though it often eludes them, they continually seek this deep sense of inner satisfaction by constantly striving to be "perfect." When that high target can't be reached, they at least need to know they did their best and tried as hard as possible. Because of this relentless focus on perfection, it is often hard for them to appreciate the good they do, understand that few things are ever perfect, and see their considerable efforts as "good enough."

What Do Ones Pay Attention To? The Type One "Radar Screen"

The strategy of monitoring themselves to be responsible, do the "right" thing, and improve things focuses Ones' attention on determining what the right thing is and how they can do that right thing. Ones naturally envision the "perfect" and notice how what is happening measures up to their ideal of quality (or not). Thus, their attention typically goes to detecting errors and correcting them, knowing the rules and following guidelines of proper behavior, and avoiding bad behavior and mistakes. Ones focus a lot of attention on judging how well or poorly they are doing whatever they do, as well as whether the people around them are doing the right things, and how those things could be refined or improved.

At work, Type Ones are very results-oriented, rational, and logical. They focus on working hard to do a good job and making sure others are doing their part. They may be concerned with how others are falling short and holding people accountable to make sure they are following the proper guidelines and doing the work they are responsible for.

Ones also focus attention on the details and processes that structure work so that all the little things get done well and according to the right procedures. They appreciate rules and structure because rules and structure provide information about how work should be done and how people are held accountable. And as leaders, they have a talent for seeing what structures are needed and knowing how to provide structure to help things go more smoothly.

The View from "Planet One": How Ones See the World

Generally, individuals with a Type One style want very much to make the world a better place and often dedicate themselves to social causes or movements. Ones can be like "moral white knights," unselfishly working to improve life in different ways, often getting involved in efforts like curing diseases, protecting the environment, and educating the poor. They notice what's wrong in the world and feel driven to fix it—both as a natural consequence of automatically seeing the flaws in how things are and because they feel responsible for (and satisfied by) doing good.

Ones believe in the social compact: they think that if everyone would just follow the rules of civilized society, everything would run smoothly. When they perceive that others are not doing the right thing—not doing their jobs the way they should, or failing to follow the rules or proper procedures—they can be critical and even punitive. This is because for Ones, if you are not doing what you are supposed to do, you are doing something wrong. And if you are doing something wrong, you should admit it or be called out and censured so you can reform your bad behavior. However, when people admit to their failings, Ones can be very forgiving, believing that people who are willing to admit their mistakes deserve compassion.

Their clear inner sense of right and wrong, and good and bad, may mean Ones see things in terms of absolute, black and white categories. They tend to think it's good to be good—or to try their best to be good—and it's bad to be bad, to make mistakes, or to act immorally. They believe certain behaviors are categorically wrong, such as lying, cheating, acting selfishly, or engaging in corruption of one form or another. And while many Type Ones learn over time to see shades of grey and forgive people's moral failings, they tend to focus on whether someone has integrity and may judge people they view as "morally flexible."

The Type One Leader: Core Characteristics

The following character traits help to define the Type One leadership style:

- ▶ *Conscientious and concerned with integrity.* Ones are methodical, detail-oriented, and ethical. They tend to be moral people who follow the rules.

- ▶ *Tendency to be judgmental.* Not only do Ones judge almost everything they do in terms of how perfect it is according to an inner ideal of quality, they may also criticize and judge others.

- ▶ *"One right way" of thinking.* Ones often think they know *"the* right way" to do something, and if you believe you know *the* right way, you want to do it your way. Therefore, it can be difficult for Ones to adapt to others' ways of doing things.

▶ *Control and over-control (and micromanaging).* Because Ones think they know the best way to accomplish a task, they want to be in control of how work gets done. This can help everyone meet high standards of quality, but can also cause people to feel micromanaged, even when the One sincerely intends to be helpful and supportive.

▶ *Results-oriented.* High-quality results feel like a personal "must" for Ones—a reflection of their integrity or personal character. They tend to focus on whether their efforts produce the kind of results they strive to create and can work very hard to make sure their work product matches their high standards.

▶ *Hard to please.* Ones want everything they do or touch to be the best—which can be both a professional strength and a potential stressor. Their clear vision of quality can inspire, but it may be hard for them to realize that setting the bar so high can be unrealistic or stressful. It also means Ones may have difficulty delegating (when they perceive others won't do it as well as they will).

▶ *Virtuousness (being good and avoiding blame).* "Being good" and focusing on what is virtuous or moral provides Ones with a set of guidelines they rely on to get along in the world. They believe if they are doing the right thing and following the rules, no one can criticize or blame them for anything.

▶ *Perfectionism and criticality.* Trying to make things perfect is a way for Ones to prove their worthiness while improving everything for everyone. If they can see it, they want to achieve it. However, this focus on perfection sometimes fuels them to be hypercritical, and perfection is often not possible or desirable or readily achievable.

Mental, Emotional, and Behavioral Patterns: Why Do Ones Think, Feel, and Behave the Way They Do?

Mental

Because the Type One outlook is based on the need to be good, right or perfect, Ones believe that it's their job to make the world a better place through striving for perfection and engaging in virtuous behavior. Although they are "body-based" types whose personality is shaped by an important connection to their kinesthetic sense or "gut knowing," they usually appear highly intellectual. They automatically apply their own high standards to others and the way they conduct themselves, so they often think in terms of "shoulds" and "musts" and may have some rigidly held ideas about what constitutes good and bad behavior. People with a Type One style also believe that work must come before pleasure, so it is often hard for them to relax before all their work is done.

Emotional

The One personality is fundamentally shaped by the experience of anger, both as a result of their early, natural response to outside pressure to "be good" and their perception that the rest of the world doesn't act from that same pressure. But because they think expressing anger (and other emotions) is "bad," they tend to hold back and over-control angry feelings. They tend to experience an inner conflict with regard to their anger. As a result, sometimes these feelings leak out in pressurized forms like irritation, frustration, resentment, or self-righteousness. At other times, Ones' belief in the virtue of "right behavior" may lead them to express emotions that are the opposite of what they are actually feeling—so if a One is mad at you, he may appear excessively polite. In psychological terms, this is called "reaction formation," a defense mechanism that automatically helps someone avoid feeling one emotion by magically turning it into its opposite. This tendency to repress or overcontrol their feelings also means Ones may inadvertently avoid good feelings when repressing the "negative" feelings they fear.

Behavioral

The endless quest to make things right or perfect can lead to work habits that make Ones effective and successful. However, it can also result in procrastination, as Ones may put off finishing or turning in work because it's not perfect enough. Ones may engage in passive-aggressive behaviors that reflect the fact that they feel angry inside, but don't want to acknowledge or express it. They may appear rigid and inflexible, go silent, or withdraw but implicitly communicate a mood of tension, resentment, or irritation. While they may think they are successfully containing and hiding their annoyance, it shows up in their non-verbal behavior, as tightness in their face and body or a frustrated tone of voice.

The Main Strengths and Superpowers of the Type One Style: What Ones Are Really Good At

- ▶ *Doing the right thing.* Ones almost always focus on doing what's correct. They take the high road. This makes Ones responsible, reliable, trustworthy, and dependable.

- ▶ *Being ethical and responsible.* Type Ones believe everyone should act according to socially agreed upon standards.

- ▶ *Working hard and being improvement- and detail-oriented.* Types Ones are motivated by a deep desire to achieve an ideal of perfection in themselves and everything they do.

- ▶ *Quality control.* It is a baseline assumption and a core value for Ones that the things they do should be done right. They are very good at providing a roadmap for achieving excellence.

- ▶ *Creating process and structures (that support work and productivity).* Ones are good at providing clarity. They are clear thinkers who see when there is a need for structure and they excel at providing it. This quality helps assure that things will be done in the right way, according to clear expectations and precise plans.

- ▶ *Making significant, well-intentioned efforts.* My brother is a One, and while his wife may have some complaints about some of his behaviors, she often says, with great affection, "No one tries harder than he does."

When Too Much of a Good Thing Becomes a Bad Thing: How Ones Can Go Wrong When They Try Too Hard to Be Right

Like all people of all types, when Type One leaders overuse their biggest strengths (and don't consciously develop a wider range of specialties), they can also turn out to be their Achilles' heel.

- ▶ *Doing the right thing.* Ones can become rigid and unyielding about their way being the *only* right way and may not see that there may be other ways of doing things that are equally good or better.

- ▶ *Being ethical and responsible.* Ones can stress themselves out by working too hard and become resentful of coworkers they perceive as not working hard enough.

▶ *Working hard through being improvement- and detail-oriented.* Type Ones may think they need to keep the pressure to improve on—that if they aren't constantly criticizing, everything will fall apart—but their unrelenting criticism can create a negative work environment in which people feel micromanaged.

▶ *Quality control.* Ones can focus on an ideal of perfection that is not realistic and push for impossible or undesirable standards, which can result in missing deadlines, overstressing themselves, and pressuring colleagues in unreasonable ways.

▶ *Creating process and structures (that support work and productivity).* However helpful those guidelines may be, they may also lead Ones to prioritize routine over spontaneity and inadvertently stifle innovation, enthusiasm, and creativity.

▶ *Making significant, well-intentioned efforts.* While my Type One brother almost always operates from a genuine intention to help others and do the right thing, he can sometimes get pushy, argumentative, impatient, or judgmental when he puts too much pressure on himself to get everything right or enlighten others about their errors and imperfections.

Fortunately, Ones' sincere interest in self-improvement can mean they are open to seeing the downside of some of their personality tendencies. They will often make good use of constructive feedback to correct themselves, even when the needed course correction means recognizing when the problem is being too focused on what is correct.

"When I'm stressed…" and "At my best…": Understanding the "Low Side" and the "High Side" of the Type One Personality Style

When stressed to the point of going to their "low side," Type Ones are less able to manage their habitual reactions and can seem critical, harsh, and judgmental. They may be unaware of their anger and the impact of their angry feelings, and are sometimes rigid and inflexible. Since Ones are naturally detail-oriented and perfectionistic, when they are under pressure they may worry that other people can't be trusted to do things right. They may have a hard time collaborating, delegating, and trusting that their coworkers are capable of matching their high standards. And then they can become resentful that they take more responsibility than others for doing the work in the right way. Meanwhile, their coworkers may experience them as control freaks who want to micromanage every little thing.

Type Ones acting from the lower side of the consciousness spectrum may become self-righteous, insisting that others conform to their view of good behavior and assuming that everyone "should" be judged (or punished) for their bad behavior. In line with this, stressed-out, overly defensive Ones may focus a great deal of attention on whether other people are doing what they should be doing, and can blame others excessively for what they see as wrong or imperfect.

On the "high side," when Type One leaders do the work of being self-aware and conscious, they can be supportive, admirable, inspiring, funny, and even heroic. Ones strive to be virtuous, and they are often deeply good people with the best intentions and little "ego"—they want to do a good job for the sake of doing a good job and don't care if they get the credit or "look good." (Though it would be nice if people acknowledged them when they are right or do something perfectly.)

Emotionally intelligent Ones temper their seriousness about quality and standards with humor and levity. They dedicate themselves to the things they do fully and display a strong commitment to hard work and the success of the team or organization, but they can moderate their need to be right and listen to others deeply. Personal growth work teaches Type Ones to be in touch with their anger, not judge themselves for it, and channel it constructively. When Ones are more aware of their tendencies and live from the high side of their personality style, they can laugh at themselves, soothe their inner-critic, and have compassion for themselves and others.

The Three Kinds of One Leaders: How the Three Instinctual Biases Shape the Three Type One Subtype Personalities

According to the Enneagram model, we all have three main instinctual drives that help us survive, but in each of us, one tends to dominate our behavior. The Type One style is expressed differently depending on whether a person has a dominant bias toward *self-preservation*, establishing *social* relationships and position in relation to groups, or *one-to-one* bonding.

The Self-Preservation (or Self-Focused) One

While the Type One style is often described as "perfectionistic," the Self-Preservation One is the true perfectionist among the three kinds of Ones. Motivated by fear about stability and security, the Self-Preservation One is the One that worries and frets the most. These Ones are often the most responsible person in their family, even from a young age, and develop a habit of wanting to control everything, usually because they feel like their survival or well-being is at stake. They can be ultra-responsible and super-competent, but also tend to feel anxious about things going right. They may work too hard, pay too much attention to every little detail of everything they do, and try to fix things that don't need fixing.

While Self-Preservation Ones are the most self-critical of the three Ones, they tend to be warm, friendly, and kind to others. They hold back their anger the most of the three Ones and may not be very conscious of feeling it at all. However, they tend to be angry underneath, and that anger may leak out as resentment, irritation, or self-righteousness, or be held as tension in their bodies. Self-Preservation Ones see themselves as being very imperfect and in need of improvement and are less critical and more forgiving of others' faults and mistakes.

As leaders, Self-Preservation Ones tend to be gentle, benevolent, funny, and appreciative of people's efforts. When less self-aware, they may want to micromanage everything and wear themselves down from the inside through their harsh and relentless self-criticism. They may also criticize others excessively and believe that people are intentionally doing things wrong and should therefore be punished (after all, don't they really know better?). When healthy, Self-Preservation Ones lead through modeling a high ideal of hard work and dedication. They tend to be tireless in their efforts to produce the best possible outcomes, do the best job they possibly can on everything they do, and support others in thoughtful ways.

The Social (or Group-Focused) One

In contrast to the Self-Preservation One, who feels very not-perfect and so actively strives to be more perfect, the Social Ones act as if they are perfect already, as if they have studied how to do things the right way and can relax a bit because they found the best, "rightest" way to do the things they do.

These Ones not only try to learn and do things the right or perfect way, they automatically take on the role of showing others what they have learned. This gives Social Ones a teacher mentality, and while this can lead the people around them to perceive them as taking a superior position to others (and in some ways they are), this motive usually remains unconscious, as Social Ones want to be seen as good and wouldn't want to intentionally assert that they are better than other people.

Social Ones are intellectual types and are usually very knowledgeable. They also hold back their anger, but instead of appearing warm, like the Self-Preservation One, they can be cool or cold, in line with their more intellectual way of relating. While most Social Ones try not to express anger, they do express a kind of anger in needing to be the "Owner of the Truth" (as in knowing the right or perfect way), and they can explode periodically when triggered.

As leaders, Social Ones can enjoy and take pride in helping others through modeling good behavior and the best way to do things. They tend to like researching the perfect way to do something and teaching others how to perform at their best. However, when they are less self-aware, they may become angry or frustrated if people aren't doing things "the right way," or ignoring or rejecting their efforts to enlighten them. Others may perceive the unaware Social Ones as acting superior, viewing them as "know-it-alls" who patronize or argue with others who don't acknowledge their expertise. When healthy, Social Ones can be humble, thoughtful, responsible, and intelligent. They typically serve as inspiring mentors and supporters who guide others with the best of intentions to do their best work in the best way possible.

The One-to-One (or Relationship-Focused) One

One-to-One Ones focus their energy and attention on perfecting other people—they are less critical of themselves and more critical of others. More reformers than perfectionists, they often zealously try to improve society and the people around them, from their community to their colleagues to their significant others.

This One is the most openly angry of the Type Ones, although the anger can often be expressed as passion, zeal or energetic support of a cause. One-to-One Ones can be more demanding of others than the other types of Ones—they may insist on their needs being met, as if they are entitled to special treatment because they are aligned with a higher moral calling or position. One-to-One Ones can also be good at lobbying or evangelizing for the things they believe in.

As leaders, One-to-One Ones bring lots of energy to a cause or professional effort. They can work tirelessly to enact reforms or create change or engage in a campaign they think will improve others or the social environment. When less self-aware, One-to-One Ones can be entitled, heavy-handed, and harsh. While claiming the moral high ground, they can blame others for what's wrong, while (unconsciously) absolving themselves of fault and ignoring their own mistakes. Some One-to-One Ones actually focus so much on what others need to do to reform their behavior that they engage in bad behavior on the sly—as a way to get their needs met while releasing themselves from the burden of their own excessive (internal) moral pressure. Enneagram experts call this the "trap door" One.

When healthy, however, One-to-Ones can energize others with their strong beliefs, endless zeal, and moral ambitions. Like Gandhi, they can quite literally change the world through their vision, their principles, and their efforts. They can push an agenda and empower others in the strongest possible way behind a cause they believe in or to meet a societal need.

The Type One at Work

Type Ones sometime feel like working with others is hard because:

- ▶ They might not do it as well as I want them to. They may not share my high standards. It can be hard to trust others to do the job the right way.

- ▶ Sometimes I assume somebody else won't do the job the right way, so it's easier to do it myself. This can lead to me working harder (and longer hours) than others, and then feeling resentful.

- ▶ Others may not like structure or respect the rules, routines and processes as much as I do. When this happens, others may engage in what I see as "bad behavior," which can lead to me judging them.

- ▶ It's hard not to judge my colleagues when I see so clearly that everything would be better for all of us if we all followed the rules and strived harder for quality.

- ▶ Sometimes when I try to help others by giving them constructive feedback, they perceive it as criticism. My intention is only to help, but my input sometimes gets experienced as harsh and judgmental.

> ▶ I tend to believe we should approach problems in a logical, rational way, and that it's unproductive to share my feelings. But this can sometimes lead to my intentions being misunderstood.

Type Ones' workplace pet peeves may be:

> ▶ When people break the rules.

> ▶ When people litter or don't clean up after themselves.

> ▶ When people violate what I view as courteous behavior, such as arriving late to meetings (consistently) or turning work in after the deadline, or not saying please, thank you, or sorry.

> ▶ When people behave in a way that is inconsiderate of others.

> ▶ When people don't follow established processes and procedures.

> ▶ When people make excuses instead of taking responsibility for their mistakes.

> ▶ When mistakes are not corrected and therefore get repeated over and over again

> ▶ When people act unethically or irresponsibly

> ▶ When people don't park right between the lines—when they behave in ways that have a negative impact on others and don't realize what they are doing and correct their behavior

> ▶ When people don't acknowledge my competence or capacities

Here's What Type Ones Can Do to Be Easier to Work With

As leaders, Ones can clearly spell out the standards they apply to evaluate the people they work with, taking care to remember that their standards may be higher than average. They can communicate expectations clearly, and provide clear processes for holding people accountable and celebrating successes while measuring what needs improvement. They can have compassion for people, understand that different kinds of people have different ways of doing things, and try to forgive people for their minor indiscretions.

Most of all, One leaders can benefit from taking into account their own biases and preferences and realizing that not all types of people have the critical eye for detail or the drive to make things right (or perfect) that they do. It will also help them enormously if they can become more aware of their own anger and reactions and learn how to own and express their feelings more consciously.

As subordinates, it helps Ones to understand that others don't necessarily value rules and processes the way they do. It can help them to be aware of feelings of resentment that might arise and give themselves some space to understand the source of these feelings and how best to channel them. Learning to communicate openly about the things that bother them, to make an effort to take some things more lightly and to be more flexible when teaming with others will also make a Type One's work life much easier.

Working with Ones

Typical Type One Behaviors in the Workplace

You *might* be working with someone who has a Type One Enneagram style if you see them doing several of the following behaviors on a regular basis:

- ▶ *He's the guy who keeps insisting that people follow rules and procedures.*
- ▶ *She expresses irritation or resentment if people do not behave according to ideals of good behavior such as being punctual, turning things in on time, or acting ethically.*
- ▶ *He works to make sure expectations, instructions, and communications are precise and planned out.*
- ▶ *She sometimes micromanages and doesn't always trust that others can do the job as well as she can.*
- ▶ *He wants to make sure the work is being done in the best way possible, according to clear and precise ethical standards. He speaks out against practices that seem fraudulent, insincere, or dishonest.*
- ▶ *She can seem tense or angry, but doesn't readily talk about what's bothering her.*
- ▶ *He can focus or over-focus (in your opinion) on the details.*
- ▶ *She can be very critical and at times even harsh, though she may not be aware of the effect of her criticism.*
- ▶ *At his best, he can be funny, but is often serious, especially about getting things done right.*
- ▶ *At her best, she inspires the team to achieve high standards of quality through her sincere desire to improve the product, the company, or the world.*

What's Great about Working with Conscious One Leaders

▶ They have a great work ethic and will try hard to do their best in everything they do.

▶ They want to contribute their best effort, but don't usually have big egos so they don't need to take all of the credit.

▶ They can work independently and strive to be self-sufficient.

▶ They can be objective and diligent problem-solvers.

▶ Most of the time, they are well intentioned and sincerely want to do a good job.

▶ When others admit to mistakes, they can be very forgiving and understanding (especially if they know you did your best).

▶ They have a strong sense of morality and ethics, and so (most of the time) respect authority and do the right thing. They don't easily fall prey to the temptations of self-interest and corruption.

Typical Challenges for People Who Work with Ones

▶ They seem mad, but they aren't saying anything.

▶ When they do get mad, they can be self-righteous and unbending.

▶ They withdraw and don't communicate—they give you the silent treatment.

▶ They get tense and seem stressed when discussing a point of disagreement.

▶ They criticize or judge you, your work or the things you are doing (a lot).

▶ They don't allow for the possibility that you may be more right than they are every once in a while.

▶ They insist that you do it their way and aren't open to multiple or better options.

▶ They don't trust you to do as good a job as they think they can.

▶ They can be rigid and inflexible when it comes to following rules and adhering to proper procedures.

▶ They can take the moral high ground in debates and so assume they are right.

Type Ones and Leadership

A Type One Leader Speaks About How Knowing Your Enneagram Type Helps You at Work

Chris Houlder is chief information security officer at Autodesk Inc., a software company based in San Francisco that makes software for the architecture, engineering, construction, manufacturing, media, and entertainment industries.

"When I got introduced to the Enneagram, I assumed it was another Myers-Briggs. But when I heard the description of my type [Type One] it was as if someone had been following me around my entire life, recording my life. Not just recording my actions, but being able to really understand the 'why' behind what I was doing. For me it was it was a profound experience.

"The insights I gathered about myself and my type were valuable, and the insights I gathered about other people were equally or more valuable.

"One of the specific insights I had about myself as a One was getting a better understanding of the inner-critic. I thought everyone had that. I thought that was a normal and natural thing for everyone. I didn't have a very strong understanding that the inner-critic was a process that was running and that it wasn't me, because it uses the same voice. It's in my head, but it's not actually me, it's not the true me. And so that was interesting. Spending some time understanding the motivation of the inner-critic was important—what it's working to actually achieve.

"My original approach was, 'I'm going to beat the crap out of the inner-critic; I'm going to show this guy.' But I realized that that's not the right approach—that gives even more power to the inner-critic. It's more about trying to understand it and see the value in it, asking, 'How do I partner with it without being overly influenced by what the inner-critic is trying to achieve for its purposes?'

"What I worked on from a skill development perspective was delegation. At first I took a very head-centered approach: Let me learn how to delegate. How do I track it? What should I delegate? Why should I delegate it? And it wasn't working. So then I sat down with a coach and she asked, 'What does 80 percent look like to you, and when do you tell people that 80 percent is okay?' I didn't have language for that. I didn't

understand that. I understood the question, but I didn't understand how somebody could answer that because my response was, 'How could you take pride in your work if there's an opportunity to do more? Why would you ever come up 20% short on a deliverable?'

"That was eye-opening for me with regard to my own work. I've always phrased it as the 'pursuit' of perfection. It's not that I expect perfection, but the pursuit of perfection gets excellence. As a leader that translated into, 'If that's my expectation for myself, that's clearly going to be the expectation that I have for others, and if I don't feel like they can do that, then it reduces my level of trust.'

"The biggest thing I struggle with today as a One is 'virtuous anger.' It's about curbing the 'virtuous anger,' where if I feel like I'm truly on the side of right and not being heard, then my anger feels justified."

When You Are the Manager and You Are a One

People who have a Type One personality style make great natural leaders when they can consciously support high standards and produce high-quality results without being too critical or overly controlling.

If you are a One, you may feel uncomfortable in leadership roles, because you typically aren't motivated by a need for power or recognition. Your leadership style tends to rely on creating good plans, designating responsibility for each step, and putting processes in place to assure that standards of quality are met or exceeded. It can be hard for you to ignore or accept when people don't do things correctly or act irresponsibly or unethically, but you will try not to express your feelings of anger or dissatisfaction directly. As a Type One leader, you may struggle to handle situations in which people are not performing, and you may criticize others in a way that demoralizes rather than motivates them while holding a conscious intention to help them. You will usually suppress their own desires to get the job done, and will set a high bar for the level of work and diligence they expect from others.

When Your Manager Is a One

The great thing about having a Type One as a boss is that you can trust that their intentions are good—they will usually try to do the right thing and treat you with respect and thoughtfulness, especially when they are emotionally healthy. They can be dedicated to good causes, have a high level of personal integrity, work hard to support others, and act as good role models. They make excellent, natural teachers, because they typically have a sincere desire to inform and help people succeed through understanding the best ways to do things.

If your boss is a less self-aware Type One, they may do too much of the work themselves, while simultaneously getting mad at you for not pulling your weight. They may criticize and judge a lot, but not realize the demoralizing effect this has on you. And they may freeze you out at times and avoid telling you what they are thinking and feeling if they judge that you can't do something right. Finally, they may not put enough thought and energy into delegation or succession planning, as they may not be comfortable giving up the reins and passing on the responsibility for guiding work processes. It may be hard for them to believe that others can do it right and be as responsible as they are, which can have the effect of undermining others' efforts.

When your Type One boss is a more conscious leader, they find ways to provide constructive feedback that supports improvement without focusing too much of their attention on mistakes and imperfections. They can channel their desire for quality in ways that inspire people to do their best. And they model the good behavior they expect from their employees by striving always to be fair, humble, considerate, and responsible.

When Your Subordinate Is a One

When your direct reports have a Type One style, they may project their own inner-critic onto you (their boss) and imagine you are criticizing them when you are not. If you give them both positive and negative feedback, they may only hear the negative and ignore the positive, or forget it even happened.

They may try hard to please you by doing good work, and silently resent you if you don't recognize their efforts and good intentions sufficiently. They may work too hard (even if you don't ask them to or ask them not to) and then become angry or irritated when others aren't doing as much as they are.

They may be too detail-oriented and not get things done in a timely fashion, but have a hard time seeing this as a problem since they think the top priority is getting it right or making it perfect—no matter how long it takes. It may be hard for them to see or accept when something is "good enough."

On the plus side, they respect the chain of command and readily obey and appreciate a good authority. They place a high value on working hard, solving tough problems, and being diligent in the things they do. They tend to be reliable, trustworthy, and dependable. They can be very loyal and dedicated, especially if you recognize them for their efforts and high ideals.

Getting Along with Ones: Tips for What to Do to Work Well with Ones

▶ *Be clear and precise.* Ones believe working together to get things right means being clear about goals, processes, and who's responsible for what and how they will be held accountable.

▶ *If you make a mistake, admit it and take responsibility.* This inspires trust and assures them that you will come forward and own and fix whatever you do wrong. Ones don't like mistakes, but they can forgive people who take responsibility for them.

▶ *Demonstrate that you value quality.* Ones will feel more comfortable collaborating with you if you are aligned around this central goal.

▶ *Have compassion for their drive for perfection.* Understanding Ones' need to get things right and the pressure they put on themselves to be perfect can help you recognize what motivates them to hold themselves and others to high standards. It may also help you be patient with them if they get tense or resentful.

▶ *Understand their tendency to criticize and empathize with how hard they can be on themselves.* If you need to deliver critical feedback to a One, remember how much they want to do quality work and that they are already very tough on themselves internally.

▶ *Emphasize positive feedback (and deliver constructive criticism very gently).* Ones will feel supported if you can help them really hear it when you want to communicate how well they did something. When offering constructive criticism, it will lessen the blow if you also mention their strengths.

Actionable Growth Tasks and Suggestions: How Type Ones Can Become More Self-Aware, Effective, and Happy at Work

All the types can learn to be less reactive and better at collaborating with others through first *observing* their habitual patterns, then thinking about the things they think, feel, and do to gain more *self-insight*, and then making efforts to *manage* or moderate their automatic reactions to key triggers.

When Ones can watch what they do enough to "catch themselves in the act" of doing the things that get them in trouble, and then pause and reflect on what they are doing and why, they can gradually learn to moderate their programming and knee-jerk responses.

In general, Ones grow through observing and learning to moderate their habitual reactions to key triggers like mistakes (their own and others'), "bad" behavior, and the obstacles they encounter while trying to meet their own high standards. Here are some ideas to help Ones be more self-aware, more emotionally intelligent, and more satisfied at work.

Self-Observation: Things for Ones to Watch Out For

▸ *Try to notice when you are being too hard on yourself. Notice when the costs outweigh the benefits of self-criticism.*

▸ *Try to own your anger. Notice if your anger rises but if you judge it, push it down or rationalize why you shouldn't be angry. Notice what happens to your angry feelings if you try to suppress them or talk yourself out of them.*

▸ *Notice if you rationalize your anger as "virtuous anger." Under what conditions do you get self-righteous or hold onto your angry feelings because you are right?*

▸ *Observe how you react in the face of positive feedback. Is it hard to take in? How do you handle compliments?*

▸ *Notice how you deal with things not being perfect. How do you put pressure on yourself and others to do everything right all the time—even when it's clear that achieving perfection is impossible?*

▸ *As a leader, notice what gets in the way of delegating. Do you trust others to meet your high standards?*

▸ *How do you relate to rules, processes and structure? Can you break the rules? What happens when other people break the rules or operate outside established procedures? How do you react? Can you lighten up?*

Blind Spots: What You Don't Know Can Hurt You!

Becoming conscious and aware of these blind spots can help Type Ones be less defensive, more open to feedback from others, and more peaceful and content through being more fully aware of all that they think, feel, and do.

What blind spots Ones often don't see in themselves:

▶ *The presence and impact of anger.* Ones often think, "I'm not angry" at the same time they are talking with a clenched jaw, or tightening every muscle in their body, or using a tone of voice that drips with annoyance. By noticing how they defend against feeling their anger, Ones can learn to be more open to understanding it and consciously channel it in productive ways that don't undermine their effectiveness or their happiness.

▶ *Overdoing criticism and the impact it has on others.* Becoming aware of and moderating their inner critic helps Ones to be less sensitive to criticism from other people (which can feel like "piling on"), and to recognize and adjust how much they focus on the negative (what they see as needing improvement) while avoiding taking in what's positive. When Ones offer criticism to others, while they usually intend only to help and support them, they sometimes fail to realize how much anger they are holding back, or that they sometimes hurt and undermine the very people they aim to help.

▶ *The downside of self-criticism.* Ones often believe they need to be tough on themselves to make sure they engage in good behavior and avoid mistakes or blame. However, they may not see how much damage their self-criticism does to their self-confidence. Instead of "keeping themselves in line," they may be undermining their sense of their own inherent goodness.

▶ *The repression of feelings and impulses.* People with a One style often claim they don't experience a lot of emotion—they tend to be practical, pragmatic and sensible. However, the degree to which they stifle their naturally occurring emotions and impulses may prevent them from drawing important information from what they feel and want.

▶ *Rigidity and "one-right-way" thinking.* Ones may not notice that other people perceive their insistence on adhering to certain "right ways" of doing things as rigid. It is important for Ones to remember that different people view rules and procedures differently, that there can be more than one "right" way to complete a task, and that being open to adapting to others can create more positive and fruitful working relationships.

▶ *The need for relaxation, pleasure, play, fun.* The habit of not acknowledging the value of rest and relaxation can be very dangerous for Ones. Their drive to be good and prove their worth through hard work can lead to working too hard and putting too much pressure on themselves.

Self-Insight: Things for Ones to Think About, Understand, and Explore

▶ *Why do you go overboard in criticizing yourself or others? What drives that?*

▶ *What kinds of things cause you to feel angry? Why do you react the way you do? Are there times when you are angry but you don't know you're angry?*

▶ *Why do you value structure and processes? What do they do for you?*

▶ *Where do your high standards come from? Why are they so high?*

▶ *Why does work have to come before play? Where does your sense of responsibility come from? Can you relax it?*

▶ *Why is it so important to be right? Why is it so important to avoid making mistakes? What happens when you are wrong?*

▶ *What feels challenging when it comes to things like delegating and succession planning? Why?*

▶ *How can you develop more compassion for yourself?*

Strengths to Leverage

It helps Ones to be aware of, actively pay attention to, fully own, and leverage:

▶ *Their dedication to working hard to do good in the world.* I tease my Type One father that he is the quintessential "do-gooder." While they have a tendency to be self-critical, Ones feel motivated and confident when they can consciously own the positive effects of the good they do in the world and the good people they are.

▶ *Their high level of personal integrity.* Ones are people others can count on to do the right thing and who often contribute to an enterprise by being the conscience of the organization.

▶ *Their high standards of quality.* This can help Ones realize that they play an important role in advocating for excellence.

▶ *Their strong sense of responsibility.* Ones will seldom leave early, shirk their duties, or try to get away with doing less than a very good job on something.

▶ *Their good intentions and extreme efforts.* Ones can defend against their inner-critics by remembering that they tend to give their best effort in nearly everything they do.

▶ *Clear thinkers who provide clarity and supportive structures.* Ones are very good at communicating complex ideas in simple language, seeing where structure is needed and building it in.

Self-Management: Challenging Tendencies for Ones to Moderate

▶ *Needing to be right.* It will be vital for you to really question if it's always so important to be right. It may help to remember this question: "Is it more important to you to be right or to be happy?" Notice when you choose being right over being happy.

▶ *Seeing things in terms of black and white.* Many Ones know intellectually reality is more about shades of grey. But in practice, and in the heat of the moment, sometimes Ones forget this—and it can be good to remember to help you reduce rigidity and impatience.

▶ *Being overly critical of yourself or others.* Notice when the inner- or outer-critic is out of control. It can be painful to watch Ones punishing themselves when they are trying so hard and doing so well. When Ones can consciously ease up on themselves and show themselves compassion, they can free up a lot of energy.

▶ *Working too hard to make things perfect.* The reality is, most things are imperfect, and "good enough" is often exactly that. It can be liberating for Ones to learn they don't have to drive themselves (and others) crazy chasing impossible standards when they don't have to.

▶ *Rigidity around rules and processes.* Ones can tend to think that everyone knows the rules and see them the same way they do—the only way to see rules, as guidelines defining exactly what to do! But, it helps Ones if they remember that people really don't see rules and procedures the same way they do, so they aren't misbehaving when they don't follow them—they just have a different perspective and are likely focusing on something else.

▶ *Righteous anger and resentment.* Allow yourself to feel, understand, and work with your anger more. Anger doesn't go away just because you don't acknowledge it—and unacknowledged anger has an impact. It helps Ones to learn to befriend their anger as a sign that something important is getting triggered that needs attention.

Consciously Manifesting Your Higher Potential: Being Aware of the "Low Side" and Aiming for the "High Side"

Ones can also grow through consciously becoming aware of the self-limiting habits and patterns associated with their personality style and learning to embody the higher aspects or more expansive capacities of the Type One personality:

▶ Learn to accept and work through angry emotions so you can find more peace and serenity in your everyday experience.

▶ Observe how you can limit yourself by focusing too narrowly on one right way or "the perfect" outcome and practice opening up to many right ways and the beauty in the imperfect or the unexpected.

▶ Notice if you are viewing things in a "black and white" way and allow for more shades of gray.

- ▸ Observe when the defense mechanism of reaction formation is happening—notice when you act and speak in a way that's contrary to how you really feel. Then practice getting in touch with the truth of your emotion and finding ways to express it honestly.

- ▸ Notice how you can slip into a serious mood when you are driven to criticize what is happening, and consciously open up to more levity and playfulness. Find ways to use humor more to rise above whatever's bothering you.

- ▸ Recognize what kinds of experiences make you tense and practice relaxing (physically) and finding opportunities for pleasure and fun.

- ▸ Notice how you can get rigid around routines, structure, and processes and practice being more spontaneous and creative.

Overall, Type Ones can fulfill their higher potentials by observing and working against their habit of focusing on how they are failing to meet an ideal standard of perfection. They can learn to be more comfortable with the perfection of their imperfection, have more compassion for themselves, and allow for their sense of lightness and humor to play a larger role in their everyday experience. When they can lean into their higher capacity for fun and relax the need to "be good," they can infuse their life and their leadership with confidence, creativity, and the deep sense of integrity that is so natural to them.

CHAPTER 5

The Type Two Leadership Style
The Power of Pleasing People

"The noblest art is that of making others happy."
> P. T. Barnum, businessman, showman, and politician

"There just isn't any pleasing some people. The trick is to stop trying."
> Robert Mitchum, actor

"Leadership is unlocking people's potential to become better."
> Bill Bradley, basketball player, Rhodes scholar,
> and former U.S. Senator

The Type Two archetype is that prototypical person who wants more than anything to be liked and appear likable. Though sometimes called "the Helper" or "the Giver," these names can actually be misleading, because the Type Two style is not so much about altruistic or universal "giving" as it is about strategic support in the service of establishing friendly alliances and connections. A Two's attention automatically goes to the people around them and how to best forge positive relationships by managing impressions and interactions.

A Two's programming tells them that the way to meet their own needs or achieve success is to be liked by as many people as possible, so their style is shaped by a primary focus on how much (or little) people like them and how they might shape-shift, turn on the charm, or offer help to create rapport or ingratiate themselves with others. They can achieve a subtle kind of power through generosity as a way of positioning themselves with important people, although this power motive is usually unconscious. Twos tend to be wired to want to be service-oriented to the point of becoming indispensable to others—and having your help considered "indispensable" can be a potent form of power.

Like everything else they do, Twos try to communicate in ways that will endear them to others. Their speaking style tends to be warm, personal, and amiable. They may focus on the other person to the exclusion of themselves and ask a lot of questions to show interest with whomever they interact.[15] They compliment and flatter others as a way of winning them over and discern what others like and give it to them—whether it's attention or privacy or a specific kind of support. They extend their influence and feel a sense of well-being through knowing they are pleasing the people around them.

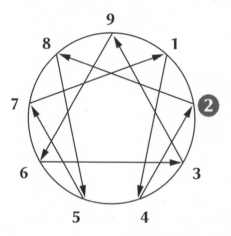

Leaders who have a Type Two style will tend to be empathetic, concerned about the human or "people" aspect of work, and sensitive to people's needs and feelings.

They can specialize in being charming and kind, powerful and competent, or attractive and exciting. But whether they gain influence through generosity and charm or they appeal to others through their drive to connect, they tend to combine a focus on people with an ability to be productive in the service of what is needed most by the team, the organization, or society. They seek to impact tasks, work products, and teams through supporting others, cultivating relationships, empowering people they like, and inspiring coworkers through flattery, warmth, and positive regard.

How to Tell if You Are a Type Two: The View from the Inside

If most or all of the following characteristics apply to you, you may have a Type Two personality style:

▶ *You see the work you do through the lens of your relationships.* You think of work as based on (and happening through) good relationships and seek influence through doing things to gain positive regard, admiration, and approval.

▶ *You are motivated by pleasing, impressing, or wanting to support others.* You work hard, and you want positive feedback that validates your efforts and reassures you that you are doing a good job. Helping seems like the quickest road to being liked and valued.

▶ *You seek to excel so that the important people in your life will think well of you.* It's crucial for you to be appreciated by others—especially others you like or view as important, but also by people you don't like.

▶ *You believe you can make others like you.* You make friends easily, know how to appeal to others, and take pride in the fact that you can win anyone over.

▶ *You are able to relate well to a wide range of people.* You're confident you can establish rapport with anyone you seek to impress or connect with, regardless of rank or position.

▶ *You find satisfaction in being supportive and helpful to others and may occasionally use this as an indirect way to get what you want or need.* As you read this, you may be thinking, *I would never do that!* However, you do think that giving should be mutual and reciprocal. It's also easier for you to give than to receive, and while receiving can be awkward, you will often do things for others in the hope that they will like you or do something in return.

▶ *You place a high value on being considerate, empathetic, and unselfish.* You believe people like people who are easy to get along with. Making others feel comfortable feels natural and important, and it bothers you when others act selfishly or treat people badly.

▶ *You can be emotional or oversensitive and will try to hide your feelings at work.* While you may attempt to hide your emotions (even from yourself) to maintain others' positive regard, sometimes you become so emotional that you can't help expressing it. (Though if you are a guy, you may be more locked down emotionally.)

▶ *You have a talent for sensing the feelings, needs, and preferences of others, but may be unclear on what you need or feel afraid to ask for it, lest you impose on others or risk rejection.* This can lead to people feeling supported by you and appreciating you, but it can also lead to you over-giving and exhausting yourself to the point where you may resent others, especially those who fail to reciprocate.

▶ *It can be hard for you to give candid (and especially critical) feedback.* You empathize with others so much that you worry straightforward constructive criticism will make them feel bad.

▶ *It bothers you (a lot) when someone doesn't like you.* You consider it important to always try to do your best and make things (and potentially yourself) more perfect so that people will evaluate you positively.

▶ *You avoid conflict because you fear it will hurt your relationships, but you will at times feel relieved to get a problem out on the table so you can fix it.* You may also have a hard time expressing contrary opinions because you fear they will alienate others. You may avoid confronting people or actively addressing conflict so that everyone can be happy again.

▶ *You have a natural ability to see the good in others and can truly enjoy helping people manifest their potential.* You can't help loving it when you hear someone say, "We couldn't have done it without you." This usually comes out of an altruistic desire to help and produce positive results, but it can also be a way to assure your value in others' eyes so you can feel good about yourself.

The Central Adaptive Strategy of the Type Two Personality Style

Early on in life, Twos come to believe that love and approval are contingent upon them doing things for people, acting nice, or being who others want them to be. They sometimes have a history of being told that they are "too sensitive" or "too much" or "too emotional," which proves to them that their needs are too much for others or that they must suppress their needs and emotions to be liked.

Motivated by the desire to create positive connections with people, Twos' coping strategy involves sensing and meeting others' needs, pleasing others, and presenting themselves as likable to gain the affection and approval of others. They become adept at emphasizing parts of themselves they think people they want to impress will like and downplaying the parts they think will interfere with establishing a connection. They worry about the potential disapproval of others and so try to appear attractive and pleasant so people will want to be around them.

Twos are at their most relaxed and happy when they know others like them or approve of what they are doing or want to connect with them. They read the people they interact with to sense what they like and then try to become what they like to create a positive impression and a friendly rapport. They avoid rejection (which feels intolerable) through being pleasing and easy to be with and not asking too much of people. They tend to gravitate to people they regard as important and become indispensable to those individuals in the hope they will return the favor and meet their needs in a reciprocal fashion. This strategy helps them to get their needs met without having to ask directly (which opens them up to the risk of rejection).

What Do Twos Pay Attention To? The Type Two "Radar Screen"

The strategy of presenting themselves in a way that will please others focuses Twos' attention on other people. They have an automatic and finely tuned radar for picking up the subtle signals that reveal people's moods and preferences, and they use this skill to decide how to manage the impression they are making to ensure they are liked. Often without even thinking about it, they adjust their presentation to match what they believe other people want or need them to be. This focus on shape shifting to orchestrate positive relationships may be so deeply ingrained in the Twos' way of being that they may not even be aware they are doing it.

At work, Twos focus attention on the "people" aspects of the job—how they can best collaborate with, support, and contribute to what people in the organization are doing. Whatever their title or position may be, they focus not only on the work at hand, but also how work tasks and processes affect people, and they have a talent for doing all they can to make sure the relational aspects of work go smoothly.

As a result, Twos can be extremely productive, especially if they like the people they work with. But focusing so much of their attention on other people and attuning so completely to what others are feeling, wanting, or needing means Twos may have no idea what they are feeling, wanting, or needing.

The View from "Planet Two": How Twos See the World

Generally, individuals with a Type Two style want to keep other people happy and improve the experience of their fellow humans. They sincerely like people and usually want to see the best in others (unless they have a reason not to), and when they don't, they are really good at acting like they do. Most of the time, they enjoy interacting with others—they are the "people people" of the Enneagram.

Twos tend to think they need to make everyone like them (by force, if necessary). They believe that there are two kinds of people in the world: those who like them and those who don't know them well enough yet to know that they like them. They feel confident that they are just one charm offensive away from winning everyone over. Twos have many weapons at their disposal to create a positive impression; however, when they fail to forge an alliance or inadvertently piss someone off, they will feel extremely bothered, get self-critical and obsessively second-guess themselves. They tend to look outside themselves to decide how they should feel about things (including themselves), and can think: *If you like me, I'm okay, but if you don't like me, there's something wrong with me.* In the psychology business, we might describe this as having an "external locus of control."

Twos believe in reciprocal giving—*I scratch your back, you scratch mine*—even if this is not always conscious. They believe everyone should help others out and have a hard time saying "no," even to things they don't want to do. They focus more on the people around them than themselves and then have an expectation that others will focus their attention on supporting them. Sometimes this goes well, like when they are generous, selfless, and fun-loving companions and the relationship is mutual. Sometimes it can go badly, like when they neglect themselves and then blame you because you took up so much of their time and attention and didn't give back (even though you didn't ask them—or want them—to give you so much).

The Type Two Leader: Core Characteristics

The following character traits help to define the Type Two leadership style:

▶ *Strategic help to create indispensability.* Giving for Twos isn't always altruistic (though they may want to think it is). It can be a strategy to ensure their position or power or influence. The more you need them, the more secure they feel in the knowledge you won't be able to exclude them.

▶ *Charm and warmth.* Much of the time, Twos will be exceedingly nice because they feel motivated to be liked and accepted and to avoid rejection of any kind. Their charming presentation is usually sincere and authentic, and when it isn't, they might not be aware that they are being false because they are programmed to believe it's good to be nice.

▶ *Empathy and emotional sensitivity.* Twos often readily feel what others are feeling and are willing to listen and offer emotional support without being asked. However, the emotional sensitivity that makes them good friends and partners can also make them take things personally or feel offended when no offense is intended.

▶ *Relationship-oriented.* Relationships are front and center on the Type Two view screen and nurturing important relationships is their top priority. The saying, "It's not what you know, it's who you know" conveys their belief that work gets done through relationships.

▶ *Other-oriented.* Twos pay more attention to what's going on with other people than what might be going on inside themselves. This means they may be more aware of how you are feeling and what you need than how they are feeling and what they need.

▶ *Self-elevation and self-deflation.* Believing they need to be all things to all people means Twos may unknowingly walk around with an inflated sense of who they are and what they can do. If this elevated sense gets punctured by negative feedback, they can feel very hurt, believe they have failed to convey a positive sense of themselves, and may go to the other end of the spectrum and feel quite deflated and bad about themselves.

▶ *Giving with the expectation of reciprocity.* Twos usually believe they give to others without expecting anything in return; in reality, sometimes this is true and sometimes it isn't. Because they are sensitive to rejection, asking someone to meet their needs can feel humiliating, so, Twos sometimes (unconsciously) "give to get." They get generous hoping others will reciprocate and give them what they need without them having to ask directly.

Mental, Emotional, and Behavioral Patterns: Why Do Twos Think, Feel, and Behave the Way They Do?

Mental

Because the Type Two outlook is about forming and enjoying mutually supportive relationships, Twos spend time thinking and strategizing about impression management, the achievement of positive connections, and whether people like them. While they can apply just as much intellectual focus to work tasks as others, the people around them and the important people in their lives are regularly in their thoughts. When they focus mental attention on doing a good (or great) job, this is often motivated by the desire to look good to specific people they want to impress or inspire.

Emotional

Although they sometimes hold back their feelings so their emotions don't repel people they want to attract, Twos are essentially very emotional people. One of three "heart-based types" within the Enneagram system, they tend to react emotionally to things, whether they show it in the moment. People with a Type Two personality style tend to be happy people who may repress their negative feelings to get along with others. They may think that sharing their real feelings of anger or sadness may alienate people who may not be comfortable with shows of emotion, and so they may feel more emotions on the inside than they reveal on the outside. And while Twos tend to be genuinely upbeat people who try to lift the general mood, they often feel sad underneath, as they may be aware of the ways they fall short in their efforts to be liked or appreciated by others. They can also be angry and resentful, especially when people they have supported do not support them in return.

Behavioral

Twos work hard to prove their worth and gain acceptance and approval. They can be driven to support others' success, to accomplish and achieve for their own sense of satisfaction, and to look good to people who matter.

Twos tend to "merge" with others and can feel so connected to or aligned with people they care about that that they can share in (or over-empathize with) their emotional experience. They may work very hard to please their boss or support a favorite coworker, their best friend, or their spouse or children. Since they have a hard time saying "no," they often overwork in an effort to meet all the needs of the people around them. They may also act to orchestrate experiences for others—either to connect people they like, or provide positive experiences for other people, or (and this is a big blind spot for Twos) manipulate someone into giving them something they want, but don't want to ask for directly (because they fear rejection).

The Main Strengths and Superpowers of the Type Two Style: What Twos Are Really Good At

▶ *Energetically supporting others.* Twos can move mountains to help their allies be successful in the things they do.

▶ *Empathically understanding others feelings, needs, and experiences.* Twos excel at being right there to give you exactly what you need right when you need it. They really do feel your pain as well as your triumphs along with you.

▶ *Service orientation.* Twos automatically attune to their audience and have a strong ethic about the value of selfless service. A team that lacks Twos may have a blind spot when it comes to taking full account of the needs of their customers.

▶ *Having fun and lifting the mood.* Twos think, "*What better way to have fun with people and make them want to be around you than to be fun to be around?*"

▶ *Orchestrating positive experiences and connections to please others.* Twos enjoy being the person who connects people, the host of a great party, or the supporter someone couldn't have succeeded without. They like doing powerful things behind the scenes—that way they won't get blamed if things don't go well and they can express their people power in subtle, less risky ways.

▶ *Appreciating what's best in others.* Twos feel enlivened when called upon to help people manifest their gifts and leverage their strengths to be happier and more successful.

When Too Much of a Good Thing Becomes a Bad Thing: How Twos Can Go Wrong When They Try Too Hard to Be Liked

Like all people of all types, when Type Two leaders overuse their biggest strengths (and don't consciously develop a wider range of specialties), they can also turn out to be their Achilles' heel.

▶ *Energetically supporting others' efforts.* Doing too much can leave Twos feeling exhausted, overburdened, and resentful of the people they support for taking up all their time, energy, and attention.

▶ *Empathically understanding others' feelings, needs, and experiences.* It's so easy for Twos to "feel your pain" that they may feel yours more than they can feel their own.

▶ *Service orientation.* Too much focus on meeting others' needs can mean Twos overlook important elements of the bigger picture or neglect their own needs and opinions. When less self-aware, Twos' "selfless service" can lead to playing the martyr if they don't receive the support they want from others.

▶ *Having fun and lifting the mood.* Feeling like they have to put on a happy face to make others feel good, even when they don't feel particularly happy, is a recipe for self-abandonment and resentment.

▶ *Working hard to orchestrate positive experiences and connections.* Twos can go too far to enhance others' experiences and not attend to the quality of their own—or those of other people they aren't focusing on as important.

▶ *Appreciating what's best in others.* Twos' tendency to support or appreciate what others do well can make it hard for them to provide honest feedback about what needs improvement—they can sugarcoat the truth to the point where they can't deliver critical feedback at all.

Fortunately, Twos' sincere interest in you (and making a connection with you, through which you can express interest in them) means that at some point they will realize that in order to really connect with you, they will need to connect more with themselves. When this happens, they get more motivated to ask the questions *But what do I need?* and *How am I feeling?* more often, balancing out their natural inclination to focus on others as a way of creating alignment and rapport.

"When I'm stressed..." and "At my best...": Understanding the "Low Side" and the "High Side" of the Type Two Personality Style

When stressed to the point of going to their "Low Side," Type Twos can finally get angry that they have spent so much time, attention, and energy giving others what they need that they haven't gotten anything *they* need. They may have been (unconsciously) hoping that focusing on others' needs would somehow eventually lead to those others focusing on their needs, but bitter experience eventually shows them that this often doesn't happen. And at that point, cracks appear in the usually ultra-friendly Two's façade—while the people around the Two are often mystified by their distress, because the Two never actually asked for what they needed. Instead, they're so accustomed to "reading" others for clues to what they need and rushing in to provide it that Twos assume other people will do the same thing for them.

Type Twos on the Low Side can express resentment (*After all I've done for you, you treat me like this?*), can get controlling and bossy (as opposed to hinting or being overly polite and indirect about what they think you should do), or they can punish others by withdrawing their support entirely (*Let's see how you do now without my help!*). They may believe they know what's good for you better than you do and may become irritated if you don't take their advice or acknowledge and appreciate them for their efforts. They may also become highly manipulative, secretly forcing things to go the way they want them to without recognizing what they do is manipulation.

On the "High Side," when Type Two leaders do the work of becoming more self-aware and conscious of their habitual patterns, they can be diplomatic, authentically generous, and deeply supportive—without expecting anything in return. At their healthiest, Twos do for others simply because it's the right thing to do, or it feels great to provide just the right kind of support, or because it's what the person or team or organization needs to succeed.

Emotionally intelligent Twos know who they are and feel good about themselves, so they don't rely so much on being affirmed by others. When they stop denying their own needs in an effort to win others over, they can take care of themselves instead of subconsciously expecting others to do it. Self-aware Twos learn how to get their own needs met, understand how to have healthy boundaries with others, and don't have to make other people happy as an indirect way of inspiring reciprocity. Healthy Twos retain their emotional sensitivity and deep commitment to others, but don't abandon themselves in the effort to create rapport with others. When they give, they give from the heart.

The Three Kinds of Twos: How the Three Instinctual Biases Shape the Three Type Two Sub-Type Personalities

According to the Enneagram model, we all have three main instinctual drives that help us survive, but in each of us, one tends to dominate our behavior. The Type Two style is expressed differently depending on whether a person has a bias toward *self-preservation, social* relationships within groups, or *one-to-one* bonding.

The Self-Preservation (or Self-Focused) Two

Self-Preservation Twos lead with charm and sweetness. They can be more fearful and mistrustful than the other Twos, which makes them more hesitant to own their power, more guarded with others, and more shy and adaptable. They appear youthful, playful, and enthusiastic, tend to be fun loving and self-indulgent, and may also be more ambivalent about connecting with others and more irresponsible if they feel incapable or overwhelmed. These Twos can be quite emotional (though they will try not to express feelings at work) and can be oversensitive and take things too personally. And while they can be very capable and competent, they are less willing to "take charge" and less comfortable being the leader or "the authority."

While all Twos feel compelled to take care of others as a way of inspiring mutual bonds of affection, the Self-Preservation Two often expresses a greater need (that runs counter to the focus on others)—sometimes in hidden or indirect ways—to be taken care of by other people. This makes them the "counter-type" subtype of the three kinds of Twos. This (often unconscious) desire to be supported by others can take a more benign form, like needing help to figure out how to do something, or a more serious form, like neglecting their own welfare—all stemming from an unconscious hope that someone else will step in and provide resources or material support (so that they don't have to). And while these Twos will want to be seen as strong and independent and hard-working, they may also be more tentative when it comes to "stepping up to the plate," or taking an active role in leading projects and exerting power in a decisive way to get things done.

As leaders, Self-Preservation Twos pride themselves on being able to relate to people at every level of the organization. They excel at doing the planning and strategizing necessary for making sure the work gets done in a structured way that succeeds and are humble when it comes to getting credit for their contributions and leadership. However, these Twos may feel more at ease in support roles and show less pride at being at the top of an organization. They often need to learn how to access and exert power and leadership in concrete ways, and may have mixed feelings about being in the spotlight and getting attention. They will likely be deeply gratified by positive feedback, but may struggle to take it in and let it feed their sense of competence and power. At their best, they will seek to support people through sincere expressions of friendliness and helpfulness and try to make work fun and enjoyable.

The Social (or Group-Focused) Two

In contrast to the Self-Preservation Two, the Social Two is more of a leader type. This Two is the "Power Two" who gravitates toward leadership roles and likes to be in charge of making things happen. They can often be found in high-level executive positions or as small business owners or entrepreneurs.

Social Twos tend to be ambitious and enjoy being influential. They seek to be seen as super-competent and capable of taking on and succeeding at any task or project. They like to feel their power in groups, to take the lead to see things are done the way they should be done and that the right people are being supported. Highly strategic thinkers, they excel at making things happen through their give-and-take relationships with people. Others may experience them as controlling and manipulative, but in their view, they may believe they are just "being strategic" or "getting things done behind the scenes" when they trade favors to win support or maneuver behind the scenes to attain a power position. They may believe they know how things should be done better than other people and so will take on a lot of work and produce a lot—and want to tell others what to do and how to do it.

As leaders, Social Twos tend to be decisive, visionary, and committed to the organization and its people. They feel comfortable in leadership positions and will work diligently to win over the crowd. Savvy and strategic when it comes to solving problems through leveraging the right relationships, Social Twos enjoy the power that comes with being the boss and will be very supportive of people who support them or provide something they need. They can appear magnanimous and warm on the outside, but may be more focused on their individual success than they appear. And while they may show vulnerability as a way of connecting with others, they may not really be as vulnerable as they look (or intend to look). At their best, Social Twos act in bold ways to do ambitious things by mixing a clear reading of what's needed in the situation with a deep understanding of the people involved.

The One-to-One (or relationship-focused) Two

One-to-One Twos focus their energy and attention on being appealing to others and creating mutually supportive relationships, one at a time. They generate a lot of forward momentum in moving toward people and presenting themselves in an attractive way to others so that others will want to be connected to them. They can also be highly emotional, but this may take the form of expressing their opinions forcefully, taking the lead in having fun or organizing social events, or lobbying passionately in support of important others.

A naturally emotional and vibrant person, the One-to-One Two brings a lot of energy and a sense of fun and excitement to interpersonal interactions. When they want to befriend someone, they can turn on the charm and impress the other person with their generosity and their attention. Good at reading people, they can pick up on the clues about what someone likes and "become that" as a way of engineering positive rapport or allegiance. However, when the object of this Two's pursuit doesn't respond in the way the Two would like, the Two find this frustrating. They may turn up the volume on the charm offensive even higher, or may become angry and insistent.

As leaders, One-to-One Twos will focus on aligning themselves with key colleagues and making sure they have the support of people they like and respect. They tend to prioritize relationships generally and focus a considerable amount of their attention on the people they regard as the most important to their success or the success of the team or organization. However, while One-to-One Twos may have favorite people within the organization, they will bring passion and emotional intensity to everything they do. They will seek to charm specific individuals so that they will know they can count on them when they need them. They may also act on impulse and get carried away if they feel excited by a particular idea or plan. When conscious and self-aware, One-to-One Twos can make big things happen, motivated by their deep caring for others and their energetic commitment to working with others for the benefit of the people they are connected to.

The Type Two at Work

Type Twos sometime feel like working with others is hard because:

▶ If I don't get any feedback or affirmation, I can feel anxious and uncertain because I don't know where I stand.

▶ They don't try to read me, figure out what I need, and meet my needs (without my having to ask) in the way I do for others.

▶ When something happens that makes me angry or upset it can be difficult for me to contain my feelings or just get over it, but I also worry people will judge me for being too emotional.

▶ I can feel burdened by meeting others' needs, but at the same time, I have a hard time knowing how to create boundaries or say "no." I often take on more than I can handle because it's easier to just do it myself than do the hard work of saying "no."

▶ It bothers me when people are inconsiderate and don't take other people's feelings into account, or when the corporate culture doesn't value team cohesion, loyalty, and putting people first.

▶ Sometimes I don't feel free to do whatever I want because I worry so much about what others will think.

▶ I can feel very hurt when people don't recognize me for my efforts or include me in social outings.

Type Twos workplace pet peeves may be:

▶ When people put their own self-interest above that of others.

▶ When people do things without considering how it will impact other people.

▶ When people give negative feedback without also providing positive feedback.

▶ When people don't reciprocate when I've done so much for them.

▶ When people withhold information and don't let me know where I stand.

▶ When people leave me out of meetings or social gatherings that I'd like to be included in.

▶ When managers patronize other people or treat others with disrespect.

▶ When people don't work as hard as I do—or when others ask for or take vacations they haven't earned.

▶ When people won't listen to me or take my advice.

▶ When people insult or personally attack me or other people.

▶ When people haven't done their part or have been lazy about their work and then I have to work harder to do what they should have done.

▶ When people take advantage of my flexibility and generosity.

Here's What Type Twos Can Do to Be Easier to Work With

As leaders, Twos can take time to understand their emotions and process their feelings mindfully (by stopping to think or talk with trusted friends) so they can moderate their reactions. The business world is becoming more and more aware of the importance of emotional intelligence; however, strong emotions are still often frowned upon in the workplace. So it's important for Twos to be aware and accepting of their emotions and their emotional triggers so they can be conscious about when and how they express their feelings.

It will also help Two leaders to remember that other types of people don't prioritize relationships the same way they do. Other types may prioritize information and data, or achieving goals, or being able to exercise power. While to a Two acting on these other preferences may appear insensitive or harsh, in reality they're just focused on different things. When Twos can own their own bias around the way they see work through the lens of relationships, they can value this as a strength, while having compassion for others who see the world differently.

Most of all, Twos will get along better with others if they do the work it takes to notice and express their own needs and the expectations they may have of others when it comes to meeting those needs. Twos' own needs tend to be a blind spot for them—and when they know what they need, it can be difficult for them to prioritize those needs or make direct requests of others. Making an effort to take note of what they need and communicate that to others in clear ways can help Twos avoid scenarios in which they become resentful.

As employees at any level, it will also be important for Twos to learn to give honest feedback—and include both the bad news and the good news, instead of focusing on the positive out of a fear of injuring the other person (but then stewing silently about what's not working).

Working with Twos

Typical Type Two Behaviors in the Workplace

You *might* be working with someone who has a Type Two Enneagram style if you see them doing several of the following behaviors on a regular basis:

▶ He's the person who always makes a point of asking how you are doing and making a comment to connect with you as a person, not just a coworker.

▶ She seems impossibly nice and exceedingly friendly, which can be really pleasant or kind of suspicious.

▶ He jumps in to offer his time when anyone needs help with something.

▶ She always says "yes" to requests and has a hard time saying "no," even when you know she wants to.

▶ He often takes the lead on planning the office happy hour or social event.

▶ She has a hard time asking for help, and can get irritated when over-worked and underappreciated.

▶ He has a hard time feeling motivated when he doesn't know where he stands with the people above him.

▶ She has a hard time being direct and tends to sugarcoat her opinions to avoid having conflicts with people she likes or wants to impress.

▶ He is highly responsive to approval and disheartened by disapproval and can be self-critical and second-guess himself when he thinks he displeased someone.

▶ At her best, she's selfless and generous, doing whatever she can to empower people and mentor people in just the right ways to help them develop.

▶ At his best, he's upbeat, positive, and supportive, and willing to work overtime to help the team be successful.

What's Great about Working with Conscious Two Leaders

▶ They are friendly, positive, and tend to be fun to be around.

▶ They can be very inspiring because they bring enthusiasm and passion to their work, especially if they find meaning in it.

▶ They make people feel valued and sincerely want people to enjoy their work and each other.

▶ They try to set a positive tone at the office and will find a strategic way to ease someone out if they create problems or undermine the team.

▶ They value work-life balance, and will place a high priority on making the workplace more humane and compassionate.

▶ They want to foster collaboration and mutual support within teams.

▶ When Twos really like you, they make excellent friends and colleagues. Naturally interested in what makes people tick, they like to listen to your problems and will want to make you feel better (even if you don't want to).

▶ They can bring large amounts of dedication and energy to supporting the organization, the team, or their coworkers, and experience a deep sense of satisfaction when their support has a positive impact on the project, their manager, or their peers.

Typical Challenges for People Who Work with Twos

▶ They seem mad, but they aren't saying anything.

▶ They work hard, but then act like a martyr and resent others for not working as hard as they do.

▶ They believe that they can do it all themselves—and then get resentful that they are doing so much and others aren't helping (even while they actively reject offers of help).

▶ They become obsessed with winning over the one person in the office who doesn't like them (because he doesn't like anybody).

▶ They can't deliver negative feedback and often tolerate bad behavior.

▶ They have a hard time being honest and direct about what isn't working for them, but they vent about it to others.

▶ They may act friendly and believe they are open and receptive to people, but have walls up out of a fear they won't be liked.

Type Twos and Leadership

A Type Two Leader Speaks About How Knowing Your Enneagram Style Helps You at Work

Teresa Roche is Chief Human Resources Officer, City of Fort Collins, Colorado and former Vice President and Chief Learning Officer at Agilent Technologies:

"Some of the downsides of being a Two are, I can want to play the rescuer and lose balance by assuming others have needs when they don't. Also, if not present fully, I can assume ALL the needs of the world are mine to meet. I can get overwhelmed sometimes because I am extremely attuned to the emotional domain of others, and I can become disoriented by picking up on conscious or unconscious information about others' feelings. If I can't accomplish results or attend to the needs of others, I can become exhausted and lose my self-confidence. I can become resentful if I am taken for granted or not acknowledged for a prolonged period of time. Also, I can spend so much time thinking it is my job to 'help' the other, I do not help myself. I can struggle to say 'no' to people and say 'yes' to customer requests when my team doesn't have the capacity to fulfill them.

"But knowing I'm a Two also helps me own the gifts and power of my type. I can look at a challenging situation and see the good in it and why it's going to get better. I can provide an immediate assessment of how people feel at a visceral level, including their inherent goodness, gifts, and opportunities. This drives my ability to inspire and lead others to deliver meaningful results where learning and growth are accelerated. My gift of sensing and delivering the power of emotion and support creates a compelling environment for myself and others to celebrate the best of ourselves and our work. I can lead teams to achieve results that tend to surpass everyone's expectations.

"Also, I am respected for my ability to 'see' people at a deep level. Through my intense and fierce loving style, I can be a powerful change agent who provides precise and accurate feedback to empower others to take the risk to grow, learn and contribute at their highest levels. And I have a high level of resilience and adaptability. I can respond quickly as required and lead others well by providing context and an extensive support system."

When You Are a Manager and You Are a Two

People who have a Type Two personality make enthusiastic leaders who can impress clients and inspire their teams because they care about their work and their people. They can read a room, perform, relate to people at a personal level, and do their homework so they don't look bad when they need to look good.

If you are a Two, you may believe you aren't a natural leader and feel more comfortable being "the power behind the throne." (Though if you are a Social Two, you may find being a leader to be easy and fulfilling.) However, it would be a mistake to stereotype Twos as always wanting to be "number two," because you can make energetic leaders who enjoy using your influence to create a quality product or experience. As a Two leader, you may feel challenged when you don't have the time to make personal connections, when you overcommit yourself, or when you need to deliver tough feedback. At times, you may exhaust yourself and resent the people around you for not supporting you enough or in the right ways. At your best, however, you are sensitive to others' needs and preferences, can listen deeply to your colleagues, and focus on developing people to create a cohesive community of good people that prospers.

When Your Manager Is a Two

The great thing about having a boss that's a Two is you can trust that they will want to have a good relationship with you. Two leaders place a high value on working with the right people and cultivating relationships. They are likely to be warm and friendly and unintimidating, and they will be concerned with looking good and doing a good job (so they can look good). Two bosses may delay or avoid conflicts and have difficulty giving you less-than-positive feedback, and may even sugarcoat their communications out of a fear of offending you. Some Two leaders can be uncomfortable with their power, while Social Twos may enjoy it.

When stressed or less self-aware, Type Two leaders can have an inflated sense of themselves on the outside to mask fear and insecurity on the inside. They may lack a sense of self—a sense of really knowing who they are and feeling good about who they are. This may mean they can't make decisions or are out of touch with how they're feeling. It can also lead to their feelings erupting periodically in fits of resentment or blame.

At their best, conscious Two leaders are thoughtful and warm, and sincerely interested in empowering you and supporting your success. They deeply enjoy the people aspect of the job and seek to inspire others to do great things. While they may be giving and generous with their time, they also have good boundaries (self-aware Twos can say "no" and make clear who's responsible for what) and know how to take care of themselves.

When Your Subordinate Is a Two

When your direct reports have a Type Two style, you can count on them to want to support you in the strongest possible way in everything you do. They feel very comfortable in most support roles, and they will try to do things the right way to make sure you like them and approve of the job they are doing. While Twos can be stereotyped as extreme helpers to the point of being overly subservient, they can actually be quite strategic in ways they support others. They can attune to others to a fault, and when they know what they want and are more in touch with how they feel, they can be generous and strong, diplomatic and driven to succeed.

Twos do avoid conflict and can be indirect. Especially in a subordinate role, they may not want to be honest about how they feel and what they think for fear of offending or alienating you. It may be hard for them to ask for what they need, so they may end up appearing needy. (Though if they knew you ever perceived them as needy, they would feel humiliated.) It may be difficult for them to express their feelings for fear of being overly emotional, so they may hold their feelings in and overwork and become angry or sad, or act out in disruptive ways. If they feel unappreciated or disrespected, they may rebel, get passive-aggressive, or leave the job.

On the good side, however, if you work with healthy Twos, they will be extremely dedicated and committed to supporting your success. They will do everything they can to make you look good and ensure that you approve of the job they are doing. They will have a hard time hearing negative feedback, but if you say it sensitively and are clear about your preferences, they will strive to improve.

Getting Along with Twos: Tips for What to Do to Work Well with Twos

> ▶ *Offer support.* Twos want to know that you're on their side and you have their back—that they can trust you to support them when they

need something. If a Two knows they can trust you to be generous with them, they will be willing to do anything for you.

▶ *Give them space to do their best.* If you want a Two to do something well, don't rush them. Twos want to do their best and add value and not let anybody down, so they need time to prepare and figure it out.

▶ *Match their level of passion and dedication* to the work and the team. Show equal commitment and enthusiasm and they will see they are not alone in putting their heart into the work they do.

▶ *Be upbeat and positive.* Twos want to enjoy people and have fun at their job, so they appreciate others who will join them in shouldering the burden of keeping people's spirits up.

▶ *Handle with care.* Learn to deliver negative feedback sandwiched between two pieces of positive feedback. Resist the impulse to ask too much of them, and encourage them to say "no" if they need to. Be direct, and support them in being the same way with you and others. And above all, let them know you like and care about them.

▶ *Affirm them and their efforts.* Let Twos know when what they are doing is working. They are highly responsive to encouragement and positive feedback. They need to know where they stand in terms of how others feel about them, and they may feel lost if people don't let them know how they're doing and how they can do better.

Actionable Growth Tasks and Suggestions: How Type Twos Can Become More Self-Aware, Effective, and Happy at Work

All the types can learn to be less reactive and better at collaborating with others through first *observing* their habitual patterns, then thinking about the things they think, feel, and do to gain more *self-insight*, and then making efforts to *manage* or moderate their automatic reactions to key triggers.

Twos grow through first observing and then learning to moderate their habitual reactions to key triggers like not being liked (enough), people's feelings not being considered, or not being seen and affirmed for their contributions.

When Twos can watch what they do enough to "catch themselves in the act" of doing the things that get them in trouble, and then pause and reflect on what they are doing and why, they can gradually learn to moderate their programming and knee-jerk responses. Here are some ideas to help Twos be more self-aware, more emotionally intelligent, and more satisfied at work (and at home).

Self-Observation: Things for Twos to Watch Out For

▶ *Notice when the habit of meeting others' needs can go beyond simple generosity and become too much—or even intrusive. How and why do you tune in to the needs and feelings of others? How aware are you of your own feelings and needs?*

▶ *Observe your connection to your emotions: When are you more aware or less aware of how you are feeling? What kinds of feelings do you tend to feel more often and less often?*

▶ *Notice when you are over empathizing with others and not taking your own feelings and needs into account.*

▶ *How comfortable are you asking for help? What happens when you need help but don't ask for it?*

▶ *Notice when you need everyone to like you and the consequences of that. Notice what kinds of things you do to ensure others like you. Notice what happens when you aren't sure if someone likes you or you get the message that someone is not happy with you.*

▶ *Notice when you shape-shift to adapt to others and lose touch with who you are and what you need and want.*

▶ *Observe what happens when you want to say "no" but you say "yes." What thoughts and feelings are behind this? How comfortable are you saying "no"?*

Blind Spots: What You Don't Know Can Hurt You!

What blind spots Twos don't see in themselves:

▶ *"Giving-to-get" (and how giving can be about control).* Twos often think they like to give in a generous, selfless way without expecting anything in return. While this is often true, sometimes Twos give as a strategy to get people to like them or to get something they need or to exert control. But many Twos may not be aware that their own denied needs may motivate their offers of help or support—especially because receiving can feel awkward and uncomfortable. It's very important for Twos to become conscious of their potentially hidden motives related to giving and helping so they can learn to ask for what they need directly.

▶ *Manipulating things to get what you want without having to ask.* When I work with Twos, they usually relate to much of the description of the Type Two personality—until we get to the part about Twos being manipulative. But if we think about the definition of "manipulate" as a more benign shifting things around behind the scenes for a particular purpose, this word does describe what Twos often do. Out of a desire to avoid rejection, they try to get what they want indirectly by orchestrating what's happening on the down low to meet their needs in a covert way.

▶ *What you are feeling and needing in the moment?* Twos often lose contact with how they are really feeling because others' feelings seem more important. While Twos can be very emotional, they can also unconsciously avoid their feelings as a way of aligning with others. When Twos deny their own needs in favor of proving their value through meeting others' needs, their unacknowledged needs will inevitably leak out in their behavior in ways they don't see. This may lead others to perceive Twos as needy—the absolute last thing a Two wants to be! So it will be good for them to consciously focus on their own needs to avoid this troubling scenario.

▶ *The presence and causes of sadness or anger.* Twos may not notice how they really feel because they naturally lean toward being in a happy mood. Most people want to be around people who are upbeat and pleasant, so Twos endeavor to be just that. However, beneath their perky exteriors, Twos often harbor feelings of sadness (and can feel depressed) because people may not regard them as highly as they would like them to, or they may believe people appreciate them for what they give and not for who they are. Also, Twos can deplete themselves by giving too much and then get resentful that others don't take care of them the way they take care of others.

▶ *Dependence on others.* Twos like to believe that they don't need or rely on others the way others rely on them. And while this may be true to an extent, it also represents a way that Twos tend to lie to themselves.

We all need people, but because Twos may have had a history of being hurt by people they depended on, they want to believe they don't need anyone.

▶ *Blind spot: self-elevation and self-deflation.* Twos usually don't recognize the way they may need to see themselves as better than they are to impress and attract others or the way they feel bad about themselves when they fail to impress and attract others. They have a kind of false pride about all they can do and be for others that leads to a puffed up self-image and can feel humiliated when the puff gets popped.

Self-Insight: Things for Twos to Think About, Understand, and Explore

▶ *How and why do you lose touch with yourself when you are trying to please important others?*

▶ *Why is it so important to be liked? What do you do to ensure others think well of you? What happens when someone doesn't like you?*

▶ *Why is it hard to give honest feedback to others without sugarcoating any criticisms you might have? What are you afraid of when you avoid offering coworkers a candid assessment of how things are going?*

▶ *How and why do you "shape-shift" to align with others? What motivates you to alter your presentation depending on whom you are with?*

▶ *Why is it hard to ask for help? What do you fear might happen?*

Strengths to Leverage

It helps Twos to be aware of, actively pay attention to, fully own, and leverage:

▶ *Natural ability to empathize with others' feelings.* Understanding how others feel and focusing on the emotional impact of things on other people allow Twos to be powerful advocates, considerate collaborators, and loving human beings. Since "being emotional" can still get a bad rap in the workplace, it's important for Twos to own their sensitivity as a strength.

▶ *Dedication to nurturing relationships and taking impact on people into account.* Twos often play an unsung role at work in understanding the importance of knowing how to relate to others and nurture working relationships. In many corporate environments, work tasks are often prioritized above relating, so it helps Twos to recognize and value the work they do to establish, maintain, and improve relationships.

▶ *Willingness to work hard.* Type Threes often get most of the credit for being "hard workers," but Twos also bust their asses to get work done. The difference is, where Threes get motivated by looking successful, winning, and getting to the goal, Twos want their efforts to have a positive impact on others.

▶ *Interest and skillfulness in collaborating with others.* Twos genuinely like the process of teaming with others, and feel an inherent enjoyment in working with people to achieve common goals. They bring a great deal of enthusiasm, positive energy, and commitment to the things they do on a team.

▶ *Generosity in giving to others.* Much of the time, when Twos give, they have the best of intentions to support and uplift others. They tend to be unselfish, thoughtful, and considerate.

Self-Management: Challenging Tendencies for Twos to Moderate

▶ *Responsibility.* Take less responsibility for managing how others feel and more responsibility for your own needs and feelings.

▶ *Boundaries.* Manage boundaries with more awareness. Learn that it's okay to say "no" and expend more energy on your own priorities and less on others.

▶ *Welcome but moderate emotions.* Accept your emotional nature as a strength, but also learn what you need to do for yourself to have your feelings, process them, channel them with awareness, rein them in when necessary, express them in conscious ways, and let them go when appropriate.

▶ *Let go of your need to be indispensable.* Develop your sense of self-worth so you don't need to be needed by others to prove your value.

▶ *Build confidence in yourself.* Learn to value yourself more from the inside so you don't need so much validation and approval from the outside to know you are okay (or fantastic). Own your power and authority in conscious ways.

Consciously Manifesting your Higher Potential: Being Aware of the "Low Side" and Aiming for the "High Side"

Twos can also grow through consciously becoming aware of the self-limiting habits and patterns associated with their personality style and learning to embody the higher aspects or more expansive capacities of the Type Two personality:

▶ Learn to become conscious of false pride (when you think you need to be better than you are to be appreciated) and aim for humility—knowing and feeling good about exactly who you are and not seeing yourself as more or less than who you essentially are.

▶ Learn to become conscious of when you over-give such that you can offer support appropriately on the outside and give more to yourself on the inside.

▶ Learn to recognize when you are exhausting yourself through your efforts to prove your worth to others and develop a deeper awareness of your personal value and qualities aside from what you do for others.

▶ Learn to be aware of any fear of dependence you might feel and develop your ability to receive (and really take in!) love, support, appreciation, and acceptance.

▶ Learn to be aware of avoiding certain emotions and develop an ability to embrace your emotional nature and deploy it for good.

▶ Learn to be more conscious of any negative beliefs you hold on to about yourself and own your competence, beauty, and power, and try to embrace what's really true.

Overall, Type Twos can fulfill their higher potentials by observing and working against their habit of focusing so much of their attention on others and learn to tune into their own feelings, needs, and wants. When they begin to value their own contributions more consciously, they can balance out their sincere caring for others with a greater degree of self-support. When they can lean into their higher capacity for validating who they are from the inside—for valuing themselves for who they are and not for how they please others—they can express more of who they are in the world and bring more confidence, decisiveness, and productivity to their work as leaders. When they can balance their concern for the welfare of others with a deep appreciation of what they bring to the table, they can lead from a grounded sense of their emotional intelligence and sensitivity and their personal power.

CHAPTER 6

The Type Three Leadership Style

The Compulsively Productive Professional, or Getting to the Goal and Looking Good Doing It

"Competition brings out the best in products and the worst in people."
David Sarnoff, broadcasting pioneer

"Choose a job you love, and you will never have to work a day in your life."
Confucius

"The only place success comes before work is in the dictionary."
Vince Lombardi, iconic American football coach

The Type Three archetype is that prototypical person who wants to do the best job possible to achieve a given objective and look good doing it (and because of it). Sometimes called "the Performer" or "the Achiever," the Type Three style is all about creating an image of success through working hard to achieve the best results, competing to win, and accomplishing tasks to gain status. A Three's attention automatically goes to work tasks and projects and how to accomplish them in the quickest, most efficient, and most direct way possible to look good in the eyes of others.

A Three's programming tells them that the way to feel good is to be as successful as they can be according to the surrounding culture's definition of "success"—and to get seen doing it. Their style is shaped by a primary focus on doing and working to achieve success so others will view them as winners. By focusing their attention intently on goals and tasks, they accomplish a great deal, enabling them to attain the possessions, titles, and other markers of material success that will let people know that they have value. Threes usually identify strongly with their work persona, say they enjoy working, and are, in fact, the biggest workaholics of the Enneagram. They are strongly motivated to do everything they can to succeed in everything they do because they believe being the best makes them appear attractive and admirable.

105

Not surprisingly, Threes' communication style matches their work style: their manner of speaking tends to be straightforward, to-the-point, on-topic, and bullet-pointed. Threes focus their communication on work and tasks, usually without a lot of extraneous chitchat that could slow things down and distract from making progress toward the goal. Natural performers, they will tune into their audience enough to be able to impress them and collaborate if the situation requires it, but not so much as to stir up emotions or get bogged down in unnecessary conversation.

Leaders who have a Type Three style tend to be work-focused, task-oriented, goal-driven achievers. You will find them (in copious amounts) at the highest levels of most organizations, as work climbing the corporate ladder or being the best at whatever they are doing is exactly what motivates them. America itself is a Type Three country, so it's not surprising that Threes do well in the business culture of America. The ideals of success, making a profit, working hard to get things done, and competing to win (and being able to buy things that reflect a winner's status) is what America—and the Type Three style—is all about.

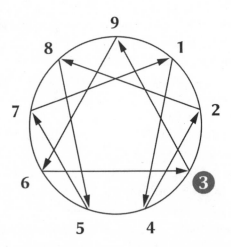

Type Three leaders tend to enjoy being the leader and the perks associated with the position—particularly having a say in how work gets done. They specialize in executing a plan to get things done and get results, and may focus on producing quality results through relentless hard work while appearing modest and humble, or by competing to win at all costs or by becoming the ideal of personal appeal and charisma. But whether they want to be deeply good at what they do, appear good at whatever they are doing, or look good as they support others in being successful in what they do, Threes usually succeed at attaining whatever goal they decide to focus their considerable energy on.

How to Tell if You Are a Type Three: The View from the Inside

If most or all of the following characteristics apply to you, you may have a Type Three personality style:

- ▶ *You see the work you do through the lens of how to do the best job possible in the most efficient way.* You strive to be productive, effective, fast, and efficient. You are driven to work hard to achieve success in whatever you do.

- ▶ *You focus like a laser beam on goals—you always think in terms of "what is the goal and how can we get there in the most direct way?"* You naturally see work in terms of specific goals to be achieved and the steps and tasks that need to be accomplished to get to the goal. And if someone or something gets in the way, you work around them or it (no matter what the cost).

- ▶ *You are good at reading an audience.* You tune in to what the people around you see as admirable, effective, and attractive, and automatically assess what others view as the best way to be or appear or do things.

- ▶ *You are skilled at discerning what people in different contexts view as successful and then becoming that.* You have a talent for matching any image you decide to turn yourself into. One of the ways you strive to be successful is by looking the part. You are a bit like a chameleon in that you can shift your image to suit your surroundings.

- ▶ *You are motivated in the work you do by wanting to look successful to others, according to how others measure success.* You automatically sense what the people around you view as successful in all the different contexts in your life, and (often automatically) seek to match that ideal.

- ▶ *You want to win and be the best.* Second place is unacceptable. If you can't win, you probably won't do it.

▶ *You identify with your work—you think you are what you do.* You find value in getting things done and achieving the rewards and status that go along with having the power to get so many things done.

▶ *You work really hard and have a hard time slowing down.* You tell yourself that you enjoy your work (and mostly you really do), so when you work 24/7 there doesn't seem to be anything wrong with this.

▶ *You get impatient with people who slow your progress toward your goal.* You have a hard time dealing with people who you see as incompetent, indecisive, or untrustworthy when it comes to delivering on their commitments on time.

▶ *You are a high-achiever or an overachiever.* You have a crazy long résumé of huge accomplishments, but you may still worry about someone who has done more than you looking better than you do.

▶ *You love checking things off your "to-do list" as done.* You keep lists, and one of the reasons you move so fast is that it feels so good to complete tasks and revel in how productive you've been.

▶ *You can be out of touch with your emotions or consider them a waste of time.* You believe that it's "not productive" to feel all those pesky feelings and they just slow you down anyway, so you usually avoid them.

▶ *You enjoy being in leadership positions and having a say in how work gets done.* You excel at meeting goals, doing work quickly and well, and aligning with the company's culture and vision—so you naturally gravitate toward leadership roles. You like being in charge of how the work gets done and making sure the work gets done, and since you are so good at it, people want you to be in charge.

The Central Adaptive Strategy of the Type Three Personality Style

Early on in life, Threes often receive the message that they are appreciated or loved for what they do, not for who they are. Perhaps well-intentioned parents who praise them for their accomplishments teach them that "doing" and performing gets rewarded. Or, they may have an absent or ineffectual parent—usually the father or other archetypal protector and provider—and so must learn to be a "doer" to survive. Threes in American culture may also get reinforced for their habit of seeking to prove their value through doing because "achieving" and "looking good" are behaviors that are encouraged by the norms and values of the U.S.A.

Motivated by a need to be seen as successful, appealing, and competent, Threes come to believe they can accomplish whatever goal they set and win whatever contest they enter. They are good getting things done and achieving "success" as defined by an American dream mind-set: owning a house, having resources, and being attractive to others. And since performance, status, and looking good seem to assure both material security and recognition from others, Threes develop the ability to work hard to achieve any goal they set their sights on. Without even thinking about it, they identify with (and become) the image of a person who will impress most of the people most of the time.

Since threes believe being the best is the way to gain acceptance, positive regard, and respect from others, failure is something to be avoided at all costs—to the point where some Threes say that if they think they might not succeed at something, they just won't do it. Failure means you didn't win and don't look good, so Threes quickly move away from any whiff of defeat by either reframing it as a success or switching their focus to something they do well. It's as if Type Threes' essential value as a person rides on their ability to overachieve, so they feel compelled to prove they are worthwhile by excelling and performing flawlessly in whatever they do.

What Do Threes Pay Attention To? The Type Three "Radar Screen"

The strategy of presenting themselves and the things they do in a way that assures others perceive them as successful leads Threes to focus their attention on reading people. Like Twos, Threes pay a great deal of attention to other people; however, when they read other people, they index success rather than likability, conforming to what others find attractive in terms of achievements, presentation, and social or professional status.

Threes look for clues about what others see as proof of "success," and are highly skilled at calibrating their presentation to match that image. They turn themselves into whatever they intuit the people in their specific social context view as successful as a way of being recognized in a positive light by others. Threes are skilled at determining exactly the right clothes to wear in specific settings, how to behave, and what to do and not do to fit in and look good in whatever environment they find themselves in.

After Threes detect what people value, they seek to become that through a laser-like focus on tasks, goals, and doing, working relentlessly to realize the achievements that will fulfill the image of success they want to create. This powerful and overarching focus on doing allows them to successfully accomplish whatever goal they set, while avoiding the emotions and deeper personal needs and desires that might get in the way of all the doing they have to do to look the way they want to look in the eyes of others.

The View from "Planet Three": How Threes See the World

Generally, individuals with a Type Three style view the world in terms of tasks to be done, goals to be achieved, and the appearances of things. They automatically align themselves with external markers of success, including the material possessions and signs of status that signify prosperity. Threes excel at shifting their presentation to look appropriate, "together" and competent at all times and in all cultural realities. Like chameleons, they adapt their outer skin to blend in (in a positive way) in all social settings and work environments.

Type Threes also see life through the lens of their "to do" lists. They love (!) the feeling they get when they can check a task off as finished, so their everyday experience is shaped by what needs to be done and their perception is structured by tasks to be accomplished (in order of priority) and what they need to do to operate at maximum productivity. They're sometimes called "human doings" instead of "human beings," because Threes can get so caught up in "doing" that they hardly leave room for just "being" (or feeling).

Believing the world loves a winner, Threes work to ensure they are perceived as people who can achieve any goal, always come out on top, and always look good doing whatever they do. While some Threes are extremely competitive and driven to win, others prefer to measure themselves against their own past levels of productivity. In either case, a Three's perspective is fundamentally shaped by a keen understanding of what needs to be done—and how they need to look—to create an image of being the best at whatever they do in whichever arena they are in. They will have whatever degree, title, clothes, car, vacation home, or achievement they require to let the world know they embody the definition of success in whatever milieu they live or work in.

The Type Three Leader: Core Characteristics

The following character traits define the Type Three leadership style.

▶ *Ability to read their audience.* Often without even knowing they are doing it, Threes "read" the people around them to know how to adjust their presentation to achieve the maximum impact in terms of impressing people with their competence and attractiveness.

▶ *Goal-oriented.* Threes want to be productive, and knowing what the goal is helps them to focus their efforts in the right direction for realizing whatever they want to achieve.

▶ *Focus on doing/achievement orientation.* Threes understand that people evaluate people in terms of their achievements and accomplishments, and they are more than willing to do whatever hard work they need to do to be successful and achieve their goals.

▶ *Image management.* I once had a lengthy and energetic conversation with a group of Threes about the process of choosing what to wear in the morning. They continually adjust their presentation to be whatever others will value as successful and professional—and looking the part in terms of the exact right shoes and outfit is a big part of that.

▶ *Competitiveness and the drive to win.* Threes want to be seen as the best, so they tend to measure themselves against other people's success or their own track record. The desire to win and come out on top in whatever they do motivates them to do all the hard work they do.

▶ *Avoidance of feelings.* Although they are in the "heart-centered" triad of Enneagram types who are connected to the emotional center of intelligence, Threes tend to be out of touch with their emotions much of the time. They consciously turn down the volume on their emotions because feelings get in the way of doing, so emotions become uncomfortable and unfamiliar territory for busy, fast-paced, doing-oriented Threes. Of course, underneath, as they find out when they do some inner work, Threes have big hearts and can be very emotional. But in the course of the workday, they tend to tune them out.

Mental, Emotional, and Behavioral Patterns: Why Do Threes Think, Feel, and Behave the Way They Do?

Mental

Unsurprisingly, Threes' thinking focuses mostly on doing and working. They think about their lists of "things to do" (some Threes have multiple, cross-referenced to-do lists) and how to be productive and efficient in getting things done. They usually enjoy their work and find a sense of identity in what they do, so much of their mind space is filled with thoughts of work and how to get work done in the quickest way possible. They may also think about the people around them, especially in terms of how to appeal to or support those people, or how others can support them in doing their work. However, they tend to prioritize work over people, which can get them into trouble when they fail to listen and take people's feelings into account on the way to getting things done.

Emotional

One of my Type Three friends says "emotions are not aerodynamic"—they slow you down or stop you. Since Threes don't like to slow down or stop, they don't dwell on their emotions. They use their emotional intelligence to read people and create relationships based on identifying with and becoming what other people feel good about or admire, but tend to avoid feeling their deeper emotions, especially pain or sadness. The most frequent emotions Threes do experience are impatience and frustration, often as a result of getting slowed down by others on their way to getting things done. Underneath, however, Threes do occasionally feel sadness, if they let themselves, especially when they think they have to be someone other than who they really are to ensure people value or admire them.

Behavioral

As you may have gathered by now, Threes do a lot. They work very hard and usually like their work—or can suspend their need to like it enough to get the job done anyway. Motivated by the desire to earn others' admiration, they accumulate accomplishments and climb the social ladder to be recognized as a super-competent, can-do person. Threes like to move fast, and can get bored or impatient if they can't move on to the next thing. They avoid failure, can smell it a mile away and will change course if necessary to make sure it doesn't happen. In organizations, Threes rise to high levels and frequently occupy top leadership roles because their ability to set goals and get results fits well in a corporate environment that prizes productivity, hard work, and the drive to accomplish.

The Main Strengths and Superpowers of the Type Three Style: What Threes Are Really Good At

- ▶ *Setting and meeting goals.* Threes excel at making things happen and producing results.

- ▶ *Working hard to get the job done/Execution.* Threes generally like to work long hours, and put work at the center of their life.

- ▶ *Marketing orientation.* Threes know how to sell—they understand what it means to tune in to an audience and shape their message to suit the interests and preferences of their "target market," which could mean their friends, family, and colleagues.

- ▶ *Projecting an image of success and competence/Looking good in every context.* Threes are experts at looking like they know what they are doing, and put a considerable amount of attention and energy into fitting the part and presenting an image that people will admire. Type Three is the prototype of the practice of adopting a persona—or social mask—to look appropriate in the social world.

- ▶ *Competing to win/Striving to be the best.* Threes tend to want to be the best at whatever they do, and they work so hard that they tend to become the best at whatever they seek to become really good at.

- ▶ *Inspiring others to drive for results.* Both through modeling an ethic of hard work and encouraging people to do what it takes to execute on a plan, Threes make inspiring and effective leaders.

When Too Much of a Good Thing Becomes a Bad Thing: How Threes Can Go Wrong When They Try Too Hard to Do It All

Like all people of all types, when Type Three leaders overuse their biggest strengths (and don't consciously develop a wider range of specialties), these strengths can also turn out to be their Achilles' heel.

▶ *Setting and meeting goals.* Threes can become aggressive and run over people on the way to a goal if they become overly focused on reaching their destination no matter what the cost.

▶ *Working hard to get the job done/Execution.* Threes may get so work-focused and so driven to be executing all the time that they overwork to the point of physical or psychological breakdown.

▶ *Marketing orientation.* Threes are so focused on skillfully reading their audience and packaging the product to make the sale that they may sometimes stretch the truth, cut corners, or craft a false presentation in the process.

▶ *Projecting an image of success and competence/Looking good in every context.* Threes' talent for adjusting their image in every circumstance can lead them to prioritize style over substance (or knowing their true identity).

▶ *Competing to win/Striving to be the best.* Threes may get so focused on winning that they engage in unethical or aggressive practices, or exhaust themselves, to prevail in the competition. They may get so focused on being the best that they will do anything to avoid failure, even when accepting and learning from failure can actually help them grow.

▶ *Inspiring others to drive for results.* Threes may get so caught up in the pursuit of the goal that they may not listen to valuable input from others about potential problems, and may damage relationships by pushing others too hard.

Fortunately, Threes' sincere interest in collaborating with others (when possible and desirable) to accomplish tasks motivates them to evaluate how they are doing. When they can slow down and check in with their colleagues, they can combine their effectiveness with a more reasoned and broad-minded assessment of how things are really going. By learning to moderate their desire for success with an openness to the lessons of failure (or at least some healthy self-doubt or self-examination), Threes can put their natural focus on getting the job done to work in support of achieving a worthwhile personal or organizational vision.

"When I'm stressed..." and "At my best...": Understanding the "Low Side" and the "High Side" of the Type Three Personality Style

When stressed to the point of going to their "low side," Type Threes can become pushy, impatient, and (vocally) intolerant of (what they view as) incompetence. They may withdraw and believe they need to work alone because no one can do the job as well or as quickly as they can. When Threes operate from the low side of their personality style, their addiction to work can get even more intense and hard to manage. They may not allow themselves time to rest or relax or recharge, which can lead to an inability to manage stress, and ultimately a physical or emotional crisis. Many Threes have stories of working themselves to the point of becoming sick or injured—which was the only way they could be forced to stop working.

Threes visiting the low side may feel increasingly emotional, as sadness, pain, or other feelings they habitually push away begin to surface as their normally strong "just work harder" defenses begin to weaken. The discomfort of feeling their emotions may drive them to work even harder, which can make them dangerously insensitive to both their own feelings and the emotions of others. They may strive even more aggressively toward their goals, or to put on an "appropriate" or happy professional face to hide their stress and not look bad, which adds even more stress and anxiety. When living on the low side, Threes can develop tunnel vision, focusing so intently on their goals that they can't listen to anyone or accept any support.

On the "high side," when Type Three leaders are more self-aware and conscious of their habitual patterns, they make time to slow down, reflect on how they are feeling, and engage more deeply with the people around them. Consciously balancing their work efforts with intentional self-inquiry can take the edge off of their single-minded focus on "doing" so Threes don't have to work so hard to avoid their feelings. They become more empathetic with others, more compassionate with themselves, and (ironically) more effective in their work.

Emotionally intelligent Threes feel good about themselves for who they really are instead of who they think they need to be to impress people. They can work productively by focusing on tasks and deepen their insight into the work they do by consulting their feelings. Healthy Type Threes collaborate skillfully with others because they know when to lead people forward in meeting goals and when to focus more deeply on communicating with the team and listening to others' input.

The Three Kinds of Three Leaders: How the Three Instinctual Biases Shape the Three Type Three Sub-Type Personalities

According to the Enneagram model, we all have three main instinctual drives that help us survive, but in each of us, one of the three tends to dominate our behavior. The Type Three style gets expressed differently depending on whether a person has a dominant bias toward *self-preservation*, *social* relationships and positioning within groups, or *one-to-one* bonding.

The Self-Preservation (or Self-Focused) Three

Self-Preservation Threes want to be both productive and quality-oriented; they care about being both effective and deeply good at what they do. This makes them the hardest workers of the notoriously hard-working Type Threes, because they feel driven to do the job and do it well in the service of security. Self-Preservation subtypes are generally concerned with getting the resources that support survival, so an anxiety about material security turbocharges this Three's workaholic tendency. Self-Preservation Threes also believe they need to be a good model of doing things well in a moral sense—in addition to the already high Three standard of getting a lot done—and that this must happen to ensure their survival.

Wanting to *be* good in addition to looking good means Self-Preservation Threes are more modest than the other Threes, especially the Social Threes. They have "vanity for having no vanity"—that is, they want to be seen positively by others, but they don't want to appear to want to be seen positively by others. They want to be recognized for their accomplishments, but they don't want to be caught bragging or engaging in blatant self-promotion.

In addition, Self-Preservation Threes can be more self-sufficient than the other Threes—they have a hard time depending on others and may work more independently to provide a sense of security for themselves and the people who depend on them. These Threes tend to look very put together while feeling anxious underneath, as they put so much pressure on themselves to do so much by themselves to take care of themselves and others.

As leaders, Self-Preservation Threes will set an example by working harder than anyone else and being humble when it comes to taking credit for things. They will likely be the first person at the office in the morning and the last one to leave. They tend to be solid, self-assured, good people that others seek out for advice. However, Self-Preservation Threes may work so hard and feel so much pressure to do a good job, they may deprive themselves of the support that relationships can provide when they "go it alone." In this way, they avoid the vulnerability they might feel if they asked for help and over-focus on what needs to get done all by themselves. When Self-Preservation Threes learn to slow down, go easier on themselves, and receive more support from others, they can be particularly powerful leaders who seek to do a good job in the best way without having a big ego or needing to be the center of attention.

The Social (or Group-Focused) Three

In contrast to the Self-Preservation Three, the Social Three enjoys being on stage and receiving recognition and applause for the work they do. Social Threes care a lot about "winning" and are the most aggressively competitive of the Threes, although they often claim they don't compete with others as much as they do with their own past performance. These Threes are more comfortable displaying signs of status and success like wearing high-end clothes and driving an expensive car. (If a Self-Preservation Three has a nice car they usually feel embarrassed about being seen in it. I've heard more than one Self-Preservation Three say they felt so awkward driving their Mercedes that they traded it in for a Prius. This kind of self-consciousness is not a problem for the Social Three.)

Social Threes shine in all kinds of public situations and know how to ascend the corporate ladder. They have a keen sense for how to get the job done and look flawless doing it, even if they occasionally cut a corner here or there. They make excellent salespeople and enjoy having power and influence, like to be recognized for their achievements, and know how to frame the things they say for maximum benefit.

Social Threes are commonly found in the highest leadership positions. They are natural leaders in the sense that they relish having a prestigious title, directing work processes, and wielding power. They have a corporate mentality in that it's easy for them to represent the interests of the company in getting things done in the most effective and efficient way to compete to be the best and maximize profit—both for themselves and the organization. They intuitively align with what's best for the company or the team and feel strongly motivated to move things forward decisively and successfully so that everyone ends up looking good and getting rewarded—both with fame and wealth. This Three may have a hard time showing vulnerability, because it's so important to look good and not show any faults, but at their best, they are strong leaders who will want to find a way to master any job and create results.

The One-to-One (or Relationship-Focused) Three

One-to-One Threes can be strong leaders and productive workers like the other two Threes, but they prioritize relationships with others more. One-to-One Threes want to look good to others more in terms of personal appeal than morality like the Self-Preservation Three or by winning like the Social Three. This Three also strives to achieve more in service to other people, and focuses on attracting others and then energetically supporting their success (instead of just their own). One-to-One Threes feel like they've won when the people they support win. And they can feel frustrated when the people they support fail, as they feel those failures as their own.

One-to-One Threes are also competitive and hard working, but they are shyer about being the center of attention and getting recognized for the work they do. They would rather promote the people they like and work with and feel close to. They have a team mentality and can be enthusiastic cheerleaders for the people they work to support, whether at work or at home. One-to-One Threes want to look good and are very aware of their image, but for them it's more about being attractive to their significant other or being appealing and charismatic so they can easily establish bonds of support with people they seek to please. They can bring a large amount of energy and work very hard for the causes or people they support. This Three can be more emotional than the other Two Threes, though like the other Threes, they tend to turn down the volume on their emotions generally.

As leaders, One-to-One Threes tend to be attractive, likable, and helpful. They try to put the focus on others rather than have the spotlight on themselves, and tend to express a great deal of concern about the welfare of the people they work with. These Threes tirelessly promote and support people on their team or in their organization who they believe deserve credit. With a softer presence than the other two Threes, leaders with a One-to-One Three style will move things forward more through the force of their personal relationships and bonds with teammates. Content to take a backseat when prizes are handed out for a job well done, these Threes enjoy working hard to make others look good—and seeing the people they like and support succeed can be the biggest reward of all.

The Type Three at Work

Type Threes sometimes feel like working with others is hard because:

▶ *I like to move fast, and sometimes others can't keep up. It can be very difficult for me if I have to slow down and wait for them to catch up.*

▶ *I can get bored and stop listening (in meetings and in conversation) if people talk too long, take too long to get to the point or the discussion gets repetitive or bogged down.*

▶ *I know it's important to do research before we decide the best course of action, but I can get irritated if we get caught up in "analysis paralysis."*

▶ *When I'm working toward a goal, I can become impatient when people ask a lot of questions, offer objections, or disagree with me.*

▶ *It can be hard for me if the goal we are working toward isn't spelled out clearly.*

▶ *It's important to me that I look good and that the team looks good, and so I really dislike it when someone does something that makes me or us look bad.*

▶ *I can become angry if people don't deliver on their commitments, especially if it reflects poorly on me or they aren't held accountable for their incompetence.*

▶ *I hate to fail, so if someone on the team thwarts my efforts and we fail, that can be difficult for me to handle. I like being in control of achieving success—for myself and the team—so it's frustrating when I don't have enough autonomy to control things and get the win.*

Type Threes' workplace pet peeves may be:

▶ Inefficiently run meetings.

▶ Meetings that drag on and on and don't get anywhere.

▶ When people block my path to my goal.

▶ People who don't deliver on what they said they'd do.

▶ When people move slowly (especially if they are in my way or I need something from them before I can move forward).

▶ Dead weight: people who are incompetent or not on board to help us move forward and execute on our plan.

▶ When people waste my time.

▶ When people don't recognize my efforts and hard work.

▶ When people go on and on and don't communicate in bullet points.

▶ When people take credit for someone else's work.

▶ People who engage in conversations about trivial, inconsequential bullshit when they should be working like I am.

▶ People who distract me when I am working.

▶ People who miss deadlines (especially if it affects my work).

▶ People who do shoddy work.

▶ Having to manage people's feelings instead of focusing on the task at hand.

▶ People who I have to explain things to over and over.

Here's What Type Threes Can Do to Be Easier to Work With

As leaders, Threes can understand that not everyone sees work tasks, goals, and success the way they do. Threes excel in a work environment because they work so hard, focus on delivering results, and prioritize being productive, but these same work habits can get them in trouble when they move too fast and leave others behind, don't take the time to communicate about what their plans are, and stop listening if they think someone isn't adding enough value. If Threes can learn to tolerate slowing their pace enough to talk through things more with others, they can bring people along with them more purposefully as they work to achieve their goals.

It can help Threes to notice when they are not listening to others—when they are having a difficult time being present. Threes often feel challenged to listen deeply to people because they are paying more attention to the "to-do list" in their heads. Threes may also fail to hear people out because they already have a plan firmly in mind and don't want to change course just because someone else has other ideas. However, it can be good for Threes to learn that sometimes the overall project is more successful when they slow down enough to take in others' concerns, insights, and contributions. If Threes charge ahead too fast or ignore problems in their rush to the goal, they can actually be less effective than if they moderated their pace and were open to listening to other perspectives.

Threes can also be easier (and more enjoyable) to work with when they take the time to connect with people on a personal level. Threes can be so work-focused that they forget that it's good to make room for the social niceties that strengthen working (and other) relationships. If they can pause at the beginning of the conversation about that supplier or the paperwork they need to ask how someone is doing, or what's happening in the rest of someone's life, they can establish a deeper kind of contact that can be an important support to the work they do with others.

Working with Threes

Typical Type Three Behaviors in the Workplace:

You *might* be working with someone who has a Type Three Enneagram style if you see them doing several of the following behaviors on a regular basis:

▶ He looks impatient during the weekly staff meeting and is the first person to look at his watch or check his phone.

▶ She's already been at her desk for an hour when you arrive in the morning (and doesn't complain about working long hours).

▶ He looks impatient when you remind him about the processes that need to be completed before he can move forward on his intended plan.

▶ She smiles politely while you tell her about the trip you took with your kids last weekend but you sense she's thinking about something else entirely.

▶ He's the guy who asks you to speed up your presentation and get to the "good part," and frequently asks you to "bottom-line-it for me" or "give me the bullet-point version" when you are having a discussion.

▶ She can't find time in her schedule for the team-building session and thinks "getting in touch with feelings is a waste of time." (Unless she is in the Organization Development department.)

▶ He has a difficult time staying motivated and engaged when the goals and task assignments aren't clearly stated.

▶ She quickly reframes a team failure into a success to avoid facing the embarrassment associated with not reaching the goal (which reminds you of the time she introduced herself to you saying, "I've successfully completed two marriages").

▶ He doesn't stop working overtime, even when he has a health scare.

▶ She never, ever misses her regularly scheduled workout.

▶ At his best, he knows exactly what to say to motivate the team to work together to achieve success.

▶ At her best, she takes the lead on energetically formulating action steps when the team feels stuck or isn't sure what to do.

What's Great About Working with Conscious Three Leaders

▶ They actually like working and their enthusiasm can be infectious.

▶ They always feel confident they know how to reach the goal and achieve success, (which makes you feel more confident).

▶ They will always do more than their share of the work.

▶ They move things along and speed up the pace when slowdowns occur.

▶ They help keep everyone on-task and focused.

▶ They communicate in a way that is concise, efficient, and succinct.

▶ They don't waste your time.

▶ They know how to read an audience and can help clarify what will sell and what won't.

▶ When they can slow down and make the time to connect, they are good at engaging with people.

▶ They will easily step in when needed and take the lead to provide direction.

▶ They stay engaged with their work as a key focal point of their life, so they usually stay available and accessible if you need them.

Typical Challenges for People Who Work with Threes

▶ They seem impatient when you are talking with them—like they would rather be doing something else (and they probably would).

▶ They can become frustrated and dismissive in meetings if they think their time is being wasted.

▶ They can't stop working or slow down, which may lead to mistakes when they overwork and can't take time to relax or de-stress.

▸ They can become so competitive that the drive to win clouds their judgment.

▸ They may leave or quit a project if they think they can't do it well or achieve enough of a success.

▸ They may do things to protect their image that aren't good for the team or the project.

▸ They may not be open to learning from failures because they need to move on so quickly (because it's so hard for them to experience failure).

Type Threes and Leadership

Type Three leaders Talk About How Knowing Your Enneagram Style Helps You at Work

Jean Halloran is the principal at Halloran Consulting LLC and former Senior Vice President of Human Resources at Agilent Technologies.

"I think the single most useful thing to me as a leader was understanding how disruptive my anxiety was to leading. That was huge. Once I understood that I was a Self-Preservation Three, and I saw that I was completely identified with my personal success, and that anything that would cause me to believe my image as a successful person was threatened made me very anxious, I saw more clearly how my anxiety about my image affected my leadership.

"And so now, at my best, I am comfortable at taking the lead. I can inspire by saying to people like, 'let's go there,' 'this is going to be so great,' 'what we're going to accomplish is phenomenal,' 'here's what it's going to look like—are you in?' 'If you're not in, don't come, seriously, but this is going to be fantastic,' 'It's going to work because I say it's going to work.' I have the ability to infuse in people a belief that we will be successful, that we can do something hard or stand up to power. It's all about getting stuff done—that's the strength of it.

"But, oh boy, if I was in the monthly staff meeting, and they were talking too long about something like, 'Should this development program include 360 feedback for everybody or only for some people?' and people were going on and on and on, quoting the pros and cons—I could get

really bored and anxious. What I used to do was act out and start getting impatient and interrupting people and saying disrespectful things like, 'Come on, let's get back to the main point here.'

"After I learned my type and I shared it with my staff, I then had the awareness to say things like, 'I'm really sorry, but my performance anxiety is about to kick in and I can't listen to very much more of this in this meeting. If somebody can sum up where we are, I'd love to hear it. But first let me ask, is there anybody who has something really new to add?' I was still impatient, I was still saying I had enough, but I was calling it what it was."

Steve Jurvetson is Partner at Draper Fisher Jurvetson, a venture capital and growth equity firm.

"The way the Enneagram has helped me has largely been in allowing me to understand and respect cognitive diversity in the workplace. I now actually appreciate how there can be a diversity of styles on a team. Seeing the different types is like having a perceptional prism that helped me understand differences in a way I was unaware of before. I thought personality traits were either correct or incorrect, healthy or devious. Now I understand there can be a mixed array of very consistent, perfectly reasonable points of view that are very different from my own.

"As for myself, it's been about being able to realize some of the obsessions I've had as a Type Three, from the preoccupation that I have with achievement to my obsession with social media and getting positive feedback from people at large. I might have been largely oblivious to that before [learning my Enneagram style and] realizing, 'This isn't really the normal level of engagement that people have with these kinds of things,' just thinking about the next affirmation and the next achievement.

"Now I'm aware, and there are more times where I might choose not to behave in the usual way. I see more: 'that's what I usually do,' or 'that's the way I typically respond to things.' I notice how as a Type Three I prioritize the easy things I can get done to tick boxes off my to-do list, above the important things. I have to consciously force myself to back up and focus on what's most helpful for my overall work-life balance.

"I've also found that it helps for me to do—and I resisted this like the plague initially, just given who I am—things like meditation and mindfulness training. Before, I wouldn't have thought it was worth the

effort because it's completely anathema to what I would spend time on. But part of what helped me was when I'd stick with it a bit longer than I might otherwise, and I'd think, 'Oh, yeah. It really does help shift me into more right-brain thinking and focus more on self-awareness tasks that I normally don't give myself time for.' In short, it's helped with healthier living, not just in the workplace, but in an overall life balance."

Richard Stone is Founder and Chairman of Private Ocean, a financial services and wealth management company, based in San Rafael, California.

"I was exposed to the Enneagram very late in my career. So it was an opportunity to reflect on how I got to where I am. And when I looked at my trajectory, I saw the Type Three patterns, which helped me observe some things I didn't like about the traits of the Three. Then I went to work immediately trying to work on those and tone them down—the negatives, if you will.

"One of the things about us Threes is we have a real need for being accepted. The words that are sometimes used to describe the Three are 'competitive achiever.' I realized that I was very competitive—to a fault. There were certain situations where I would think, 'time to let go and move on,' but I wouldn't. I would stay in the fight because I wanted to win. And one of the other things that I saw that I didn't like was that Threes tend to exaggerate things to make themselves look more important.

"Right out of college I started in the financial planning business, which at that time was in its infancy. It wasn't even developed yet. And when the credential, the 'certified financial planner,' was developed, I was a graduate of the first class of CFPs. And I obtained some other professional designations as well, in addition to having a college degree in business. As the business evolved over the years, it started to get more and more accepted as a profession and the standards moved upwards. And for the business that I wanted to build, I personally didn't have the credentials, the full credentials, to stand on my own. So I went to work surrounding myself with people who had those credentials. I almost lived vicariously through the people that I worked with. To the point that today, it's crazy. In a firm of our size—we manage just under a billion dollars of assets—I'm not aware of any firm in the country that has the academic horsepower we have. We have three PhDs on staff, and something like eight engineering degrees, including a masters in nuclear engineering. Just

top, top people. And I found myself talking and bragging too much about that. And so my colleagues have said, 'Richard, tone it down.' And so, now I realize that that was not good. It wasn't showing well for me. So I consciously worked on toning that down.

"Learning about your Enneagram type is a 'good news/bad news' story. The competitive side of the Three can be negative sometimes—competing when I didn't need to be competing. The flip side of that is that my competitive nature really helped me accomplish a lot of goals. Once I got my mind set on something, I pretty much accomplished it. I would just stay on it."

When You Are a Manager and You Are a Three

People who have a Type Three personality are natural leaders who like to be in a position to drive work forward and accomplish big goals in a way that works for everybody. If you are a Three leader you will likely rise to the top levels of organizations because your habitual mind-set aligns perfectly with conventional business practices. Threes are programmed to focus on a goal, find the most effective plan to get to the goal, and do whatever it takes to execute the plan. As a Three, you tend to view emotions as unproductive, and may focus on the work more than on people. You can be emotionally deep inside, but may avoid your own feelings as part of the effort to get things done.

Threes' tendency to prioritize work above everything may be amplified when they are in charge. As a Three leader, you tend to make sure you are working harder than anyone else and usually have high expectations for the people who work under you—both in terms of your level of productivity and dedication to the work—and you may have a low tolerance for people who don't meet those expectations. At their best, you take the big picture into account and demonstrate a thorough understanding of how to motivate people to do their best to achieve their goals.

When Your Manager Is a Three

The great thing about having a Three boss is they will be very dedicated to the work and the goals of the organization—and you, if you do good work. They will set a clear vision and model a strong work ethic, even if they sometimes overdo it (and want you to overdo it too). If you meet goals, and contribute to the success of the organization, your Three boss will be very happy with you.

If you slow things down or do things your boss perceives as a waste of time, things may not go as well.

When stressed or less self-aware, Threes can be insensitive to people's feelings and the human problems that at times interfere with work. They can be so focused on meeting goals that they can run over people or fail to pay attention to feedback. If they see that something is not working, or you aren't doing what they believe you are meant to be doing, they may question you. Underperformers will be managed.

At their best, Type Three bosses can be really awesome—they can be supportive, helpful, and will let the team get on with it and do their work without interference. One-to-One Threes particularly want to have strong working relationships so they can encourage people to fulfill their potential. Self-aware Threes will make a point of talking with people to sort things out when problems crop up. They will still be very task-driven, but will take more time to be friendly.

When Your Subordinate Is a Three

When your direct reports have a Type Three style, you can count on them to focus on implementing your plans and goals, and if you communicate your objectives clearly, to enjoy the challenge of doing the work to make them happen. Threes can thrive whether they are the boss or not; as long as they believe in and understand how success is defined, they will devote themselves to achieving it.

A Three who does not respect his or her boss may have a hard time hiding it, and the boss can feel disrespected. Threes have clear ideas about how things should be done, and if they don't agree with the way the boss is doing things, they may challenge them. Conflicts are likely if Threes feel micromanaged or their input is not taken into account. They also move really fast, and it can become awkward if the boss can't keep up.

If you have a good relationship with your Three employees, they will try to do everything they can to make you look good, just as they would want someone to do for them if they were the boss. Threes really appreciate leaders who listen to their ideas and let them do whatever they want to do, and things work well when the boss trusts their Three direct reports to get the job done well with little supervision.

Getting Along with Threes: Tips for What to Do to Work Well with Threes

▶ *Be competent and get shit done.* Threes like coworkers who they can trust to do a competent job and do what they say they are going to do. Meet your deadlines, do quality work in a timely fashion, and be accountable when your work is not up to par.

▶ *Leave them alone to do what they do.* Threes like to have the freedom to get things done quickly on their schedule. It's best not to bother them with stuff they don't find meaningful or relevant to the work that needs to be done.

▶ *Be mindful of Threes' preferred pace.* Threes move fast. Your work pace may not be as rapid as theirs may, and sometimes there will be unavoidable slowdowns, but it will help you to help them if you understand how very much they like things to move along quickly.

▶ *Don't waste their time.* Be on time to meetings, don't make meetings longer than they have to be, don't engage in too much small talk, and don't spend a lot of time explaining stuff to them that they don't need to know to do their job. Communicate in bullet points.

▶ *Recognize that relationships may be secondary to work.* The Three in your office may or may not need to be your friend. Relationships are important to Threes, but they are more open to relating to others when they don't have a lot of work to do. If you befriend your Three teammate, don't be too offended if the Three prioritizes work above your relationship (or has a hard time listening to what you did last weekend).

▶ *If you want their attention, get on their calendar.* Threes often have their whole day and week planned out and scheduled, down to their morning workout and the mid-week social hour. If you want their undivided attention, make sure you've blocked out some time in their schedule so they can make their best effort to be present.

▶ *Don't expect them to spend time dealing with your feelings.* Threes habitually avoid feeling and managing their own emotions, so they certainly don't want to deal with yours. If you feel hurt, angry or disappointed by something at work, Threes will want you to suck it up, act like a grown-up, and get on with getting things done.

▶ *Help them to avoid "the f-word."* Threes have a very difficult time with failure. (Some of them will have a hard time even considering the possibility of it.) So they will appreciate it if you do everything in your power to help them succeed—or be kind when things don't go well and help them slow down long enough to learn from it.

▶ *Recognize their efforts and achievements.* Although some Threes may show it more than others may, Threes do all that they do to gain the respect and admiration of others. They will feel supported and appreciated if you make a point of acknowledging key wins and all the hard work they do.

Actionable Growth Tasks and Suggestions: How Type Threes Can Become More Self-Aware, Effective, and Happy at Work

All the types can learn to be less reactive and better at collaborating with others through first *observing* their habitual patterns, then thinking about the things they think, feel, and do to gain more *self-insight*, and then making efforts to *manage* or moderate their automatic reactions to key triggers.

Threes grow through first observing and then learning to moderate their habitual reactions to key triggers like being slowed down by others' "incompetence," having to deal with others' emotions, and having their efforts thwarted by other people's agendas or needs.

When Threes can watch what they do enough to "catch themselves in the act" of doing the things that get them in trouble, and then pause and reflect on what they are doing and why, they can gradually learn to moderate their programming and knee-jerk responses. Here are some ideas to help Threes be more self-aware, more emotionally intelligent, and more satisfied at work (and at home).

Self-Observation: Things for Threes to Watch Out For

▶ *Observe your need to move quickly in getting things done. What happens when you get slowed down? Notice how you resist slowing down or stopping. What's behind your need for speed?*

▶ *Notice how much you love to check things off your "to do" list. Why do you get such extreme satisfaction from getting stuff done? What kinds of things do you do to prioritize checking something off your list?*

▶ *Notice how you keep yourself busy all the time. Observe what motivates your need to stay in motion and work so hard. Notice especially what you might be avoiding.*

▶ *Observe how you relate to your own emotions. What is going on when you do so much you don't leave room for them? Under what conditions do you feel more and less?*

▶ *Observe your desire for recognition. To what extent does this motivate you to perform and succeed? What is this about for you? When you receive recognition, can you take it in?*

▶ *Notice how you read the people around you and the social context for clues to how to present yourself for maximum benefit. Become conscious of how you shift your presentation to fit your audience and what's behind that.*

▶ *Observe what you do to avoid failure. Why is failure such a bad thing?*

▶ *Notice what happens when something gets in the way of your path to your goal. What feelings arise? What is this about?*

▶ *Notice how you tend to prioritize work above relationships. Why? What are the consequences?*

Blind Spots: What You Don't Know Can Hurt You!

What blind spots Threes often don't see in themselves:

▶ *Your emotions and the value of emotions generally.* As a part of their drive to get things done, Threes often avoid or ignore or minimize their emotions. Yet, as heart-based types, they use their sometimes-neglected emotional capacity to read people to determine in part how to present themselves. It helps Threes to develop if they can connect more with their unacknowledged feelings because their emotions help them to know who they really are, what they really want, and what things are really worth doing.

▶ *The value of slowing down (and occasionally stopping).* Threes risk their health, their psychological well-being, and often their relationships if they don't look at how and why they move so fast and do so much. It helps them to recognize the value of consciously slowing down and taking better care of themselves.

▶ *Your real self—who you really are apart from your image.* What usually gets lost in all of Threes doing and achieving is themselves. Threes focus so much on the image they want to create and the accomplishments that help them look good that they often don't know who they are, what they really want, and how they want to live. Discovering who they are can literally save their lives.

▶ *The importance of relationships.* Often without meaning to, Threes sacrifice their relationships—or the quality of their relationships—by putting all their energy into their work. It can be hard for them to be present with people, and it can be difficult for them to be present enough to see that they are not present. When Threes work to become self-aware, it is important for them to examine the state of their relationships and create enough room to consciously choose prioritizing being present with people instead of unconsciously sacrificing their personal life.

▶ *The need for love—what's behind the image management and the need for recognition.* Threes do all they do to be loved and appreciated for who they really are. So, it's kind of ironic that they strive to be recognized and valued, but then they get so busy and so focused on living from an image that they aren't home inside themselves to receive real warmth and positive regard from others. Threes on a growth path benefit from realizing that what really drives them is the need for affection and doing what it takes to open up to actually getting it.

Self-Insight: Things for Threes to Think About, Understand, and Explore

▶ *How and why do you resist slowing down so much? What might you be afraid will happen if you slow down or stop?*

▶ *Why are you so driven to do tasks and realize goals? What motivates this drive, and what would happen if you resisted it?*

▶ *Why do you avoid feeling your emotions? What feels threatening about opening up to a more conscious awareness of what you are feeling?*

▶ *In what ways do you create an image that differs from who you really are? Reflect on instances in which you presented yourself in a way that misrepresented how you really feel, what you really think, or who you really are. How and why does this happen? Explore the differences between the image(s) you create and who you really are.*

▶ *What gets in the way of being present with the people in your life? What feels difficult about engaging more deeply more often with the people you are in relationships with? Is there something you are missing out on when you are working so hard?*

Strengths to Leverage

It helps Threes to be aware of, actively pay attention to, fully own, and leverage:

▶ *Ability to get the job done well and quickly.* The world already rewards you for this, and it gives you a lot of power. Growth doesn't mean you have to change what works, it just means being able to moderate when appropriate.

▶ *Confidence and determination when working toward a goal.* Other types suffer because they can't take action to make things happen—so celebrate this as a big strength and find creative and interesting ways to put it to work to make the world a better place.

▶ *Ability to read people/Ability to relate to people.* You may not be giving yourself enough credit for how well you relate to people. Ask people for feedback about how your relationship is going—and what they value about you—and notice if you find any clues to what's extraordinary about the real you that you need to embrace.

▶ *Resourcefulness and tenacity.* One of the perks associated with being someone who gets shit done is that you can almost always find a way to make important things happen. The world needs this quality—so own it and teach others how to do it.

▶ *Emotional sensitivity.* You probably don't give yourself enough credit for how sensitive you can be to people's emotional struggles when you want to be. Allow yourself to be touched by people more often and see how it opens you up to the beauty and richness of your emotional capacities. Getting past your fear in this area will enhance your life.

Self-Management: Challenging Tendencies for Threes to Moderate

▶ *Fast pace.* Part of what drives Threes to move so fast and do so much is an unconscious desire to avoid feeling inadequate or unloved. Threes may subconsciously fear that if they stop or slow down, feelings like these will arise that they don't want to feel. But it's crucial for Threes to learn to moderate the pace so they can be more present to their lives and who they are.

▶ *Drive to compete.* The need to win at all costs often comes with a large price tag. Threes develop through learning they don't always have to win to have value. Balancing the desire to succeed with a conscious effort to embrace the lessons in failure helps Threes to grow and accept all of themselves.

▶ *Doing.* Similarly, Threes benefit when they can moderate their compulsion to always be doing. They become more whole and happy through balancing doing with a greater openness to feeling and just being.

▶ *Image management.* At a deeper level, Threes may believe that it's their image that people love and not who they are as unique individuals. The more Threes do to become someone others will admire, the more they potentially become less of themselves.

▶ *Overworking/staying busy.* At some point, when you can't slow down or stop working ever—even on vacation (!)—it may dawn on you that this is a problem. Develop the ability to moderate your workaholic tendencies so an illness or some other sort of breakdown doesn't have to do it for you.

▶ *Over-identifying with your work or your image.* If you are a Three, you may think that you are what you do—but you are much more than that! If you have the idea that you would be no one without your job, it's time to get to know yourself! You are so much more than your image or the work you do.

Consciously Manifesting Your Higher Potential: Being Aware of the "Low Side" and Aiming for the "High Side"

Threes can also grow through consciously becoming aware of the self-limiting habits and patterns associated with their personality style and learning to embody the higher aspects or more expansive and balanced capacities of the Type Three personality:

▶ Learn to become conscious of the need to look good to impress others and try to present yourself more as yourself. Realize that the real you is better than any image you create could ever be.

▶ Learn to be aware of why you drive yourself so hard and do so much work, and consider that you don't have to do it all or be successful to be the valuable, lovely, awesome competent person you already are.

▶ Learn to be conscious of not being present and learn to take your attention off your to-do list and put it on what's happening in the moment.

▶ Learn to be more aware of what compels you to do, do, do, and work so hard and then try to interrupt that compulsion by slowing down, relaxing more, and luxuriating in feeling and being.

▶ Learn to observe the way you index (or over-index) success as the measure of who you are and develop the ability to index other yardsticks, like how you feel, what you desire, what has meaning, and how people react to you when you are being honest about who you are.

▶ Learn to notice when you are over-identifying with your work or your image and do what it takes to get in touch with the real you—who you really are, how you really feel, and what you really want.

Overall, Type Threes can fulfill their higher potentials by observing and working against their habitual focus on doing and performing to create an image of being a winner and learn to focus more deeply on how they feel, what they really want, and who they really are. When they can moderate their tendency to drive forward in the fastest way possible to get to the goal and do the hard work of slowing down, they can access more support from their inner being as well as the people around them. When they can lean into their large and often untapped capacity for feeling the richness of their inner experience, they can enhance the things they do and produce in a way they may never have imagined by putting more of the unique gifts and emotional truth of their real self into the mix. When they can combine their amazing ability to take action with the depth of who they are as individuals, they can be powerful leaders who do big things well in a way that benefits everyone.

CHAPTER 7

The Type Four Leadership Style
The Power of Authentic Self-Expression

"Don't worry about being good... aspire to be authentic."
Yann Martel, author

"Everyone is so obsessed with themselves nowadays that they have no time for me."
Louise Rennison, author and comedian

"I don't think there's anything worse than being ordinary."
Angela Hayes (played by Mena Suvari), in the movie *American Beauty*

The Type Four archetype is the prototypical person who wants to be seen as unique and special in the things they do and the way they relate to others. A Four's attention automatically goes to his or her connectedness (or lack thereof) to others, to noticing and sometimes idealizing (or complaining about) what's missing, to evaluating the authenticity and aesthetics of things, and to making comparisons to other people. Sometimes called "The Artist," or "The Romantic," Fours are one of the most emotional types in the Enneagram system, and are sensitive to both their inner world and their outer surroundings. They see translating their emotional depth into creative acts of self-expression as the way to be understood by others and form meaningful connections.

A Four's programming says the way to have value in the world is to be recognized and affirmed as a unique and special individual. So, their style is shaped by a focus on expressing themselves—through their creativity or through their feelings—and being seen and appreciated for that authentic "specialness." They seek to communicate their internal experience through the things they do in meaningful and aesthetically pleasing ways, and are highly attuned to how they are received and validated (or not) by the outside world. And while Fours have a special talent for accessing and empathizing with deep emotions, they may suffer when they do not receive the understanding

135

and affirmation they seek from others, as they may struggle to provide it for themselves.

Fours try to communicate in ways that will engender connection and understanding, but they also often experience the pain of disconnection and misunderstanding when others do not see them as they want to be seen. There can be a lot of "I" and "me" in their communications—their speaking style tends to be self-referential, as they seek to be understood on the basis of how they are feeling and what they are thinking.[16] They like forming deeper connections through conversations based on sharing emotions and personal experience, and tend to dislike superficial exchanges.

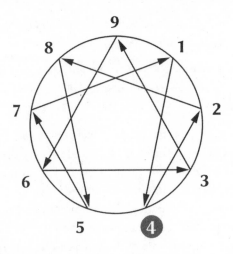

Leaders who have a Type Four style tend to be attuned to people's emotions, passionate about the things they do, and dedicated to providing an environment where people feel welcome to express themselves authentically. They can be hard-working humanitarians, soulful artists, or passionate visionaries. But whether they inspire others through their dedication to important human causes or their romantic and idealistic temperament, they combine a sensitivity to emotional experience with a drive to make an impact through the depth, creativity, and meaning they create and promote in the world.

How to Tell If You Are a Type Four: The View from the Inside

If most or all of the following characteristics apply to you, you may have a Type Four personality style:

▶ *You see the work you do through the lens of your internal experience.* Your work is based on (and happens through) your connection to your emotional life and your inner experience of the things you do and the people you interact with.

▶ *You want to be seen and understood as who you feel you uniquely are.* It's crucial for you to be appreciated by others as who you understand yourself to be on the inside, not as who others might perceive (or misperceive) you to be.

▶ *You seek to connect with others in meaningful ways and disdain superficiality.* You have a hard time doing small talk because you seek depth and meaning.

▶ *You can't help comparing yourself to others and dwelling on how you are lacking or how you are special in relation to other people.* You may feel envious of people you think have something you don't (that you want), and may feel superior to people who don't have what you do. Or, you may work hard to get what you want so you don't have to ward off envious feelings.

▶ *You are sensitive to the experience of not being connected when you'd like to be.* Sometimes, you may feel like you don't fit in—like you are on the outside looking in.

▶ *You find satisfaction in expressing yourself in a way that communicates your unique experience of the world.* Self-expression is very important to you; you enjoy the richness of the challenge of translating your inner experience into art or other creative work projects.

▶ *You place a high value on being authentic.* While some people avoid expressing emotions, especially at work, you believe that as long as the emotion is authentic, there's nothing wrong with having your feelings.

▶ *You can be emotional, oversensitive, or moody, and your strong emotions have at times caused problems for you in relationships.* While you may feel self-conscious about expressing your emotions, feeling your feelings is one of the primary ways you connect to yourself and understand your experience.

▸ *You enjoy connecting with people on the basis of shared authentic thoughts and emotions—and it's important to you to feel understood.* You consider it important to express yourself authentically and you hope others will too. You may have a hard time faking it, and if someone fails to understand you, you may have a difficult time moving forward in relating to them.

▸ *You can sometimes feel inadequate or deficient because you can't help comparing yourself to others and noticing what you are lacking.* You may at times feel "less than" when you believe other people have things you don't have or are somehow in a better position than you are.

▸ *It's easy for you to see what's missing in a given situation.* Your attention naturally goes to what is lacking, but when you point this out to people, they can sometimes perceive you as negative.

▸ *You have a talent for sensing what's going on at the emotional level among people, whether it's in your family, your team, or your organization.* You often play the role of truth teller, which can lead to people feeling supported by you when you name something important that may be happening under the surface, but can also lead to people discounting you when they don't want to face what is really going on.

▸ *Your comfort with deep emotions means people seek you out when they need to talk about how they feel or when they are in pain.* Your ability to feel a range of emotions and your familiarity and comfort with painful ones means you can be present when people are feeling their feelings.

The Central Adaptive Strategy of the Type Four Personality Style

Fours often report having experienced some sort of loss of connection early in life that shapes their style of coping in the world. Often, they have a memory of being loved by or enjoying meaningful contact with a parent or caregiver, and then something happened to change that important connection. A younger sibling came along, or a life event made the parent unavailable or less available, and the Four child felt this as a loss of love or a painful shift in a life-supporting relationship.

Motivated to try to regain what was lost, Fours strive to prove themselves worthy, or communicate their suffering, or assert their specialness. They develop an adaptive strategy of engaging with the feelings of loss and longing as a way of managing what happens in their connections, expressing themselves in unique ways to invite connection with the right people, and identifying with a deficient or superior sense of themselves as a way of protecting themselves from re-experiencing the early sense of abandonment.

This focus on feeling and emotion makes Fours' coping style less suited to the conventions of the western workplace than other types, and the Type Four leadership style is less obviously compatible with the typical corporate setting. It may be difficult for Fours to get the understanding they crave from coworkers with other styles, and it can be hard for non-Fours to see how feeling "bad" feelings or identifying with darker emotions like pain and sadness can serve as a self-protective strategy. But people who lead with a Type Four style bring much-needed qualities and strengths to business—they naturally see what is lacking and needed to make things more whole, more beautiful, more functional, or more balanced. Plus, their ability to attune to others and empathize with their emotional experiences makes them uniquely suited to understanding key elements of work and working relationships, including what people need to relate to each other in productive ways and how authentic self-expression can lead to visionary and innovative creation.

What Do Fours Pay Attention To? The Type Four "Radar Screen"

The strategy of presenting themselves and the things they do in a way that allows them to express themselves, connect with others, and be understood focuses Fours' attention on what is going on inside them. Fours seek to connect to themselves (and others) through an ongoing experience of their inner emotional territory. They automatically see what is missing—including what they lack that makes them feel unworthy or inadequate—and automatically focus people's attention on what is necessary that is being left out.

At work, Fours tend to focus on human interaction and the creative aspects of the job. They will usually have an opinion about how something works aesthetically and how to improve it, and will offer insights on how people are getting along and what's happening (especially emotionally) at a deeper level among colleagues. Their perceptual bias prioritizes meaning, depth, and authenticity—so they may be preoccupied with addressing or fixing people or relationships that don't feel sufficiently connected, effective, or meaningful.

People with a Type Four personality style are "self-referencing," meaning their attention goes immediately to their own inner experience rather than what other people are feeling and doing and needing. They may be more aware of what's going on in their internal landscape than what's happening to you. It's not that they aren't interested in others—they pay a great deal of attention to their relationships and can be very attuned to others when they want to be. It's more that their primary focus is on what they are experiencing.

The View from "Planet Four": How Fours See the World

Generally, individuals with a Type Four style view what's happening in terms of how it measures up against an ideal. Like Type Ones, they make automatic mental comparisons about themselves and their circumstances, but while Ones focus on detecting and correcting errors in a matter-of-fact way, Fours tend to make value judgments based on how meaningful (or not) something feels. They are attracted to the extraordinary and disdain the mundane, which can give them a "the grass is always greener..." outlook. To Fours, what's distant and unavailable is often more interesting and worthwhile than what's present in the here-and-now.

Fours want the world to see and affirm their worth as unique individuals. However, their lived experience often shows them that people misunderstand them (and each other) or fail to validate their value. Fours sometimes feel like their sensitivity to the emotions most people would rather not feel, like pain and sadness, makes them misfits, especially in the working world where emotions are not valued as a meaningful source of data. Fours understand that the information emotions bring has great value, especially when it comes to assessing what works and what doesn't or what has meaning or doesn't or who is connected to whom (or isn't).

Type Fours can't help being open and sensitive to the emotional level of things, even at work, which can sometimes lead them to feel devalued or undervalued. When naturally emotionally intuitive Fours get the message that their sense of things is not appreciated—perhaps because others want to ward off the threat of their own emotional awareness. This can confirm the Four's inner sense of inadequacy. While many Fours develop an inner strength around standing up for their emotional truth, they may also feel sensitive to the judgments and assessments of the people around them, and may doubt their worth in work settings dominated by people who believe emotions have no place in business. Conversely, where this kind of meaning is part of the work, Fours may feel comfortable in the knowledge that they contribute in meaningful ways and their contribution is valued.

The Type Four Leader: Core Characteristics

The following character traits help to define the Type Four leadership style:

▶ *Highly value authentic expression.* Four leaders tend to be very tuned in to the question, "Is what we're doing authentically communicating what we are about?" They want the things they do and produce to be an accurate reflection of the values of the team or the organization.

▶ *Emotionally intuitive and empathetic.* Fours have a special gift for tapping into the emotional level of what's occurring among people. They tend to be in touch with what they are feeling, with others' emotions, and what's happening emotionally among the people around them.

▶ *Desire to stand out as special, unique, or extraordinary.* Motivated by a strong desire to be recognized for the valuable qualities that make them who they uniquely are, fours can prioritize designing products or services that help them express their identity and attract attention as being especially beautiful or effective. They may get competitive out of a desire to outshine the competition.

▶ *Attentional bias to what's happening in relationships in terms of emotional connection.* Four leaders tune in to the "relationship channel"—they pay attention to the status of their connections and put energy into establishing and maintaining meaningful relationships, though they may not stay connected if it means being inauthentic.

▶ *Moody/dramatic.* Fours can be unapologetically emotionally expressive, which sometimes leads to other people perceiving them as moody, dramatic, or oversensitive.

▶ *An emphasis on work that has meaning.* Fours may have a hard time staying motivated if the work they do doesn't have meaning. And they can add value to an organization when they insist on doing what feels meaningful to the people who work there.

Mental, Emotional, and Behavioral Patterns: Why Do Fours Think, Feel, and Behave the Way They Do?

Mental

Fours think in terms of comparisons and relationships; how others will evaluate what they are producing, how they stack up against others, and how to infuse the things they do with meaning. Deeply connected to their own inner life, Fours fantasize a lot about what could or might happen and ideal scenarios they'd like to manifest, and may focus on the disparity between what they imagine and what is actually happening. They think deeply about what goes on among people and how to communicate with others to express what they are thinking and who they are. Fours can be insightful and intellectually creative, and when they balance their emotional sensitivity with clear and objective thinking, they can be particularly effective in the things they do.

Emotional

Fours are more comfortable with emotion than any of the other Enneagram types are—they live more in their emotions, have more emotional ups and downs, and believe in the value of emotions and emotional connections. They typically have access to a wide range of feelings, which they feel intensely, and can dwell in darker feelings like melancholy and longing, shame and inadequacy, fear (of abandonment) and anxiety, and anger and frustration. However, they may also avoid certain feelings, sometimes by focusing on other feelings that are more comfortable or familiar. For instance, Fours sometimes take refuge in feelings of sadness or melancholy (or false happiness) as a way of defending against the pain of shame or the fear of failure. Fours may also "hang out" in some emotions more than others, because they are more habitual, more aligned with their preferred self-image, or more useful as a protection against other emotions. Fours are especially attuned to the beauty that can be found in pain and the poetry and richness of deep emotional experience, and can readily feel the flipside of difficult feelings, as they deeply experience a full range of emotions, including excitement, joy, and happiness.

Behavioral

A Four's behavior varies to a large degree according to which of the three kinds of Fours (described below) we are talking about. Some Fours tend to be hard-working and focused on being tough and accomplishing tasks to prove their worth. Other Fours can over-identify with their emotions and may have a difficult time moving out of feeling and into action—they may dwell on what they don't have or a sense of inferiority that can be paralyzing. Still other Fours may actively compete to win or prove themselves superior as a way of asserting and communicating their value. Generally, some Fours can be more depressed and withdrawn, and others can be more active or even hyperactive. When overly attached to feelings of inadequacy and low self-worth, they may have trouble taking action, but when they feel good about themselves, they can be motivated to achieve high levels of excellence.

The Main Strengths and Superpowers of the Type Four Style: What Fours Are Really Good At

- ▶ *Artistic impulse/Aesthetic sensibility.* Fours see and seek to highlight what's beautiful or poetic in everyday reality. They naturally tune in to aesthetics and what can be done to make things more pleasing.

- ▶ *Emotional intuition.* Fours automatically sense how people are feeling, what tensions and conflicts may exist among them, and the status of their invisible emotional connections.

- ▶ *Large capacity for depth of feeling.* Fours make good counselors, sounding boards, and friends in that they aren't afraid to empathize with you, even if it means joining you in a painful or upsetting emotional space.

- ▶ *The courage to be authentic.* Fours value being real, and tend to be truth tellers who would rather displease someone than communicate in a way that feels false.

- ▶ *Sensitivity to the status of human connections.* Fours have an ability to see and understand how well (or not) people are connected to each other, the obstacles and challenges in the way of relationships, and how open or not people are to relating authentically.

When Too Much of a Good Thing Becomes a Bad Thing: How Fours Can Go Wrong When They Take "Being Real" and Seeking a Life Less Ordinary Too Far

Like all people of all types, when Type Four leaders overuse their biggest strengths (and don't consciously develop a wider range of specialties), they can also turn out to be their Achilles' heel.

▶ *Artistic impulse/Aesthetic sensibility.* Fours can get hung up on getting the aesthetics just right, which can slow down the process of completing something. They may become frustrated when the reality of what they create doesn't live up to the ideal they imagine.

▶ *Emotional intuition.* Fours can overwhelm people who aren't as comfortable navigating emotional territory when they insist on surfacing feelings others aren't ready to face.

▶ *Large capacity for depth of feeling.* Fours may express too much emotion for others to process, may hold up work processes when they insist on their feelings being validated and understood, and may judge others who can't access their emotions in the same way they can.

▶ *The courage to be authentic.* Fours can push others to be honest in ways they may not be ready for, and may express more authentic emotion than a situation requires. They may judge those who are unable to adhere to their high standards of emotional truth as inauthentic.

▶ *Sensitivity to the status of human connections.* When Fours focus too much on how people are relating, they can get stuck in wanting to fix relationship issues and neglect work priorities. They may have trouble accepting the real limitations of some connections or individuals.

Fortunately, Fours' sincere interest in people and forging meaningful connections means that they can often learn that in order to work well together, they may need to temper some of their requirements for mutual emotional understanding. When they can balance their own needs and feelings with a realistic understanding of what's possible in their work setting, they are able to offer their gifts and talents in a way others can appreciate.

"When I'm stressed..." and "At my best...": Understanding the "Low Side" and the "High Side" of the Type Four Personality Style

When stressed to the point of going to their "low side," Type Fours can become moody and temperamental, and tend to make everything about them and what they are feeling, thinking, and needing. Some Fours get more self-punishing under stress, while others will (often unconsciously) punish other people. They may complain more openly or angrily about what's not working for them and how they aren't getting what they need; or they may sulk and stop cooperating as a way of signaling that something is wrong and they need more attention.

Some Fours on the low side may act more withdrawn and melancholy, becoming depressed or shut down, while others may speed up and work harder in an anxious way. They may appear more reactive and respond more emotionally to things, and they may have a difficult time moderating the emotions they express. Some may try to control themselves, knowing their emotional reactivity may alienate people, others will let go of any concern about impression management and just get mad, and still others will control their feelings initially, but then explode if they get angry or hurt enough. At their worst, they can be like Eeyore, the Type Four donkey from *Winnie the Pooh*—big downers who focus only on what's negative or not working to the point where others see them as pessimistic or obstructionist.

On the "high side," when Type Four leaders become more self-aware and conscious of their programming, they can be wise, creative, and compassionate. They draw on their deep capacity for empathy to create a bold vision of the work that needs to be accomplished in a way that can inspire their people. At their healthiest, Fours balance clear contact with their inner experience—a conscious sense of their needs and emotions—with a sense of generosity and gratitude in understanding and supporting others. They learn to engage their feelings, receive the information they bring, process them or communicate them with self-awareness, and let them go.

Healthy Fours demonstrate how emotional intelligence and sensitivity can be a great strength in the workplace. They use the wisdom they develop learning to navigate their own emotional terrain to guide and mentor others, and can bring people together, sensitively mediate conflicts, and name emotional issues that need to be faced so teams can become more cohesive. Unafraid of intense feeling or interpersonal stress, they support others in communicating more honestly as a way of welcoming more of people's "real selves" at work, creating an atmosphere of authenticity and support where individuals can thrive and enjoy what they do.

The Three Kinds of Four Leaders: How the Three Instinctual Biases Shape the Three Type Four Sub-Type Personalities

According to the Enneagram model, we all have three main instinctual drives that help us survive, but in each of us, one tends to dominate our behavior. The Type Four style is expressed differently depending on whether a person has a bias toward *self-preservation*, *social* relationships within groups, or *one-to-one* bonding.

The Self-Preservation (or Self-Focused) Four

Self-Preservation Fours are the least outwardly emotional Fours. Having received the message that their emotions were too much for people (usually a parent early on), they try to keep a lid on darker feelings like sadness, disappointment, hurt, and anger, leading some people to think they can't possibly be Fours at all. In reality, these Fours connect deeply to their emotions; they just keep their negative feelings to themselves so they don't alienate the people they want to be connected to. Instead, they lead with friendliness and an upbeat, happy exterior presentation.

Self-preservation Fours tend to be more anxious than the other two Fours, although they are typically stoic and strong, and learn to endure pain without showing it. Outwardly, they are more "sunny" and helpful and work hard to prove their worth. Instead of dwelling in envy or dissatisfaction at not having enough or being good enough, Self-Preservation Fours strive to get what they want, and hope to earn others' respect and affection through doing for others and not burdening people with their pain. They can be tenacious in working toward a goal, but also reckless, throwing themselves into an effort to achieve or help others by sacrificing themselves or disregarding their own safety. They seek to earn others' admiration by showing how much they can do, sometimes silently taking on more than their share of the work and shouldering more of the burden.

As leaders, Self-Preservation Fours provide others with a heroic model of how to work hard in support of a cause or to improve conditions for others. They may resemble Threes in their dedication to their work, but they will also be attuned to what's happening at the emotional level of the group. Self-Preservation Fours tend to be humanitarians, committed to alleviating the pain of others, and typically throw themselves into whatever they do. As one Self-Preservation Four leader told me, "If someone tells me I can't do something, I don't stop until I do it." This reflects the determination and tenacity that drives the overall Four leadership style, which blends a deep concern with and compassion for emotional experience with a work style motivated by a desire to prove they can do whatever they decide to do. Self-Preservation Fours temper this intensity with a lightness and sense of fun that helps them transcend their pain and connect with others.

The Social (or Group-Focused) Four

In contrast to the Self-Preservation Four, the Social Four is more emotionally expressive and more melancholy. Social Fours wear their emotions on their sleeves, hoping to gain attention and support through communicating their difficult feelings. Social Fours are sensitive people who feel deeply connected to their emotions—and connect to themselves at a deep level through experiencing those emotions.

More than the other two Fours, Social Fours have a habit of comparing themselves to others and winding up on the bottom, viewing themselves as in some way inferior or inadequate. This can seem puzzling to people close to them because they are often (objectively) competent, attractive, successful people. Yet they can be so stubborn in their insistence that there is something wrong with them that you want to ask, "What's wrong with you that you think there's something wrong with you?"[17] As explained above, this can be understood as Social Fours' way of hiding out in a negative self-image as a way to protect themselves from the even worse feeling they might have if they go to all the trouble of taking action to get what they want—and ultimately fail.

As leaders, Social Fours have a talent for reminding people of the need to be more authentic and effective by tapping into deep feelings—even if that means facing some pain. They don't shy away from taking a strong stand for the value of emotions and emotional intelligence in informing the work people do, and their own fearlessness in the face of pain and grief allows them to be courageous and bold when they take action to express themselves creatively. Although at times they may focus too much attention on what feels challenging, at their best they make it safe for others to face their vulnerabilities as a way to develop greater strength as individuals or within teams.

The One-to-One (or Relationship-Focused) Four

One-to-One Fours are the most competitive of the three Type Four sub-types. They automatically compare themselves to others and want to come out on top, and can become so focused on getting what they need and proving their superiority that they leave impression management behind. And while they adopt this superior attitude as compensation for an underlying sense of inadequacy (that they may not be consciously aware of), others may perceive the One-to-One Four as arrogant or difficult. These Fours may project their pain outward, acting out envy through competing or by expressing anger that others aren't meeting their needs. They tend to believe "the squeaky wheel gets the oil," which can result in a vicious cycle, as the One-to-One Four gets demanding, people react negatively, and the Four becomes more assertive or insistent, which intensifies others' reactions.

One-to-One Fours' deeper motivation is a refusal to suffer the pain at feeling less than other people feel. They may focus on how the outside world doesn't measure up or affirm their worth, and may try to minimize others' accomplishments to elevate their own. More shameless than shameful, One-to-One Fours don't have a problem expressing anger, which is why they sometimes get mistaken for Type Eights, who also aren't afraid to confront someone if they need to. They may express an elitist attitude, and can have an all-or-nothing view of success—if they don't win decisively, they will be left with nothing.

As leaders, One-to-One Fours can be bold visionaries who are willing to fight to be heard and do whatever it takes to achieve success. They tend to have an upbeat, active energy that fuels them to work hard to prove their worth and demonstrate their superior abilities. When they are less self-aware, they can be hard to work with—they will complain when they don't like what others are doing, protest when they don't get what they need, and, when they feel inferior, may express anger as a way to assert power and manipulate situations. However, when they are more conscious and aware, they can be interesting and attractive, deeply engaged in their work and their relationships, and passionately committed to doing what it takes to achieve success in whatever they do. They can be innovative and artistic visionaries (like Steve Jobs) who energetically work with others to do great things.

The Type Four at Work

Type Fours sometime feel like working with others is hard because:

▶ I often don't feel understood by the people I'm working with.

▶ It can be hard to know how to collaborate with people who don't share my vision.

▶ My coworkers don't place the same value on emotional expression as I do.

▶ I feel dismissed when others won't take the time to listen to me and make an effort to understand how I am feeling.

▶ I sometimes compare myself with others and can get stuck in the emotions that are stirred up by feeling less than (or more than) other people.

▶ My bosses or coworkers won't deal with the underlying tensions within the team—and don't want to hear it when I try to surface them to urge people to address them.

▶ It's hard for me to work well with others if they haven't taken the time to connect with me and understand who I am on a personal level.

▶ I can have a difficult time relating to people I perceive as fake or inauthentic.

▶ It's hard for me to engage in small talk or superficial conversations, so I sometimes feel awkward and uncomfortable communicating with coworkers I don't know well or whom I perceive as shallow.

Type Fours' workplace pet peeves may be:

▶ When people can't slow down long enough to get to know me.

▶ When people don't value my contribution or appreciate the work I do.

▶ When people perceive me as negative or pessimistic when I am trying to help by bringing attention to what is missing.

▶ When people don't understand what I am saying or how I am feeling but keep insisting that they do.

▶ When others prioritize speed and efficiency over getting the aesthetics right.

▶ When my bosses make me spend a lot of time working on mundane tasks that don't have meaning to me.

▶ When I don't get rewarded or compensated in a way that feels commensurate with my talent or abilities.

▶ When people tell me to "just get over it" or "look on the bright side" when I am having difficult feelings about what's going on.

▶ When I'm not heard, or people don't value my feelings or intuition.

▶ When other people don't care about the aesthetics of the physical environment, or create a negative working atmosphere.

Here's What Type Fours Can Do to Be Easier to Work With

As leaders, Fours can try to have patience with people when they don't value or address emotions in the same way they do. They can consciously experience and process their feelings in whatever ways they need to, and then support themselves (or get support) in finding ways to communicate about what's happening that others can more readily understand. Type Fours will benefit from developing more inner resources for coping when they feel misunderstood and finding creative ways to communicate their perceptions without getting reactive. It helps them to remember to value their depth and emotional intelligence, even when others do not.

It is also useful for Fours at all levels of an organization to actively remind themselves to have compassion for people who have a difficult time experiencing and communicating about emotions. This can be hard in the business world, where Fours may feel devalued for their emotional strength and sensitivity, but this is why it's crucial for Fours to not buy into the cultural tendency to make anything related to emotions "bad" out of fear and discomfort.

Since most Fours have a bias toward telling the truth, even when it hurts, it can be helpful to remember that others may tend to project negative stuff onto them. When people want to avoid hearing things they don't want to hear or feeling feelings they don't want to acknowledge, they will resent anyone who stands for facing these difficulties and dealing with the attendant emotions. The more Fours can accept that they are likely to be resented for bringing up uncomfortable realities, the more they can take care of themselves when people willfully misunderstand them or don't want to listen to their perspective. As a Four, it's only natural to react defensively when people don't want to hear what you have to say or deny your feelings, but if you can learn to expect this reaction and develop healthy ways of interacting when it happens, you may end up being more appreciated and understood.

Working with Fours

Typical Type Four Behaviors in the Workplace

You *might* be working with someone who has a Type Four Enneagram style if you see them doing several of the following behaviors on a regular basis:

- ▶ She seems more intense than the average workplace professional.
- ▶ He gets sensitive and defensive if you don't like his creative ideas.
- ▶ She can be moody and temperamental.
- ▶ He always has a lot of ideas about how to improve the aesthetic elements of whatever you are working on together.
- ▶ She speaks in terms of her emotions and feelings about things in a way that seems a little out of place at work.
- ▶ He always draws the team's attention to what's missing in a plan or project in a way that can seem somewhat negative.
- ▶ She tends to look on the dark side and doesn't always appreciate what's going well.
- ▶ He can be demanding and isn't afraid to express anger.
- ▶ Sometimes it seems like she makes everything about her.
- ▶ He sometimes seems arrogant, especially if we all don't acknowledge his contribution and skill. He acts like he's the best (even when he isn't).
- ▶ She works hard to prove herself and works even harder when she's anxious.
- ▶ He brings a sense of artistry and creative thinking to everything we do.
- ▶ She says she feels like she doesn't fit in and that people don't understand her.

What's Great About Working with Conscious Four Leaders

- ▶ They bring a lot of passion and dedication to work they find meaningful or important.
- ▶ They are great people to talk with if you are having difficult or painful emotions (which can be hard to find at work).
- ▶ They make you feel deeply supported when you are going through something that's hard to know how to handle.

▶ They love the creative process, offer a lot of innovative ideas, and help you to access your creativity.

▶ They are really good at tasks that require an artistic eye or design talent or an aesthetic sensibility.

▶ They have a lot of depth and intensity, and so can be fun to talk to, especially about more substantive and meaningful topics.

▶ They make an effort to understand you and connect with you.

▶ They can be great collaborators when you are aligned with them around a common creative vision.

▶ They care about what's happening among people and have the courage to speak up when something needs to be addressed to enhance team cohesiveness.

▶ They aren't afraid of tough conversations or giving honest feedback.

Typical Challenges for People Who Work with Fours

▶ When something isn't working, they will likely confront people about it and express their displeasure openly.

▶ They can seem moody in a way that's hard to know how to deal with, and may slow down work processes when they are upset by something.

▶ They can get upset when they don't feel understood or supported. (And it can be hard to know how to make them feel understood and supported.)

▶ They may resent you if you have a big success that they haven't achieved.

▶ They may dismiss people because they judge them as too superficial or as emotional lightweights.

▶ They may harbor grudges if they feel wronged by someone.

▶ They may appear self-centered and self-absorbed.

▶ They may insist on surfacing issues people don't want to deal with.

▶ They may get mad if they think their contribution isn't valued enough.

Type Fours and Leadership

A Type Four Leader Speaks About How Knowing Your Enneagram Type Helps You at Work

Arash Ferdowsi is cofounder and CTO of Dropbox Inc., a file-hosting service company based in San Francisco that offers cloud storage, file synchronization, personal cloud, and client software.

> *"For me, what I related to in the Type Four description was the tendency to at times feel kind of different or defective, but different in both a bad way and a good way—sometimes feeling like an outsider, but also feeling this desire to feel special or distinct or unique. That stuff really resonated with me. The more I dug into it, the more I understood some of the thought patterns I had that I knew were there. It made me realize that there's not something wrong with me that I'm thinking this way, it's just this bias I have and I need to balance it out with objectivity.*
>
> *"It really helped me understand, more and more, when I have really strong emotional reactions to things, how to unpack them and become a bit more rational about them, knowing I have these tendencies in certain directions.*
>
> *"I definitely think knowing my Enneagram style has helped me to be a better leader. I think it's helped me get better at managing my emotional reactions to things. But it's also helped me to understand what I'm good at and actually leaning into that in certain ways."*

When You Are a Manager and You Are a Four

Being a boss that's a Type Four means you regularly take into account not only how well the work gets done, but also the aesthetic elements (how things look) and the human factor (how people feel) involved in producing that work. You are likely highly empathetic and sensitive to the internal human dynamics of your team and/or organization, and want to know your people, be involved in hiring decisions, and feel connected to key employees.

You may not feel completely comfortable in the role of leader. Your tendency to find fault with yourself can make you reluctant to put yourself out in front or take the lead in things on a larger stage. And, much of your experience as a leader will depend on which subtype of Type Four you are. Self-Preservation Fours will work very hard when in leadership roles, both to prove themselves and to fend off the anxiety that they may feel about not being enough or not having enough. Social Fours may doubt themselves and dwell on feelings of inadequacy, which can undermine their ability to lead, or they may infuse their organization with their deeply held values of authenticity and be a model of personal integrity. One-to-One Fours may enjoy being leaders, being natural competitors who strive to demonstrate that they are the best at whatever they do.

When you feel insecure, you may feel an internal sense of inadequacy, which can make you question your decisions and second-guess your actions. You may rely on close colleagues to provide a reality check about how you are doing and what's going well. At your best, you can be an inspiring leader— sensitive to how people are feeling and simultaneously driven to work hard to produce work product people can feel good about and take pride in.

When Your Manager Is a Four

The great thing about having a boss that's a Four is you can be pretty sure they will be interested in forming a personal connection with you. They will likely put a lot of thought into the hiring process (if they are involved) and will want to see you succeed. They also may be more emotionally available than you expect (or than bosses with other personality styles), and will probably be someone you can talk to if you are struggling. And if they have an issue with you, they will probably bring it up, especially if they feel confident that you have established a good connection.

When under pressure or less self-aware, Type Four bosses can get mired in their emotional reactions to things and may have a difficult time focusing on work or rising above their feelings. This behavior will vary depending on which subtype they are—they may disconnect from you and work harder in a self-sacrificing way, become withdrawn and self-deprecating and see things through a negative lens, or become angry and demanding about the mistakes they perceive people are making that are undermining their success.

At their best, Four bosses are open to honest input from others and deeply appreciative of your contributions. They enjoy the process of how teams interact to communicate about the work and get things done. While they may periodically doubt themselves, they will create a network of trusted associates that can support them in making tough decisions, producing work that has meaning, and celebrating people's successes.

When Your Subordinate Is a Four

When your direct reports have a Type Four style, it will help to keep the lines of communication open so you can be sure you stay connected and talk things through as they happen. Fours perform well when they feel understood and supported, and they are sensitive to feeling like they don't fit in. If they feel understood and connected to you, they can perform very well and provide valuable creative input on a team.

Depending on which kind of Four they are, they may avoid conflict and withdraw when stressed or express their feelings in an apologetic or angry way, and may even insist that you understand and validate how they feel before the work can move forward. If they lead with the Social Four style, they may have a hard time letting go of hard feelings or disappointments. If they have the One-to-One Four style, they may display competitive behavior or complain about things they don't like and ask that their needs be met. If they have a Self-Preservation Four style, they may resemble Type Threes in the work setting. If Fours feel unappreciated or believe their feelings aren't being taken into account, they can become difficult and hard to manage.

On the good side, if you work with a healthy Four, they will be sensitive to your needs and feelings—and those of others—and will work hard to prove their worth and make a high-quality contribution. They will be open to talking about problems and points of disagreement and enjoy expressing themselves creatively in the work they do. And they will be likely to demonstrate a high level of emotional intelligence and want to support the people around them and the work in a meaningful way.

Getting Along with Fours: Tips for What to Do to Work Well with Fours

▶ *Understand them.* Fours are sensitive to feeling misunderstood, so if you make a sincere effort to understand them, you will take a giant step toward getting along with them. (However, it bears repeating: They will be the judge of whether you understand them or not, not you.)

▶ *Let them express emotions without reacting or "fixing" them.* If you let them vent their emotions and make a sincere effort to hear them out, those emotions may subside and the underlying issue may resolve itself. If you don't, they won't and it won't.

▶ *Let them know you value them and their unique contribution to the work.* Fours long to be recognized for what they do that expresses their singular gifts. Take the time to tell them you appreciate them, and be specific about why.

▶ *When they have a problem, don't tell them to "look on the bright side."* If your Four coworker takes issue with something or highlights what's missing, either seriously address the substance of what they point to or let them know in clear terms why you aren't going to.

▶ *Be authentic. Affirm their desire for authenticity.* Fours have a sixth sense when it comes to detecting inauthenticity and insincerity. Be real and honest in the same way they are and it will strengthen your working relationship.

▶ *Connect with them in a meaningful, personal way.* Show them you care about knowing who they are and forming a meaningful connection by listening to them and taking the risk of sharing a bit of your own personal information.

▶ *Help them to see beyond the emotional level without devaluing their emotions.* You can support the Fours in your life by validating their expressions of emotion, but also telling them when you think they may be overdoing it. And remember: they will hear you more clearly (and not get as defensive) if you honor their feelings first.

Actionable Growth Tasks and Suggestions: How Type Fours Can Become More Self-Aware, Effective, and Happy at Work

All the types can learn to be less reactive and better at collaborating with others through first *observing* their habitual tendencies, then thinking about the things they think, feel, and do to gain more *self-insight*, and then making efforts to *manage* or *moderate* their automatic reactions to key triggers.

Fours grow through first observing and then learning to moderate their habitual reactions to key triggers like feeling misunderstood, being dismissed for being moody or difficult, or not feeling valued for who they are and what they contribute.

When Fours can watch what they do enough to "catch themselves in the act" of doing the things that get them in trouble, and then pause and reflect on what they are doing and why, they can gradually learn to moderate their programming and knee-jerk responses. Here are some ideas to help Fours be more self-aware, more emotionally intelligent, and more satisfied at work (and at home).

Self-Observation: Things for Fours to Watch Out For

▶ *Notice the difference between thinking with your feelings and just thinking in a more objective way.*

▶ *Develop an ongoing awareness of your relationship to your emotions: Do you suppress them? Over-indulge them? Amp them up to create drama as a way of avoiding something or defending against the emptiness of the mundane? Get stuck holding onto them? Use them to impact or influence others?*

▶ *Be aware of any tendency you might have to hold on to feelings past their expiration date and have a hard time rising above your emotions or moving on.*

▶ *Notice how you compare yourself to others. What is your thought process like when you do this? How does this make you feel? What motivates it? What are the consequences?*

▶ *Observe your tendency to focus on what's missing or what isn't working. Notice what motivates that and how it impacts others.*

▶ *Notice if you have a hard time focusing on what's positive in the work you are doing. Be aware of ways you may devalue what's happening that's actually good or great through longing for something better—something you may be idealizing because it's unavailable or distant.*

▶ *Observe any tendency you might have to compete with others as a way of proving your worth or combatting underlying feelings of unworthiness.*

▶ *Notice any desire you might have to need to have others see you as special or extraordinary to defend against a fear of being ordinary or inadequate. See if you can detect what's underneath that—what motivates that?*

▶ *Observe your tendency to focus on the past or old hurts or disappointments.*

Blind Spots: What You Don't Know Can Hurt You!

What blind spots Fours often don't see in themselves:

▶ *What's working well or positive in the here-and-now current situation.* People who lead with a Type Four style often display what Carl Jung called "positive shadow." That is, they focus more consciously on what isn't working or feels bad so that their "shadow," or the "dark side" elements they don't want to acknowledge, relate to *positive aspects* of who they are or what they do.

▶ *What's great about you—your gifts, strengths and positive qualities.* Fours tend to focus their attention on what they are lacking, so their strengths and positive capacities—what they do really well—may be blind spots. If they don't see what's good about what they do, they risk undermining their efforts or sabotaging themselves by not seeing the good in themselves.

▶ *Your tendency to be overly "self-referencing"—making things about you and your feelings (when it may not be about you).* Fours automatically tune in to their feelings and thoughts—their own inner experience—as a primary focus. Sometimes they may not realize that others see them as overly self-focused, that they make things all about them when they aren't.

▶ *The deeper feelings of pain, fear, and inadequacy beneath the emotions you'd rather focus on as a diversion.* Fours have more comfort and fortitude when it comes to difficult emotions, like melancholy or pain, than other types. For this reason, they may not always see how they take refuge in a specific feeling (like sadness or pain) as a way of distracting themselves from a deeper, more painful feeling, like fear of failure or rejection.

▶ *All the things you have to be grateful for—and the power of actively remembering to feel gratitude for specific things.* Gratitude can be a relatively easy way for Fours to remind themselves to see what's good in their lives. When they don't own their positive qualities (see above), they may also forget to think about how rejuvenating and uplifting something like intentionally expressing gratitude can be.

Self-Insight: Things for Fours to Think About, Understand, and Explore

▶ *Why is it sometimes difficult to let go of specific emotions, rise above your emotional reactions and move on?*

▶ *What do you get out of focusing on what's missing? What are the consequences on dwelling on your feelings relative to what's missing or lacking?*

▶ *Notice your tendency to compare yourself to others and feel "less than" or "more than" other people and try to understand what motivates that.*

▶ *How and why do you focus on feelings of melancholy or anger? What's behind your focus on those feelings?*

▶ *What is happening when you focus a great deal of attention on needing to be understood and affirmed by others?*

▶ *What is happening when you amp up your feelings to create drama, or alternatively (if you are a Self-Preservation Four) if you get masochistic and focused on toughing things out alone or needing to prove yourself?*

Strengths to Leverage

It helps Fours to be aware of, actively pay attention to, fully own, and leverage:

▶ *Their natural ability to understand the emotional level of interactions.* Like Deanna, the "empath" (psychic) ship's counselor on the television show *Star Trek: The Next Generation*, Fours' ability to understand what's going on among people at a deeper, more emotional level can provide useful insights that can help people understand what's really going on in relationships and within teams. Instead of devaluing this attentiveness to emotions, draw on this wisdom to enhance team dynamics.

▶ *Their dedication to creating a pleasing and comfortable working environment.* People with a Four style place a high value on how things look and feel—they understand that the aesthetics of their physical environment can have a positive impact on people. Fours also naturally tune into people and feel motivated to make sure they have what they need to feel supported in doing their work. By focusing on the emotional tenor of things, they try to remove any emotional obstacles to people doing what they need to do to do their work.

▶ *Valuing and championing the importance of forming connections.* Fours understand that people who feel connected to each other are likely to work better together, and that people who share meaningful experiences will have an easier time producing meaningful work.

▶ *Their fearlessness in the face of emotions many people don't want to face.* Fours tend to express a greater willingness to deal with whatever emotions might arise. A great strength of people with this style is a real willingness to meet difficult situations—and their attendant emotions—head on, and work through them.

▶ *Their intensity, passion, and the courage of their convictions.* Naturally passionate people, Fours bring a real depth to whatever they do. When heartfelt feelings and a desire for deep meaning can be channeled into the work being done, it bodes well for the quality of the results.

Self-Management: Challenging Tendencies for Fours to Moderate

▶ *Welcome but moderate emotions.* Accept your emotional nature as a strength, but also learn what you need to do for yourself to have your feelings, process them, channel them with awareness, rein them in when necessary, express them in conscious ways, and rise above them or let them go when appropriate. For Fours, this last piece is particularly important.

▶ *Build confidence in a positive sense of yourself.* Learn to value yourself more from the inside so you don't need so much validation, understanding, and affirmation from the outside to know you are valuable and good.

▶ *Temper your emotional reactions to things.* Although your emotional intuitiveness is a great strength, learn to give yourself the space you need to be with your emotional responses for a while before you express them in the work environment. Consciously combining your feeling responses with intellectual insight and an awareness of the context and the other people involved (and their capacity for emotional understanding) will help you to be more effective when you express both your thoughts and your emotions.

▶ *Noticing what's missing.* While it's a strength to be able to discern what is needed and lacking, putting too much attention on this too often can lead to others perceiving you as overly negative or unsupportive.

▶ *Going for depth, meaning, and intensity.* People who lead with a Type Four style value what feels meaningful and can disdain what feels superficial or lightweight. If they overdo this tendency, they may judge others for not being as deep and intense as they are. While meaning is important, it may also be vital to allow for levity—and for the reality that different people have different capacities for engagement and there is a value in a diversity of approaches and tones.

Consciously Manifesting Your Higher Potential:
Being Aware of the "Low Side" and Aiming for the "High Side"

Fours can also grow through consciously becoming aware of the self-limiting habits and patterns associated with their personality style and learning to embody the higher aspects or more expansive capacities of the Type Four personality:

▶ Learn to become conscious of comparing yourself to (or competing with) others and aim at rising above the mind-set of measurement. Allow yourself to feel good about exactly who you are without regard to how you stack up against someone else and remember that everyone has talents and challenges.

▶ Learn to become conscious of when you are over-identified or over-involved with a particular emotional state and intentionally rise above it. Aim for equanimity as a higher state in which all feelings are equally important, but all feelings come and go. As the saying goes, if emotions are like clouds that pass by and pass away, identify with the sky, not the clouds.

▶ Learn to recognize when you are getting overfocused on what's missing or feels disappointing and consciously pay attention to what is going well and what feels good.

▶ Learn to be aware of any fear of loss, rejection or misunderstanding you might experience and try not to take things so personally. Learn to let things (or people) go when they don't serve you.

▶ Learn to be aware of avoiding certain emotions through focusing on other emotions. Notice when dwelling on a specific pain, sadness or frustration may be a way for you to distract yourself from something deeper, and allow yourself to welcome whatever is true, knowing you will find a way to cope.

▶ Learn to be more conscious of any negative beliefs you hold onto as a way of avoiding any fears you have of what it will mean to embrace your goodness and your competence. Question old automatic thoughts about lack and substitute a belief in your own abundance.

Overall, Type Fours can fulfill their higher potentials by observing and working against their habit of over-focusing on their own interior sense of how they might be lacking or what their environment might be missing, and by learning to balance their need for deep connection and emotional expression with a sense of what is right or appropriate for the situation or the team. When they can value themselves and their own contributions more consciously, they will need less understanding and affirmation from the outside. When they can have compassion for themselves and learn to value their real strengths, they can communicate more of who they really are and have a greater impact without needing to be validated by others or evaluated according to other people's achievements. And when they can combine their dedication to meaning and creativity with an acceptance of their own and others' real capacities, without needing to see them as more or less, they can lead others by inspiring them through a kind of deep appreciation, respect, and openheartedness.

CHAPTER 8

The Type Five Leadership Style
The Knowledgeable Observer or the Quiet Authority

"Without data you are another person with an opinion."
Edwards Deming, management guru

"Try to learn something about everything and everything about something."
Thomas Huxley, biologist

The Type Five archetype is that prototypical person who "lives in their head." Sometimes called "the Observer" or "the Quiet Specialist," Fives focus on information and data and feel most comfortable engaging with people on an intellectual or mental level. A Five's attention automatically goes to data and facts, and how to produce results through collecting and analyzing the best information, while the Type Five style is all about examining human interaction from a safe distance, maintaining boundaries, and relating to people through knowledge rather than emotions or actions.

Perhaps the biggest introverts of all the Enneagram types, a Five's programming says the way to stay safe in the world is to maintain a certain distance from people—to create, maintain, and protect a sense of private space so energy isn't depleted through interacting with others. Their style is shaped by a primary focus on conserving energy and other key resources (like time and space) by limiting their level of engagement with others in specific ways. Focusing their attention on the mental level of whatever is happening and (automatically) detaching from emotions helps them avoid the stress, discomfort, and potential exhaustion associated with becoming overly emotionally entangled with other people. Fives are relatively uncomfortable sharing their personal feelings, concentrate on facts and information, and try to maintain boundaries around their personal space.

The Type Five communication style is about maintaining boundaries and focusing on the intellectual side of things. Their speaking style may seem succinct and concise, or they may not talk very much at all—and when they do, they will focus on the facts and figures most relevant to the work at hand. When they feel uncomfortable or are around unfamiliar people, they may simply stay quiet, to the point where people may find them abnormally private and read their silence as arrogance or disinterest. However, when asked to discuss something they have a deep intellectual interest in, they may talk at great length and take enormous pleasure in sharing information.

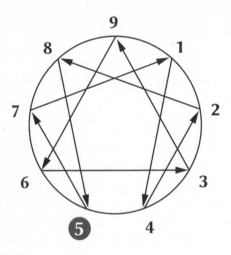

Type Five leaders can be the true "thought leaders" of the Enneagram—they enjoy gathering and assessing data and mastering areas of knowledge related to the work they do. However, when it comes to the human and emotional side of leadership, they may feel more challenged. Often self-deprecating and shy, Fives typically avoid the spotlight and are happier with the intrinsic rewards of leadership than the recognition that comes from it. They may be leading experts in their field, make innovative contributions to new technology, or combine deep knowledge with an original vision of life. Whatever their focus, Fives leaders readily dedicate themselves to drawing on intellectual insights to help themselves and others understand the world.

How to Tell if You Are a Type Five: The View from the Inside

If most or all of the following characteristics apply to you, you may have a Type Five personality style:

▶ *You see the work you do through the lens of the information that needs to be mastered to get the job done.* You enjoy doing research on whatever topics interest you or help you further clarify or do the work you need to do.

▶ *You feel more comfortable with data and facts than people and emotions.* You automatically tune in to the mental level of what's going on and detach from whatever feels overly emotional.

▶ *You enjoy being alone and need a great deal of private time.* You don't need to be around other people to be happy. Much of the time, you would rather be alone than with people.

▶ *You are skilled at looking at things objectively.* You analyze things intellectually, without any emotional response or attachment.

▶ *You enjoy working independently.* You feel most comfortable when you are alone, and you like to work by yourself.

▶ *You enjoy becoming an expert in things you have an intellectual interest in.* Reading and researching feels so much less complicated than interacting with people and dealing with their feelings.

▶ *You enjoy work most when it engages you intellectually and you can study something that interests you.* You feel satisfied and content when you can learn new things and gain knowledge.

▶ *You value your privacy (very much).* Interruptions, surprises, and people who stay in your office too long talking about things you don't care about can all feel intrusive and uncomfortable.

▶ *You feel uncomfortable in situations where you have to engage in small talk or share information about yourself, like cocktail parties and job interviews.* It's much easier to communicate about the intellectual aspects of work than it is to convey personal information.

▶ *You are not very emotional, and when you are, you prefer to feel your feelings when you are alone.* Some people may perceive you as aloof, but you mostly feel shy and uncomfortable in social situations because you don't like to talk about yourself with people you don't know well enough to trust with private information (which is most people).

▶ *You tend to be more of an observer than a participant in the social world.* You can find people interesting, but don't necessarily want to connect with them on a deep level.

▶ *You tend to disconnect from your emotions and feel much more comfortable relating to others on an intellectual level.* Although you are a sensitive person and you have keen powers of observation, it feels draining to share your feelings with others or have to deal with theirs.

▶ *You enjoy being in leadership positions that involve developing knowledge and using information in service of furthering a larger cause or enterprise.* You excel at accumulating knowledge and information, and you enjoy having an impact through pushing the boundaries on what is known about a given topic.

The Central Adaptive Strategy of the Type Five Personality Style

Fives often report that early on in life they were either intruded upon or neglected—either their boundaries were not respected by others and so they developed a need to protect their private space, or they were not given enough of what they needed and had to learn to get by on their own with scarce resources. They sometimes have a history of having to deal with others' drama or emotional upheaval and learning to withdraw, finding a sense of safety by detaching from feelings (and unwieldy relationships) and taking refuge in their heads.

This habit of retreating to a place of refuge—either a private space where they can be alone or into the comfort zone of their intellect—allows Fives to find protection from intrusion, hold on to scarce resources, and engage with the world in a way that feels both safe and interesting. I sometimes hear Fives say they believed something was "wrong with them" before they found the Enneagram, because they didn't want to be around people very much—then they realized there wasn't anything wrong with them, they were just Fives! People with a Type Five personality style experience a kind of inner scarcity because an early need to rely on others took them into what felt like dangerous territory. The need to distance themselves from people who might suck up their time and energy means they need to find ways to get by on less, since they can only rely on what they can get or do on their own.

While Fives may appear unemotional and unsentimental, they are actually highly sensitive; they feel and experience things acutely. To cope, they develop an inner program that tells them the best way to get through life (and work) is to maintain strong boundaries and focus on the mental level of things to protect against being depleted by the needs and feelings of others. When people can be held at a distance, things are kept in separate compartments, private space is protected, and work happens through focusing on data and intellectual interaction, Fives feel a sense of calm and well-being.

What Do Fives Pay Attention To? The Type Five "Radar Screen"

The strategy of maintaining a mental focus and protecting private space leads Fives to focus their attention on their own thought processes, obtaining and assessing information, and maintaining a sense of control around time, space, and energy. People who lead with a Type Five style automatically attend to their own strong needs for time and space so that they have the room they need to think, accomplish tasks, and do what they need to do.

Self-sufficient and autonomous, Fives naturally guard against intrusions from the outside and are quick to read the signs of possible disruptive forces—like needy or overly emotional people—and take evasive action if necessary. They automatically sort people into mental categories according to how much (or how little) interaction they want with them, and when they interact with others, they pay attention to how to establish boundaries and how to take advantage of natural boundaries. While they may sincerely enjoy many social interactions, they may also be keenly aware of time limits, as knowing contact will end at a particular time can help them allay any worry they may feel about how long they will have to engage (and how much energy will be expended). For instance, a Five friend of mine is a high school math teacher, and she can fully enjoy the experience of relating to her students during class because she knows that at the appointed time the bell will ring, class will be over, and everyone will leave. And she will be, happily, alone again.

Fives are also highly attuned to their own level of energy. One Five I know put it this way: at the start of the day, he imagines he has a full tank of gas, but as the day goes on, he is aware that each specific task and interaction requires him to consume that fuel. Certain life experiences take more fuel than others—and his attention focuses on which interactions take more or less of his energy, and how he might avoid larger expenditures (and so keep more energy for himself to use as he wishes) or at least be mindful about spending his fuel where he most wants or needs to spend it.

The View from "Planet Five": How Fives See the World

Generally, individuals with a Type Five style view the world in terms of interesting things to think about and get fascinated by. Five leaders tend to look for causes they can support and find meaning in. They may lead through being the intellectual force behind making an impact related to an effort they believe in, but will do so from a safe distance. They may find deep emotions alien and daunting, but they can be passionate about ideas, fields of study, and social values they find interesting, important, and meaningful.

Fives see the world through an intellectual perspective—they think deeply about things and have a strong thirst for learning and knowledge. They typically have a greater need for information and intellectual understanding than they do for people or relationships. It's not that they don't want and need good, supportive relationships—they do. Fives just have less of a need to be surrounded by people all the time, they require less of the people they are in relationships with, and they prefer to be in close relationships with just a few, trusted individuals.

People with a Type Five style also view the world with an eye toward maintaining their sense of personal space. They think in terms of how to navigate the social world while maintaining a sense of comfort and safety. At work, they may engage with people around the tasks and the mental aspects of what needs to be done, but will usually share little or no personal information about themselves. While they can develop solid relationships with coworkers, it may take a Five a while to feel comfortable enough to open up and share personal details or feelings.

The Type Five Leader: Core Characteristics

The following character traits define the Type Five leadership style:

▶ *Ability to access and assess information skillfully and with interest.* Fives' hunger for knowledge and information makes them naturally oriented to the accumulation and analysis of data. They are both good at it and enjoy doing it.

▶ *Objectivity.*Fives automatically separate emotions from thoughts, and so they are able to be neutral when evaluating or communicating about a situation.

▶ *Focus on maintaining appropriate boundaries.* Fives understand that people need space—because *they* do. They are naturally trustworthy with respect to confidences and respectful of people's privacy.

▶ *Intellectual and thoughtful.* Fives operate most comfortably on the cognitive, or mental, level of things. They enjoy gathering information and thinking deeply.

▶ *Detachment from emotions.* This makes them very objective thinkers, but can sometimes mean they lack empathy or don't want to deal with the emotional level of things.

▶ *Private and modest.* Fives do what they do without wanting to get a lot of attention for the things they do. Naturally shy and introverted, they tend to be uncomfortable in the spotlight and prefer to work from the background, or from home, or some other private space.

▶ *Tendency to compartmentalize.* Whether they are ideas or people, Fives like to keep things in cognitive "file folders" so they can exercise a sense of control of what they know and what people know about them. (For instance, they might not invite people from different arenas of their life to the same party. Then disparate individuals could share information about them with others in a way they couldn't control.)

Mental, Emotional, and Behavioral Patterns: Why Do Fives Think, Feel, and Behave the Way They Do?

Mental

Fives are "head-based" types who feel most at home in their mental space: thinking, learning, and accumulating knowledge. Thinking is a focus of living and working and a way of defending against emotions for Fives—both their own, which can feel overwhelming or hard to navigate, and those of others, which can threaten to deplete their energetic resources. They identify so strongly with their thinking function that it can feel to Fives like thinking about things that interest them and developing their understanding of those things is "who they are" and what they can contribute most to the world.

Emotional

Fives unconsciously detach from their emotions as a habitual coping strategy. This is not to say they don't have feelings—they do, but their main adaptive strategy involves separating thoughts from emotions and living from the mental level as a way of maintaining a sense of power and control in the world. Fives tend to only be comfortable feeling their emotions when they are alone—you will almost never see a Five display big emotions in public or at work, and if Fives register feelings, they will usually wait until they are alone to fully experience them. If they do show their feelings in a work setting, it will often be some sort of excitement about an intellectual point of interest. Fives may also display anger in support of maintaining boundaries (or if a boundary has been violated or is in danger of being violated)—both for themselves and others they care about.

Behavioral

Fives may delay taking action when they think they don't have enough information on which to act. They prioritize thinking over doing, and often believe they need to learn more before they feel comfortable taking a stand or executing on a plan. People with a Type Five personality style may struggle to feel connected to their feelings or their physical selves. They need a large amount of personal space—they may be quiet and keep their distance, they may avoid the office holiday party or after-work drinks, and they rarely share personal information with colleagues. It can be challenging for Fives to collaborate closely with others on a team—they tend to like to work alone, and may be wary of needing to rely on others or having their work depend upon other people's contributions.

The Main Strengths and Superpowers of the Type Five Style: What Fives Are Really Good At

▶ *Gathering and evaluating information.* Fives excel at finding the information necessary to get the job done and finding the meaning in the data they analyze that best supports the work.

▶ *Intellectual understanding and vision.* Fives live in their heads—and they tend to have really excellent heads. They are usually highly intelligent, deep thinkers, with quick minds.

▶ *Objective analysts.* Fives naturally take the emotion out of whatever they are looking at or doing, so they are really good at contemplating things thoughtfully and evenhandedly.

▶ *Giving people the space they need to be themselves or do what they need to do.* Fives like having a lot of personal space and so they naturally offer it to others. You probably won't be micromanaged by a Five leader.

▶ *Self-sufficient, autonomous, independent.* Fives feel comfortable working alone and can function independently, without needing a lot of support or supervision from others.

▶ *Humble and self-deprecating.* Fives tend to be shy and so are usually uncomfortable in the public eye—they don't seek affirmation from others or feel a need to be the center of attention or get credit for things. Motivated by learning and knowing, they do the work for the meaning they find in it, not to prove themselves worthy in the eyes of others.

When Too Much of a Good Thing Becomes a Bad Thing: How Fives Can Go Wrong When They Try Too Hard to Know It All (or Go It Alone)

▶ *Gathering and evaluating information.* Fives sometimes put off taking action when they don't think they have enough information. They may also get lost in the data—they may be so interested in what they are learning, they don't move quickly enough on what the data tells them.

▶ *Intellectual understanding and vision.* Fives tend to undervalue other forms of information, like intuition or "gut knowing," or emotions, or "reading the room." They may over-develop their intellect and under-develop their emotional intelligence.

▶ *Objective analysts.* Fives excel at separating information from emotion, but may have trouble adding the emotions back in in order to access feelings as a *source* of information.

▶ *Giving people the space they need to be themselves, do what they need to do.* It may be difficult for them to engage with people and share enough about themselves to connect with them.

▶ *Self-sufficient, autonomous, independent.* Interdependence can feel challenging for Fives. They may find it hard to connect with others to the degree necessary to establish good working relationships.

▶ *Humble and self-deprecating.* Fives' reluctance to be the focus of attention may also mean they don't show up when it's appropriate to give and receive feedback, celebrate successes, and accept credit when it's due in a way that's good for the team.

Fortunately, Fives' sincere interest in drawing on their knowledge and objective vision to have a positive impact on the work often motivates them to overcome some of the obstacles they experience in forming easy and effective working relationships. When they feel valued for the insights they bring and invited to communicate about what they are thinking, they can be active contributors despite their need for extra personal space and independence.

"When I'm stressed..." and "At my best...": Understanding the "Low Side" and the "High Side" of the Type Five Personality Style

When stressed to the point of going to the "low side" of their developmental spectrum, Type Fives can become even more remote and unreachable. Interpersonal stress, drama, or conflict can be particularly difficult experiences for the Five, who feels most comfortable working alone or with trusted others whose behavior is predictable. Since interacting with people can be stressful enough for Fives under normal conditions, tensions among people, especially emotionally charged tensions, may trigger Fives to withdraw even further or stop communicating altogether. Fives may also "hide out" when they experience feelings or emotions that they don't want to express in public.

The outward signs of a Five's stress may be relatively subtle. They may isolate themselves more and communicate less, disappear entirely and be difficult to contact, or seek refuge by working from home or being alone as much as possible. Fives dislike conflict and would usually rather leave the scene than have to deal with an emotional disagreement; however, in some cases, they may express impatience or even anger, especially if their boundaries have been violated (or threatened). Fives sometimes use anger to let you know you have encroached on their space, mistreated someone close to them, or are in danger of doing so. When a Five takes a stand like this, however, it may not be "low side" behavior—it may be a healthy reaction to the understandable stress of having someone trespass into private space.

On the "high side," Fives can be more open, engaging, and communicative. Especially when talking about an area of intense intellectual interest, they can express excitement and passion and be very engaged in sharing what matters to them. Fives can also be very funny, displaying a kind of lightness and humor (when at ease and relaxed) that's reflective of their personal insights into the things and people they observe. At their best, Fives can enjoy being alone or be more welcoming of others, expressing more warmth and being more sociable and friendly.

Emotionally intelligent Fives learn the value of accessing and expressing some emotion to establishing good relationships with people, even when it requires an effort. They develop the ability to stretch themselves to share a bit more or communicate more regularly, even though there may be times they would rather not. They work on opening up more so that others can get to know them better, and reap the rewards of having supportive relationships—even though, for the Five, that may feel uncomfortable at first.

The Three Kinds of Five Leaders: How the Three Instinctual Biases Shape the Three Type Five "Sub-Type" Personalities

According to the Enneagram model, we all have three main instinctual drives that help us survive, but in each of us, one of these three impulses tends to dominate our behavior. The Type Five style gets expressed differently depending on whether a person has a dominant instinctual bias toward asserting *self-preservation* behaviors, positioning themselves within *social* groups, or establishing *one-to-one* bonds with specific individuals.

The Self-Preservation (or Self-Focused) Five

Self-Preservation Fives focus on maintaining firm boundaries with people. They tend to feel most comfortable when they are alone at home or in some other private space, and experience a strong need to be able to withdraw to a safe space whenever they feel overwhelmed or threatened or simply want to. Self-Preservation Fives like to minimize their connections to others and tend to find safety and meaning in only a few close relationships. They may feel nervous asking others for favors because they don't want people to feel entitled to ask them for favors in return, and focus on managing the boundaries between themselves and others in a careful way, so they don't accidentally let someone in they'd rather keep out. These boundaries can take different forms—time limits, saying "no" to invitations, avoiding one's neighbors, or even a friendly attitude that acts as a camouflage so people won't push them to connect more than they want to. Much of this Five's attention goes to finding ways to hide or withdraw if someone wants to get too close or if a working relationship threatens to become excessively interdependent.

Self-Preservation Fives are the least communicative of the three Fives and the most warm (or seemingly warm). Despite being wary of people who might take their friendliness as an invitation (when it isn't), these Fives can be caring people, especially when confident that their boundaries (or escape routes) are solid. Self-Preservation Fives like being alone so much they tend to be choosy about who they decide to spend time with. They can be steadfast friends to the few people they really like, but won't necessarily want to be friends with everyone they work with.

As leaders, Self-Preservation Fives will be motivated by a concern for getting things right and making an impact through a largely intellectual contribution, but will not need to take the credit for the work that gets done. These Fives can be good leaders in that they will want to engage at the level they need to further the work—but no more than they have to. They may be tempted to keep work in silos—to compartmentalize functions or people— but will need to work against this tendency to allow for more communication than they may feel comfortable promoting. When deeply committed to the values and ideals connected to the work they do, they can be effective, involved leaders, though they may direct things from a distance and use the natural barriers associated with roles, time, and space limitations to avoid feeling overwhelmed or exhausted by what might be required of them. They won't have big ego needs for attention or recognition, and when they feel trusting of the people they work with, they can be more open and engaged.

The Social (or Group-Focused) Five

In contrast to the Self-Preservation Five, the Social Five focuses less on boundaries and more on furthering values and ideals they share with others, often at a distance. While these Fives also like private space and time to themselves, the focus of their attention is on how to know more about, become expert in, and work with others to further a cause or a system of knowledge. These Fives look to super-ideals—to overarching values that are important to them—to give their lives meaning and shape. They seek out experts in their field, may work to become experts themselves, and look to join groups that adhere to their values or ideals. They also have a strong sense of who is "in the group" and who is "out of the group."

For these Fives, the idea that "knowledge is power" is key. They strive to become experts about their topic or cause and feel very sensitive to being shown to "not know" something. They tend to feel more connected to the people who share their interests and values than the people they live with or near who are not part of the group—even people in their own family—even when those individuals are far away. And they may be more intellectually connected to their values than they are committed to actually living them out in their daily lives through their immediate relationships. For instance, they may be intellectually invested in ideas related to promoting greater consciousness or emotional intelligence as part of a professional group, but not actually work on becoming more conscious in daily life.

As leaders, Social Fives can be so passionately committed to a cause or a movement that they focus all their energy and attention on it—even to the detriment of their closest relationships. They may experience an underlying sense of meaninglessness because they may unknowingly deprive themselves of the nourishment and meaning that close relationships and emotional connections provide. So Social Five leaders may become invested in a cause as a way of acting out a desire for meaning and purpose in their lives without having to feel threatened by too much intimacy or connection with other humans. When they are less aware, this focus can cause problems, as when they put all their energy into a set of ideas without letting those ideas take root in their hearts and lived experience. But at their best, these Fives work tirelessly to further causes that can have a real positive impact in the world and create a deep sense of meaning for people.

The One-to-One (or Relationship-Focused) Five

One-to-One Fives focus more attention on feelings and relationships than the other two Fives. While they are still quite Five-ish and look like the other Fives from the outside, they tend to be more connected to their feelings and have more of a need for relationships under the right circumstances. This is why they are the "counter-type" of the three Type Five subtypes. These are the Fives who have more of an inner romantic streak, which they seek to express through some sort of artistic pursuit or creative outlet like writing, visual art, or music.

Like Social Fives, One-to-One Fives pursue an ideal or "super-value" that gives life meaning, but in the case of this Five, the ideal they want to manifest is an ideal relationship. Although they value private space and are introverted like the other Fives, they have a stronger desire to find special relationships with people they can really trust and open up to. However, while this Five has more of a need for closeness, they may fear sharing more of themselves at the same time. And the ideal of partnership or friendship they seek may be a high ideal—this Five may have trouble finding the people they want to connect with in a deeper way because they require such a high level of trust and openness from the other person.

As leaders, One-to-One Fives tend to be deeply committed and passionate about the work they do, even if it isn't always obvious. They have more of a desire to connect with the people they work with, and will want to share more of themselves in a personal way, even if they don't always find a way to do it. These Fives may make very good leaders in that they have an emotional intensity they want to express through the things they do, and so there may be a stream of passion or creativity that fuels their leadership style. In addition, they will want to create strong bonds with key people in the team or organization as a way of furthering their goals and advancing their common mission.

The Type Five at Work

Type Fives sometime feel like working with others is hard because:

- ▶ *I don't like to have to depend on other people to get work done—I like to be able to work alone and do my own thing.*

- ▶ *It can be difficult to spend a lot of time around the people I need to collaborate with—especially when the team or the collaborators are not of my choosing.*

- ▶ *Sometimes it's hard for me to know how to relate to people, or to want to get to know them enough to understand how to work well with them.*

- ▶ *I am uncomfortable dealing with other people's emotions and can become irritated if people bring their personal dramas to work.*

- ▶ *I like to have as much time as I need to review all the information necessary to support the work I do, and sometimes other people don't have the same view of the importance of fully vetting and evaluating all the relevant data.*

- ▶ *Sometimes people ask more of me than I want to give in terms of time, energy, and personal information.*

▶ *Sometimes the work and outcomes aren't clearly structured and commu-nicated (and this can lead to problems with people and messy emotional issues).*

▶ *When work processes and expectations aren't clear, it can lead to unin-tentional or accidental dependencies—and I don't want to have to end up doing work that someone didn't know they had to do or work with someone on something I didn't expect I would have to (and don't want to).*

Type Fives' workplace pet peeves may be:

▶ When goals, roles and structure are not clearly defined (so I know where the boundaries are).

▶ When things aren't efficient and the leader hasn't thought through the process.

▶ When people do sloppy work and I have to deal with their mistakes.

▶ When people interrupt me when I'm in the middle of a task.

▶ When people draw me into their personal dramas or expect me to deal with their emotional reactions.

▶ When people surprise me with a task at the last minute.

▶ When people expect me to share personal information about myself.

▶ When people don't respect agreed upon time limits.

▶ When people intrude upon my private space or private time or take up too much of my time that I would rather be spending by myself.

▶ When people don't respect my knowledge about a specific topic I have studied extensively.

▶ When people waste my time talking about personal stuff at work. Talking about personal stuff is fine, but make a date for after work.

Here's What Type Five Leaders Can Do to Be Easier to Work With

As leaders, it helps Fives to understand that not everyone sees work the way they do, with a focus on information, knowledge, and independence. In the modern work environment, where people are being asked to collaborate more and more, Fives may feel challenged because they feel so much more comfort-able working on their own and maintaining distance and autonomy in relation to their coworkers. If Fives can understand this tension in a conscious way and make efforts to bridge the gap between what they may be comfortable doing (working more independently) and what might be optimal for good teamwork (working more closely with others), they may have an easier time negotiating their working relationships.

It can also help Fives to remember that others may not understand or know how to interpret their need for distance and their tendency to be quiet or less communicative than other people are. Fives' shyness can make them seem cold or even arrogant to others, when in reality, they may just feel awkward navigating social relationships. However, not communicating creates a space in which others can project their own stories about what is going on onto the Five, who may be misunderstood as insensitive or aloof.

Fives can be easier to work with if they can find ways to be open about their natural tendencies. If they can let coworkers know that they need personal space and independence, but that they are also aware of their patterns and will try to work against them when they need to, they can create a greater sense of mutual understanding and establish more space in which they can both be themselves and be appreciated for the efforts they make. I once heard a Five leader say that just as he doesn't like to get out of bed in the morning and work out, he doesn't always want to walk around the office and talk to people, but he knows it will be good for him and strengthen his working relationships. This kind of conscious effort to wade into uncomfortable territory for a good cause can help Fives enjoy their work more and be more effective.

Working with Fives

Typical Type Five Behaviors in the Workplace

You *might* be working with someone who has a Type Five Enneagram style if you see them doing several of the following behaviors on a regular basis:

- ▶ She goes into her office, shuts the door and doesn't come out very often (and doesn't seem to welcome people stopping by to chat about nonwork-related topics).

- ▶ He doesn't say very much in meetings, even though he listens, pays close attention to what people say, and seems intellectually engaged.

- ▶ She can talk at length about high-level math or the mental challenges involved in her hobbies, but she rarely reveals any personal information.

▶ He does good work and is a key member of the team, but doesn't always want to attend social gatherings—especially during the workday.

▶ She sometimes procrastinates, explaining that she needs more time to gather more information.

▶ He is reluctant to volunteer for special projects that require extra collaboration with other people or that require him to speak in public.

▶ She is a particularly valuable member of the team because she has such deep knowledge of the topic area.

▶ He can seem disengaged at professional development events when people tell personal stories that aren't directly relevant to the work or the team.

▶ At her best, she can be relied upon to offer deep insights and an objective perspective.

▶ At his best, he has a positive impact on the work because he focuses on what's most important and always acts like a consummate professional.

What's Great about Working with Conscious Five Leaders

▶ You can count on them to provide a high level of expertise and high-quality, authoritative information.

▶ They maintain their objectivity, even in situations in which others might get emotional.

▶ They sincerely enjoy learning and doing work that involves increasing their level of knowledge.

▶ They are dependable and accountable, organized, thoughtful, and dedicated.

▶ They are improvement-oriented and want to know how they can do better.

▶ They usually don't get restless or dissatisfied with their work—they want to be the best at what they do instead of wanting to do something different.

▶ They are good listeners and open to others' ideas around work issues.

▶ They have good boundaries and honor those of others—they observe and respect time limits, personal space, and stated expectations.

▶ They are rational and logical—they have clear thought processes and will encourage others to be clear in their thinking.

▶ They are low drama, calm in a crisis and will keep their personal feelings from interfering with the work.

▶ When the boundaries are clear and Fives feel relaxed, they tend to be warm, friendly, and humorous.

Typical Challenges for People Who Work with Fives

▶ They sometimes seem to want to get away from you—or talk for the shortest amount of time possible—when you call them over to discuss a work project.

▶ It can be hard for them to collaborate when structure and processes are loose—when there are undefined roles and unclear expectations.

▶ They tend not to want to do favors for people at work, and they don't have much sympathy for people's personal issues or problems.

▶ They may become annoyed if they think people are wasting their time with irrelevant conversation.

▶ They can resist doing tasks that they think are outside of their comfort zone—that fall outside the parameters of what they feel skilled at.

▶ They may not want to follow the crowd in specific efforts or communications. They will want to register their own, individual opinion so they can avoid feeling misrepresented or getting involved in other people's agendas.

▶ They may not always want to collaborate—they may fear being tied to other people's work because it may not be up to their level of quality or they may have to wait for someone else to do their piece. They guard against feeling dependent on someone they don't trust to do the job right.

▶ They have a strong need for personal space, quiet time alone, and clearly defined work tasks.

▶ Their need for compartmentalization may feel excessive and controlling to those who don't need things to be as clearly delineated as they do.

Type Fives and Leadership

Type Five Leaders Speak About How Knowing
Your Enneagram Type Helps You at Work

Ed McCracken was the CEO of Silicon Graphics in California from 1984 to 1997. Prior to working at Silicon Graphics, he was a Group Manager at Hewlett Packard.

"I've been in business quite a while. I was at Hewlett Packard for 15 years, and it seemed like every manager had a view of what a perfect person would be like. They would try to coach you to be a perfect person—a perfect manager, a perfect engineer, a perfect whatever. In this culture, it probably means somebody that's extroverted and is out there and influencing people and all those things. I don't know how many times a manager told me that I should talk more.

"But I just didn't relate to that. I'd say, 'Ooh, how would I do that?' And so this concept of the Enneagram, where there isn't a Type 10—this perfect manager or whatever—but there is a lot of individuality, and people are different, and a group of people is a dance of different types— to me, that was a big insight, that there was no Type 10, and that I didn't need to be a Type 10 and no one else did either. When I first learned the Enneagram—and learned I was a Type Five—I thought, 'Well, I don't want to be a Five.' So I tried to act for a week like I wasn't a Type Five. I think everybody does that. Then I figured out, by myself, that the way that I was acting to not be a Five was the way that a Five would act not to be a Five. So there was no hope, in other words.

"And then I developed the concept of learning to love myself as a Type Five. And that was a pretty quick process. One of the things about me that's different from the American 'Model Manager or Leader': in the work environment, I would counsel people to work on their strengths rather than their weaknesses—that their strengths are the most powerful. I didn't have to fill in the weaknesses; mostly they needed to become more powerful in the things that are strong about them and bring them to the workplace. That's what I attempted to do with myself—to be more of who I am, flaws and all.

"And I also learned, during that same process, that the things I thought of as deviant behavior—different from the norm—were actually healthy

behaviors quite often. That it was just about the differences between people. So I became much more excited about differences, especially uniqueness in people.

"Knowing I'm a Five has made me feel a lot more comfortable with myself, using my strengths rather than trying to act like I was an extroverted Three—which I'm not very good at. I learned to work to be a good leader given that I am a Five: exposing my thinking more, working through issues verbally in a way that people could follow me and watch me, and so on."

Art Blum is Vice President of Regulatory Affairs at BioMarin Pharmaceutical Inc., a biotechnology company based in San Rafael, California.

"My tendency is to not grab the spotlight. What my coach says about me is, when I speak, people listen and they respect me. She uses the word 'gravitas.' I've learned there are times when I need to take more active control—I need to be more of an Eight when the situation warrants it. When I am the leader of a fairly good-sized group, I play that role. I can do it and I do do it. But that's not my preference to do that. That's my coach's encouragement to me: to take charge and have people look at me as the big player here. That's something I think about all the time. It's helpful, because all too often people will resort to what's comfortable, what their comfort level is, and it's not always appropriate for the occasion.

"I get a lot of kudos when I make an active effort to take those active leadership roles. It's unexpected. When I do what's expected, then I've done my job. When I do it with gravitas, then I've really done my job.

"Even though I'm a Five and I like my alone time, I don't want to be the guy sitting in my office with the door shut and lose access to people, lose opportunities to communicate, to influence. Those things are really important as a leader. Stepping out of my comfort zone is a requirement of this job."

When You Are a Manager and You Are a Five

It can be challenging to be the leader if you are a Five because it can mean engaging with people more deeply and often than feels comfortable or natural to you. You may be shy about being out in front of groups, or exerting power in active ways, or having to communicate with many individuals on a regular basis. On the other hand, you may relish the chance to be a thought leader, to help organize and clarify a team's thinking, to inspire people to be open to learning, or to reinforce organizational standards of quality, professionalism, and respect for boundaries.

If you are a Five leader, you usually want to find a logical and effective course of action based on the best available information. You tend to have an opinion about how the work should be done, informed by an objective analysis of the data, and you will want to create clear processes and be definitive about responsibilities and desired outcomes so that time isn't wasted and people don't unnecessarily replicate others' work. You believe that when boundaries are clearly defined, people can trust that their independent work can stay relatively independent, while at the same time contributing to the whole. At their best, Five bosses tend to be self-contained, but willing to share their (fact-based) thoughts and listen to those of others.

When Your Manager Is a Five

The good thing about having a boss who is a Five is that they won't bother you unnecessarily with irrelevant details or nonwork-related personal issues. While some Five bosses can be remote and uncommunicative, especially when stressed, more self-aware Fives leaders can be thoughtful, understanding, and open-minded. If your Five manager feels confident about the ability to establish boundaries and communicate safely, he or she can be supportive without being intrusive. Especially if you share common intellectual interests and perspectives, Fives can be enthusiastic and trustworthy partners in thinking through problems, structuring effective work processes, and making sure the work gets done well.

When stressed or less self-aware, your Five manager may withdraw and neglect to communicate as much as you think is necessary to stay connected to what is happening with work tasks and projects. Five leaders who feel overwhelmed or insecure may avoid engaging with people and fail to communicate in regular ways, and emotional issues within the team may cause them to isolate themselves from things that feel difficult or impossible to confront. This may cause you (or others) to perceive the Five leader as aloof, arrogant, or uncaring, so it may help to remember that Fives usually only seem insensitive because they are so sensitive on the inside.

At their best, Five managers think through what needs to be done and handle issues directly and rationally. They are straightforward and professional, without burdening their staff with any emotional reactivity. Particularly gifted at objective analysis and honoring appropriate boundaries, they study the situation and offer clear-minded suggestions about how to organize the work so that everyone can contribute their best efforts, redundancies and unnecessary dependencies are avoided, workflows are planned logically, and communications are clear and timely. They will be calm if things get tense, maintain a professional reserve, and listen to people to strategize thoughtfully about ways to bring about the best outcomes.

When Your Subordinate Is a Five

When your direct reports have a Type Five style, you can count on them to focus on the work, without inserting extraneous issues into the mix—especially additional emotional reactions. They will work well independently, and respect your private space and time. You will get along well with the Fives you work with if roles, functions, plans, and deliverables are clearly spelled out, as Fives are happiest when tasks are explicitly laid out and they are then left alone (and trusted) to do the work.

Fives usually won't want to deal with issues that are too emotional or too personal, so if you need anything more than an objective sounding board, it may be wise to seek someone else. And when there is a power differential between you and the Five, discussions involving what the Five regards as "messy" emotions (especially if they're not connected to the work) may be even more stressful for your direct report to endure. They may be open to interacting socially with you, but will want to do it in a way that is clearly separated from the boundaries around the normal workday. Speaking of boundaries, you will get along much better with your Five direct report if you respect time limits, private space, and work task specifications. Also, Fives don't like surprises, so if you have something difficult to say, give them a little warning, try to give them a say in the time and place, and be direct and kind.

If you have a good relationship with your Five employees, they can be a steadfast source of support, reliable performers, and a calm port in a storm (if the storm isn't too emotional). They will respect your boundaries and provide trustworthy information on which you can base decisions with confidence. They won't need to get all the credit for the work, they will enjoy intellectual challenges, and they will not require a lot of oversight, preferring as they do to work independently.

Getting Along with Fives: Tips for What to Do to Work Well with Fives

▶ *Respect space and time.* Fives will appreciate you if you set appropriate time limits and stick to a clear schedule. Avoid busting in on them unannounced to talk about your weekend, a personal problem or whatever you are upset about. Have the courtesy to make an appointment and don't use work time for personal issues.

▶ *Check in, but in short bursts and measured doses.* We all need to communicate on a regular basis when we work together, but when collaborating with Fives, it will go well if you check in with them periodically and briefly and stick to the point.

▶ *Straightforward, but thoughtful communication.* Fives don't like to expend unnecessary energy when communicating—so plan ahead, focus only on what's necessary for an optimal information exchange, be clear about your objectives, and stick to the agenda.

▶ *Be professional.* Fives appreciate coworkers who demonstrate the skill, manners and good judgment one expects from a person trained to do a job well in a business environment. They don't like it when people get messy, emotional, or personal—and if you accidentally do, don't expect the Five to deal with your feelings.

▶ *Avoid drama and messy emotions.* See above. Also, one of the things Fives like most about being at work is that there are usually norms against showing emotion at the office. If you really want your Five colleagues to hear you and respond well to what you communicate to them, try your best to take the emotion out of it.

▶ *Leave your personal life out of work matters.* When at work, Fives want to be at work—they want to get the job done. Some may enjoy socializing with workmates, but only after work, not during work hours. And don't expect them to be your friend necessarily, as they only need and want a few, and those slots may be filled.

▶ *Make your communications clear, concise, direct, short, and efficient.* Fives tend to believe they have limited energy to expend on human interaction. While this is part of the illusion of the Five personality, many Fives really buy into the idea that they have finite energetic resources and can be wary about spending too much energy on any one interaction. So when talking with Fives, remember that less is more.

▶ *Leave them alone to do what they do.* Fives like to have the freedom, the space, and the time they need to do whatever work they can by themselves. It's best not bother them with stuff they don't find meaningful or relevant to what needs to be done.

▶ *No surprises.* Fives want to know what the boundaries, time limits, and expectations are in advance. Surprises can also stir up emotions, which Fives would rather experience when they are alone. So, try to avoid springing things on them (or planning a surprise party for their next birthday).

Actionable Growth Tasks and Suggestions: How Type Fives Can Become More Self-Aware, Effective, and Happy at Work

All the types can learn to be less reactive and better at collaborating through first *observing* their habitual patterns, then thinking about the things they think, feel, and do to gain more *self-insight*, and then making efforts to *manage* or moderate their automatic reactions to key triggers.

Fives grow through first observing and then learning to moderate their habitual reactions to key triggers like feeling intruded upon by others' needs and demands, having to deal with others' emotions, and having their expectations or boundaries violated.

When Fives can watch what they do enough to "catch themselves in the act" of doing the things that get them in trouble, and then pause and reflect on what they are doing and why, they can gradually learn to moderate their programming and knee-jerk responses. Here are some ideas to help Fives be more self-aware, more emotionally intelligent, and more satisfied at work (and at home).

Self-Observation: Things for Five Leaders to Watch Out For

▶ *Tune in to your relationship with your emotions generally. Are you more comfortable relating to others on the mental level? Can you feel your emotions more readily when you are by yourself?*

▶ *Observe your ability or inability to access feelings in the moment. Can you notice how you go directly to thinking and detach from emotion?*

▶ *Observe how you react if the people around you get emotional or make (what feels to you like) excessive demands on your time or energy.*

▶ *Notice any beliefs you have about having a limited about of energy and emotional capacity. What fears or other feelings might be behind this sense that you can be easily depleted?*

▶ *Notice the different ways you enforce or protect your boundaries. Notice when this feels right and when it may be excessive (or isolate you).*

▶ *Observe how much and how often you share personal information with other people. Notice how many people you feel comfortable communicating your inner experience with and what holds you back when you decide not to.*

▶ *Note the consequences of not being more known to more people vs. the comfort of maintaining a sense of privacy.*

▶ *Observe any fears you have related to sharing more of yourself with others. What do you imagine will happen if you open up more to more people?*

▶ *What kinds of things do you do at work or as a leader to feel safe and grounded? What kinds of experiences feel challenging or risky?*

Blind Spots: What You Don't Know Can Hurt You!

What blind spots Fives often don't see in themselves:

▶ *Engagement with emotions and the value of emotions generally.* As a part of their drive to stay safe and conserve energy, Fives automatically and unconsciously detach from emotions, and can (conveniently) believe emotions are not important. Their main psychological defense mechanism is "isolation," which allows them to deal with the anxiety associated with navigating the social world by separating feeling from knowing. Fives automatically focus on thoughts, and may at times think they are feeling when they are really just thinking about feelings. When they are not aware of this tendency, it may be difficult to re-engage with their feelings in a way that helps them to be enlivened by and connected to their relationships and their work.

▶ *The value of sharing more personal information with others.* Fives' programming tells them it's best to keep their thoughts and feelings to themselves, as getting more involved with people through communicating about their inner world will deplete them of precious resources and threaten boundaries around time and space. They don't see that sharing more of themselves leads to stronger relationships with other humans, which leads to more nourishment and more inner abundance through accessing support from others.

▶ *The supportive and energizing function of relationships.* Fives tend to believe that relationships with others threaten to exhaust their energies, when really, they have the potential to replenish inner energetic resources.

▶ *The value of conflict.* Fives usually dislike conflict because it can involve intense emotions and unexpected personal revelations, both of which seem costly energetically to Fives. But in avoiding conflict situations, they also avoid deeper engagement with people, which can end up limiting them instead of protecting them.

▶ *Their own wealth of emotional strength, power, and abundant energy.* Fives believe in their susceptibility to depletion and overreact by protecting their boundaries and taking refuge in the mental level of life. But in doing this, they overlook what's really true—that the false belief that they can be easily depleted of energy limits their ability to manifest their own power, energy, and other inner capacities when it causes them to contract and cut themselves off from support.

Self-Insight: Things for Fives to Think About, Understand, and Explore

▶ *Why are you more comfortable relating to others on the mental level? Why is it easier to feel your emotions when you are by yourself?*

▶ *How and why do you detach from emotions, and what purpose does this serve? What is it about expressions of emotion that feel messy or threatening?*

▶ *What are you afraid will happen if you share your emotions with others? What beliefs might be behind any fears you have of being more open and emotionally connected to people?*

▶ *How does your belief in inner scarcity keep you trapped in an experience of having scarce energetic resources? Could this belief be an illusion that actually cuts you off from generating more energy in your life in different ways?*

▶ *What are the consequences of living so much of life from your head alone? How might it help you to develop more of a connection to your body and your heart?*

▶ *How do different kinds of boundaries help you to feel safe and contained? What happens when you consider relaxing your boundaries a little bit to experiment with being more available for connection with others?*

▶ *What motivates you to limit the amount of information you share with others about yourself?*

Strengths to Leverage

It helps Fives to be aware of, actively pay attention to, fully own, and leverage:

▶ *Ability to make and maintain good boundaries.* Fives naturally honor other people's boundaries around private time and space. They're attentive to the value of spelling out time limits, expectations, desired outcomes, and roles and responsibilities.

▶ *Intellectual curiosity and enthusiasm for knowledge and ideas.* Fives have the desire and capacity to gather and analyze large amounts of information—and they usually enjoy the process. This makes them content experts who can take the lead in helping people access and learn about the most important data related to their work.

▶ *Objective thinking.* Fives' automatic tendency to separate out emotions from ideas helps them to analyze what's happening from an emotional distance that can support rational, intelligent responses to difficult situations.

▶ *Professional and modest.* Fives' distaste for emotional entanglements—especially at work—makes them highly sensitized to the behaviors that constitute professional conduct. They can be good role models when it comes to how to interact with others in a way that is thoughtful, humble, courteous, and respectful of people's privacy.

▶ *Content expertise.* Fives' hunger for knowledge and love of learning often leads to them accumulating large amounts of expertise about specific fields of study. They are often valuable team members because they know so much about what they do and always want to keep learning and expanding their knowledge base.

Self-Management: Challenging Tendencies for Fives to Moderate

▶ *Distancing from emotions.* If you are a Five, you prefer interacting with others on the mental level and tend to want to separate yourself from things that feel too emotional—both your own emotions and others' emotions. Growth work for you thus usually entails getting more in touch with emotions in the moment and eventually learning to communicate more about your feelings while interacting with others.

▶ *Autonomy, independence, and preference for private space.* As a Five, you feel safest when you can work independently and control your private space. However, if you can learn to be more flexible when it comes to wanting to work alone and maintaining your privacy, you can create more possibilities for collaboration and supportive connections.

▶ *Difficulty with sharing personal information.* It can feel dangerous to a Five to share what feels personal with people—especially at work. So it's a good growth stretch for you to try to share a little bit more personal information with colleagues you trust as a way of expanding your capacity for deeper relationships and more effective teamwork.

▶ *Excessive concern with conserving energy.* You sometimes resist growth work (especially at work) because you don't see a problem with your defensive strategies. But many of them grow out of a false sense that you will become exhausted if you allow for more connection with others. Exercise and other somatic practices can help you get more in touch with more of your natural energy as a way of learning that you have more inner resources than you think you do.

▶ *Belief in scarce personal resources.* Your fears of depletion motivate you to hold yourself back from life. By questioning your assumptions about how little you have to subsist on, you open yourself up to a greater experience of abundance.

▶ *Fear of intrusion and emotional entanglements.* Recognizing, owning, and challenging the fear of intrusion and emotional demands are good first steps you can take to learn to work against your fears and open up to others. "Feel the fear and do it anyway" is a good mantra for Fives who are tired of letting fear hold them back.

Consciously Manifesting Your Higher Potential:
Being Aware of the "Low Side" and Aiming for the "High Side"

Fives can also grow through consciously becoming aware of the unconscious, self-limiting habitual patterns associated with their personality style and learning to embody the "higher aspects" or more expansive and balanced capacities of the Type Five personality:

► Learn to become conscious of the discomfort with working closely with others and the need to maintain strong boundaries and try to ease into opening up more and enjoying collaboration. Realize that the things you fear might happen if you allow for closer relationships probably won't.

► Learn to notice when you put up boundaries to keep people out and experiment with opening the boundaries more, and more often. Realize that you can maintain healthy boundaries and allow for more contact with others in measured doses and that this can make your life richer and more meaningful.

► Learn to notice when you detach from your emotions and take the risk of staying more engaged with them. Realize that developing the ability to connect with your feelings in the present moment will help you to engage with life more deeply and make connecting with others more appealing and interesting.

► Learn to be conscious of your fears on a more regular basis and challenge them when they seem excessive. Realize that the things we fear most have often already happened, and that you are capable of more courage than you may give yourself credit for.

► Learn to be more aware of what compels you to shut down, contract, or hide in the face of contact with others—especially emotional connection. Realize that you have just as much capacity to connect and collaborate as anyone else, and get in touch more regularly with your desire to make contact in a meaningful way.

► Learn to observe the way you index safety and how seeking to stay safe actually threatens to increase your sense of inner depletion by cutting you off from the support of the people around you. Realize that others may want to support and appreciate you more than you let them.

Overall, Type Fives can fulfill their higher potentials by observing and working against their habitual focus on protecting their boundaries and conserving energy out of a fear of depletion and exposure. When they can understand their sensitivity to external demands and take steps to safely experiment with contacting their own emotions more, they can learn to expand their capacities to be more open with others and allow for a deeper engagement with life, work, and people. When they can combine their excellent minds with greater access to their felt experiences in their bodies and through their emotions, they both open themselves up to a fuller experience of their life and work and expand the range of what they can accomplish through the work they do. They can develop into truly great leaders if they can allow themselves to build on their analytic strengths by learning to enjoy working with others and engaging more deeply in the people aspects of the work they do and the intrinsic rewards that come with personal growth.

CHAPTER 9

The Type Six Leadership Style
The Skeptical, Vigilant Troubleshooter

"When I use my strength in the service of my vision it makes no difference whether or not I am afraid."

Audre Lorde, writer, poet, and civil rights activist

"The most formidable weapon against errors of every kind is reason. I have never used any other, and I trust I never shall."

Thomas Paine, political activist, philosopher, political theorist, and revolutionary

The Type Six archetype is the prototypical person who seeks certainty and security, but often doesn't find it. A Six's attention automatically goes to reading people and situations to determine how trustworthy or safe they are. Primarily motivated by fear, though not always aware of it, they test and question people, continually asking, "Can you be trusted?" "Will something go wrong?" and "How can we be prepared if the worst happens?" Sometimes called "The Loyal Skeptic" or "The Devil's Advocate," Sixes focus on forecasting potential problems so they can be ready to deal with trouble or meet any challenges that might occur.

Sixes' programming tells them that the way to find safety in a potentially dangerous world is to always be on the lookout for threats so that they can be prepared if something bad happens. Their personality style is shaped by a focus on assessing risk, watching for unexpected dangers, and reading people to see if they have hidden agendas or ulterior motives. They need time to develop trust in others, but once they do trust someone, they become steadfast and loyal. Deep down, Sixes want to find a good authority, but experience leads them to believe that people with power tend to use it to hurt those with less power. They tend to question authority and identify with "the underdog," and often work to support underdog causes.

Sixes' communication style reflects their tendency to look for information with which to assess situations and locate potential problems. They ask a lot of questions (and don't answer very many), and when you present them with a plan, they will usually try to poke holes in it—looking for the weak points and determining how to challenge it or reinforce it. For Sixes, everything is context dependent, so they seek data through which to understand the situation, the players, the issues, the goals, and possible courses of action.

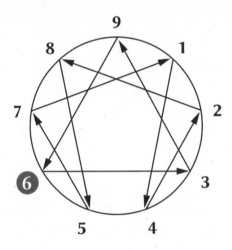

Leaders who have a Type Six style tend to be attuned to assessing threats and risks, solving problems, and analyzing what's happening with an eye toward planning for the different scenarios that might unfold. Six leaders think strategically in terms of all the issues that could arise, and how those issues might be addressed such that goals, plans, projects, and people can be protected. They can be warm and sensitive questioners, intellectual analysts, or assertive contrarians. But whether they help to solve problems through doubting and questioning, they support solid planning through precision and careful analysis, or they rebel against bad authorities with strength, they combine keen insight with a passion for supporting the "common man," and so can bring courage and a revolutionary spirit to all their endeavors.

How to Tell if You Are a Type Six: The View from the Inside

If most or all of the following characteristics apply to you, you may have a Type Six personality style:

▶ *You see the work you do through the lens of what might go wrong.* You are a consummate troubleshooter and contingency planner. You excel at noticing the problems that might occur at each stage of a work process.

▶ *You ask a lot of questions as a way of making sure products and procedures are thoroughly checked out and all goes according to plan.* You can't help doubting what people say, but your real intention is to solve problems ahead of time so fixes can be planned and disasters can be avoided.

▶ *You automatically try to poke holes in people's plans to test how solid they are.* You have a hard time just accepting things at face value—you feel motivated to think about "worst case scenarios" as a way of preventing them from actually happening.

▶ *You have a hard time trusting people in the initial stages of a relationship. You need time to get to know people before you decide they can be trusted.* You need to observe others to determine if they are trustworthy. You have a good inner "bullshit detector." Once you trust them, you really trust them—but if someone you trust betrays you, that's really bad.

▶ *While you hope to find good authorities and leaders to work with, you have a natural antiauthority streak.* You usually need to test them to see if they are trustworthy, and if they aren't, you may withdraw or rebel against them.

▶ *You usually support whichever team is the underdog.* You naturally sympathize with the oppressed and the powerless, and you can mobilize a lot of energy and passion in working on behalf of underdog causes.

▶ *Although you may work hard, you may not feel comfortable with success.* You don't like standing out from the crowd, so success can feel dangerous or awkward. If things go well, you can't help waiting for the other shoe to drop.

▶ *While you often act from fear, you may not always be aware of your fear.* You are motivated by a need for security and safety that can just seem like a good strategy for being prepared or being ready to solve problems as they occur. And so you may not relate to being "fearful"—even though you are.

▶ *Some people might view you as pessimistic, because you easily speak to what could go wrong or turn out badly, but you view yourself as a realist.* You can't help noticing and voicing potential problems but you see this as essential: You realistically evaluate the pitfalls in any plan so they can be prevented.

▶ *You often have a hard time making decisions because you can always think of another question to ask.* You may find it hard to take a stand at times, or decide on a course of action, since you can so easily find ways to doubt or question your own thinking.

▶ *You often can't help taking the contrarian view or playing the "devil's advocate."* If someone offers an opinion, you automatically want to argue the opposite position (even if you don't fully believe it). This helps you to test whether people really say what they mean and find certainty through challenging what's really true.

▶ *Your desire for certainty motivates you to look for good data to help you make rational decisions.* You naturally apply logic and reason when thinking through a problem to find the best solution. One of the most intellectual and logical of all the Enneagram types, you attempt to find safety through the thought process itself.

▶ *You are good at rationally analyzing situations and are very insightful.* You enjoy examining things with your mind and solving problems—you tend to think outside the box and read people well.

The Central Adaptive Strategy of the Type Six Personality Style

Sixes often report experiencing some sort of fear-inducing situation early on in life, often involving untrustworthy authorities. They may have had a parent who was unpredictable—perhaps because of alcoholism or mental illness, or just inconsistent, absent, or unreliable—and so to cope, they learned to try to anticipate what was going to happen next. Many Sixes report a problem with the father figure, the archetypal protector, giving them a sense that they did not have enough protection. Whether the father was ineffectual, overly strict or tyrannical, or undependable, the Type Six child had an early sense of having to find ways to feel safe without a strong protective figure to internalize to give them a sense of inner security.

Motivated to try to establish a sense of safety on their own, Sixes adapt to what often feels like a dangerous world by developing the ability to forecast the future—to pick up on subtle clues about what people will do and where problems might arise. This makes them good at detecting inconsistencies in people's behavior and sniffing out trouble before it occurs. While all personality types are essentially defensive stances, Sixes become good defensive strategists in the classic sense—they get good at scanning the environment for potential problems so they can have some lead-time in figuring out how to meet those problems and mount a defense.

At work, this makes Sixes good at getting ahead of the curve mentally and thinking through all the problematic issues that could arise so that they—or their team—can strategize about how to handle potential obstacles before they derail a project or a plan. They can be reliable employees and hard workers (though sometimes motivated by anxiety), but they can also get caught up in their tendency to overanalyze and have trouble taking action. People who lead with the Type Six style bring analytical and strategic skills to the job of managing people based on their talent for risk assessment, their loyalty, and their logical minds.

What Do Sixes Pay Attention To? The Type Six "Radar Screen"

The strategy of watching for signs of danger and seeking certainty causes the Six to scan the environment and the people in it for signs of threats. They constantly ask questions like, "Who's doing what?" "Who can be trusted?" "What does the data say about what's true?" "Who will hurt me?" and "What might go wrong?"

People with a Type Six leadership style pay a great deal of attention to how people behave and whether their actions are aligned with their stated intentions. When surrounded by people they trust, they can relax and focus on the work, but they will likely have their guard up and maintain a certain reserve in new situations. They also watch what happens in their environment closely to determine what threats exist that they should anticipate. At work, Sixes automatically see potential problems in a project or process, solve what problems they find, remember what problems have occurred in the past and learn from those mistakes, and continually keep an eye out for new and recurring threats.

Sixes apply the same kind of attention to people—it can be hard to earn their trust, and they will need time to watch your behavior to get to know who you are and how you operate, try to detect inconsistencies, look out for unstated intentions, and test you to see if you do what you say. Eventually, if they see that you are honest and forthcoming, they may become comfortable putting trust in you.

The View from "Planet Six": How Sixes See the World

Generally, individuals with a Type Six style view the world as a dangerous place. They are acutely aware that threats to their safety and security exist at all times, and use their powers of perception and sharp analytical skills to constantly evaluate the risks they detect "out there." However, because the threats they perceive outside stir up anxiety inside, Sixes may also project their fears onto their environment, making the outside world seem more dangerous than it is. The result can be a vicious cycle in which their habit of looking for threats amplifies the Six's perception of the world as dangerous, whether they are aware of being fearful or not.

Sixes seek out safety, security, and certainty in response to their sense that trouble could occur at any moment. They want to find a good authority to trust in and solid sources of outside support, but past experience has taught them that it's safer to have their guard up, remain hypervigilant, and test people to determine their trustworthiness. Their coping strategy of being wary and watchful can make them good problem-solvers, but also problem-seekers (as a way of feeling safe), and because they also tend to enjoy the process of problem solving, they can view the world through the lens of searching out problems to solve, and may sometimes find them where they don't exist. Sixes are particularly prone to suffer the effects of self-fulfilling prophecy—they may make things true by fearfully imagining they are true (when they really weren't until the Six focused so much fearful energy on them).

Sixes view reality as being context dependent—if you ask them a question about something, they will often answer, "It depends..." They have a keen awareness of the complexities and contingencies of life and see themselves as realists. Most of all, they value being prepared. They know that life can be unpredictable, and seek to foresee whatever problems may happen, and as a result of all of this forethought, they tend to remain calm in a crisis and handle threats well when they do occur.

The Type Six Leader: Core Characteristics

The following character traits help to define the Type Six leadership style:

▶ *Good analytical minds for evaluating data and doing research.* Six leaders tend to have a mental facility with the theoretical—they are not only intellectual types, but excel at anything requiring logic, reason, and abstract thinking.

▶ *Good troubleshooters.* Sixes are excellent at assessing scenarios and locating threats. They specialize in poking holes in plans and identifying potential problems before they occur.

▶ *Skill at preparation and readiness in the face of things that might go wrong.* Type Six leaders are forward thinking. They think in terms of forecasting potential dangers and being ready for any contingency.

▶ *Excellent problem-solvers.* Sixes automatically search for problems that might come up and enjoy the process of thinking outside the box and finding creative solutions.

▶ *Ability to be calm in a crisis.* Having anticipated all the contingencies and threats that might crop up, when problems do happen, Sixes are usually ready for them and adept at handling them.

▶ *Protective and supportive of team.* Six leaders are naturally motivated to protect people they trust and feel connected to. Temperamentally suspicious of authorities, they also tend to be alert to any ways their teammates or direct reports may be threatened by people in power.

Mental, Emotional, and Behavioral Patterns: Why Do Sixes Think, Feel, and Behave the Way They Do?

Mental

Sixes are "head-centered" mental types who think in terms of analyzing ideas and situations and evaluating risks. They have active imaginations and tend to think in terms of "what ifs?" as a way of finding certainty in an uncertain world. Sixes engage in "contrarian thinking" and mentally "push back," challenge others' thinking, test positions to see if they are solid, and try to strengthen group thought processes by pushing on potential weak points to see if they hold up. Highly logical people who value reason and rational thinking and want to base decisions on facts and data, Sixes also tend to have "doubting minds" that may perpetually question things. They may doubt what is going on, they may doubt themselves and they may even doubt their doubt. However, when they can step back and look at the evidence, they are good at evaluating data, thinking things through and finding good solutions.

Emotional

Type Sixes come more from their heads than from their emotions. However, the one emotion all Sixes seem to experience is fear—although they experience it in different ways. Some Sixes will be very aware of regularly feeling fear and can name many things they are afraid of. Other Sixes subconsciously find ways to manage their fear so it doesn't register in their conscious experience. Some Sixes ease their fear by looking to a good authority or a set of rules or processes to guide their actions. And other Sixes seek to become strong so they can proactively move toward the sources of their fear and overcome them. But whether they are aware of it or not, most Sixes are motivated to a large degree by fear. Some Sixes also feel guilt and shame, though their guilt is usually all in their heads—part of their defensive strategy of uncovering and fixing badness—and not based in reality.

Behavioral

Sixes behave in very different ways depending on which of the three subtypes they are (described below) and the context and conditions they are in. They often ask a lot of questions, try to poke holes in plans and presentations, and doubt and test what is happening to see what they can trust. They can be hard workers who always do their due diligence, or they may get caught up in analysis-paralysis and have trouble taking action. They may manage their anxiety by taking on difficult situations, or they may avoid challenging situations and want to hide. They may be organized, precise, and efficient, or they may be indecisive, uncertain, and disorganized. They can be caring and friendly or reserved and defensive. As Sixes themselves will tell you: it all depends on what conditions they are facing, what they are thinking and feeling, and whether they tend to respond instinctually to their fear with a "fight" or "flight" or "seek protection" response.

The Main Strengths and Superpowers of the Type Six Style: What Sixes Are Really Good At

▶ *Ability to accurately assess risks and threats.* Motivated by the need to stay safe and find certainty, Sixes have a talent for intuiting the risks and threats in any project or plan.

▶ *Good problem solvers.* Sixes' analytical minds easily focus on breaking things down into their component parts and finding the best ways to address problematic issues and situations.

▶ *Insightful and analytical.* Sixes are good at asking the right questions, gathering and analyzing the pertinent data, and generating useful and accurate insights about what is going on.

▶ *Precision and attention to process.* Germany is a Six country—and the phrase "German engineering" has become widely understood to mean German cars and other products demonstrate a high degree of precision and quality. Sixes find safety in precisely attending to the processes and principles that help achieve predictable, quality products and outcomes.

▶ *Loyalty and reliability* . Once Sixes establish trust, they tend to be extremely loyal, reliable, and trustworthy—modeling the same qualities they look for in people they trust.

When Too Much of a Good Thing Becomes a Bad Thing: How Sixes Can Go Wrong When They Can't Help Looking for Trouble

Like all people of all types, when Type Six leaders overuse their biggest strengths (and don't consciously develop a wider range of specialties), those strengths can also turn out to be their Achilles' heel.

▶ *Ability to accurately assess risks and threats.* Sixes can be so attuned to watching out for risks and threats, they may overestimate how risky a situation is and see threats where they don't exist.

▶ *Good problem solvers.* The habit of looking for problems can lead Sixes to find them where they don't exist. They may over-index negative data and underestimate the positive.

▶ *Insightful and analytical.* Sixes can get stuck in questioning, doubt, and endless analysis to the point where they don't take action. In addition, they may overvalue their analytical ability and not develop their emotional intelligence.

▶ *Precision and attention to process.* Like some German citizens, many Sixes rigidly insist on precision and process and don't leave room for flexibility or going with the flow. If you've ever tried to cross the street against the light at an intersection when there are no cars around in Germany, and you were then scolded by a helpful German, you know what I mean.

▶ *Loyalty and reliability.* Sixes have high standards for determining who is trustworthy and who deserves their loyalty. They may withhold their loyalty for a long time before they trust you, and if they aren't sure of your trustworthiness, they may not be as reliable as you might like them to be—or as they are capable of.

Fortunately, Sixes' sincere interest in finding security means they will often do the work it takes to learn to trust people and engage with their team in productive ways, even if this means maintaining a certain level of vigilance for a while. When they can focus on proactively dealing with risks and solving interesting problems, they can usually develop good working relationships where they can put their analytical skills to good use and learn to have faith that things will turn out all right.

"When I'm stressed…" and "At my best…": Understanding the "Low Side" and the "High Side" of the Type Six Personality Style

When stressed to the point of going to the "low side" of their developmental spectrum, Type Sixes can become mistrustful and paranoid. They may get caught up in fear, question people endlessly, and their requirements for evidence of what or who can be trusted may be impossible to satisfy. They sometimes project fear-fueled scenarios they make up in their heads onto the people around them without realizing they are projecting. They may also push back and rebel against others (openly or covertly), refuse to accept the opinion of the majority or those in power, or mistrust anyone in authority.

Less self-aware Sixes under pressure may also withdraw and hide. While suspecting others of hidden agendas, they may avoid conflict. They may express ambivalence, get stuck in doubt, and have difficulty making decisions. Stressed-out Sixes may also get caught up in an inner conflict between pleasing others and rebelling against them. They may get lost in fear-based abstractions or theoretical possibilities (or conspiracy theories) to the point where they have a hard time trusting anything. Depending on their subtype (described below), they may fear expressing anger and doubt themselves, rigidly adhere to rules, or get aggressive and refuse to cooperate.

On the "high side," when Type Six leaders become more self-aware and conscious of their programming, they can be observant, intelligent, and understanding. They tend to read situations and people well, intuit what the key issues are, and meet challenges with courage and confidence (after evaluating the most relevant data). They combine analytical skill with a deep interest in people, taking care to get to know the individuals they work with so they can develop strong relationships based on mutual trust. Good leaders with a Type Six personality style identify with the underdog, or the "everyman," and so establish democratic, egalitarian policies and are mindful of the needs of people at all levels of an organization.

When living more from the "high side," Sixes feel whatever fear and anxiety they have, but move forward anyway. They are able to act courageously, even under adverse circumstances, by assessing risks wisely and balancing an understanding of their fear and reactivity with a clear-headed analysis of the factual evidence and the input of trusted advisers and colleagues. Able to counter their naturally occurring fear through a careful consideration of reality, they are able to have faith in themselves and others to find the best ways to move things forward, despite the risks, threats, and problems inherent in the situations they face.

The Three Kinds of Six Leaders: How the Three Instinctual Biases Shape the Three Type Six "Sub-Type" Personalities

According to the Enneagram model, we all have three main instinctual drives that help us survive, but in each of us, one tends to dominate our behavior. The Type Six style is expressed differently depending on whether a person has a bias toward *self-preservation*, establishing *social* relationships and positioning themselves in relation to groups, or *one-to-one* bonding.

The Self-Preservation (or Self-Focused) Six

Self-Preservation Sixes cope with fear through finding allies and friends to protect them. The most actively fearful or "phobic" Sixes, they try to be warm and friendly in order to attract people, and since they fear others' anger, they become programmed to hide or suppress their own aggression. These Sixes feel a kind of insecurity or separation anxiety—they fear that they are not ready or able and have a hard time feeling powerful or accessing an inner sense of their own authority. Because of this, they tend to be the least certain of the three kinds of Sixes. They ask a lot of questions, but don't answer any, and are "proof junkies" who can never find enough proof to feel confident enough to take a strong stand. Self-Preservation Sixes see the world in terms of grey instead of black and white, and can inject doubt and uncertainty into any topic. They doubt others and they doubt themselves.

The Self-Preservation Six must cope with a double dose of fear—the usual fear associated with the Type Six style combined with the fear and insecurity characteristic of someone who is concerned with survival. They present as very openhearted, warm, sincere, and giving, but are very heady and intellectual on the inside. They can establish close bonds with others as part of their survival strategy, and may not look fearful to the people around them, but they have many fears, including a strong fear for their physical safety.

Leadership can be challenging for Self-Preservation Sixes. They may periodically succumb to fear and anxiety, have a hard time making decisions or appearing decisive, and struggle to appear strong or act from a clear sense of power and authority. They may look to others to shore them up and provide them with support or cover, which can make them feel or look weak. However, if Self-Preservation Sixes can learn to deal with their fears, they can leverage their ability to connect with others and be leaders who are thoughtful, wise and sensitive to the needs and concerns of their people. Even the most fearful Sixes can be calm and steady in a crisis. Self-Preservation Sixes have the power to rise to the occasion and deal with difficult circumstances without appearing afraid. Especially when they can learn to understand their responses and develop more courage and self-confidence in the face of anxiety, these Sixes can be approachable, considerate leaders who help others move forward through obstacles.

The Social (or Group-Focused) Six

The Social Six is more certain and less ambiguous, seeing things more in terms of black and white than grey. Social Sixes feel anxious when things are uncertain, and cope with their anxiety by finding an outside authority to guide their life choices and ease their fears. This authority can be a person, but it can also be an ideology or a system of thought, anything that provides a set of rules and guidelines about how to live. However, this can lead Social Sixes to become *too* sure of things. In seeking to calm their anxieties by adhering to an impersonal authority (often a replacement for the father), Social Sixes can become "true believers" in a cause or system of thought.

Social Sixes are highly intellectual types who feel more comfortable (and less fearful) when they have rules and reference points that tell them what to do to be safe, who the good guys and bad guys are, where north, south, east, and west are, and so on. They can look like Type Ones in that they obey the rules and want to know what their duty is—they are precise, rational, cool characters who think in flowcharts and like efficient, orderly processes. They appear stronger than the Self-Preservation Six because they find security and certainty in whatever authoritative system they adhere to. We see the Social Six character in the German culture—Germans are known for their reserved temperament and willingness to follow the rules.

As leaders, Social Sixes will want to create clear structures based on systematic, rational rules and guideposts. They tend to express their leadership through establishing and clarifying processes, norms, roles, and duties. They may have a system of thinking they adhere to, draw strength from, and use to provide coworkers and direct reports with a set of instructions to guide their work and set expectations. They will take a highly rational approach to the work they do and may not be able to be spontaneous. Most Social Sixes will want to know and act from a clear sense of their duty as a leader and will work hard to fulfill their responsibilities in the most efficient and sensible way. Although at times they may be overly intellectual and abstract and have a hard time accessing their emotions, at their best, they will have an attitude of humble service and want to model a thoughtful, reasonable, and rules-based approach to doing work and managing others.

The One-to-One (or Relationship-Focused) Six

One-to-One Sixes are the most assertive, strong, and rebellious Sixes. To cope with fear and anxiety, they adopt a stance designed to intimidate others to keep danger at bay. They believe "the best defense is a good offense" and take on a "fight" mentality in reaction to fear, moving toward risky or dangerous situations as a way of dealing with underlying anxiety. Sometimes called the "counterphobic" Six, they're the most likely Six to (unconsciously) avoid registering fear, and usually do not relate to feeling "fearful." However, at a deeper level, they are, like all Sixes, motivated by fear.

One-to-One Sixes have a very difficult time trusting others; they usually rely only on themselves, and actively take contrarian positions, pushing back on whatever the dominant opinion of the moment might be. They seek to be and appear strong (physically and otherwise), but they may only look courageous. Unconsciously overriding any awareness of their vulnerability and fear as a defensive strategy, they may act their fear out in an unconscious way to the extent that they deny it—the more aggressive and challenging they seem, the more fearful they may be. These Sixes can look like Type Eights in that they can be outspoken rebels who go against people in positions of power. They tend to be risk-takers, daredevils and "shit-disturbers" who react to their fear of being controlled by stirring things up or creating trouble within a team.

As leaders, One-to-One Sixes can seem strong and authoritative, though they may be more vulnerable and insecure than they appear. They may feel uneasy in leadership positions, since they have such a strong antiauthority attitude, and tend to be action-oriented, though the actions they take will be more effective if they become aware of their fear and learn to manage it in conscious ways. When they can own their vulnerability and act from true courage, One-to-One Sixes can put their revolutionary spirit to work in the service of good leadership. At their best, they take the interests of everyone into account and can take bold action to move projects forward in thoughtful ways, making sure their strength comes from true courage instead of just a rebellious or counterphobic impulse. The more they become aware of and own their fear, the more they can ground themselves in a deeper sense of their own authority. And the more they see the good things good authorities can do (whether they are the authority or someone else is), they more they will be able to model faith and boldness in the service of a larger vision.

The Type Six at Work

Type Sixes sometimes feel like working with others is hard because:

▶ *It's hard for me to work well with someone if I don't trust them, and it's hard for me to trust people.*

▶ *It can be hard to collaborate with people if I suspect them of having hidden agendas.*

▶ *My coworkers don't always place the same value on taking enough time to question and test every detail of a plan or project before it's rolled out.*

▶ *I feel dismissed when others won't take the time to understand all my questions and doubts, especially because I am just trying to make sure mistakes aren't made and problems don't surface that we aren't ready to handle.*

▶ *People at work sometimes expect me to make decisions, but I don't want to take the heat if it's not the right decision—and it's always the wrong decision for someone.*

▶ *I can be a bit like a computer—more data-oriented than people-oriented.*

▶ *I sometimes think the wisdom of my careful approach to work tasks is not respected.*

▶ *I don't always trust that leaders I work with will use their power fairly and wisely.*

▶ *Sometimes I'm viewed as a troublemaker or as slowing down work processes, when I am just trying to have all my questions answered and make sure we do our due diligence.*

▶ *It's difficult always being the person who asks the hard questions.*

Type Sixes' workplace pet peeves may be:

▶ When people don't take my questions and doubts seriously.

▶ When people don't value my ability to poke holes in plans as a way to strengthen them.

▶ When people perceive me as negative or pessimistic when I am trying to help them by bringing attention to potential problems and threats.

▶ When people dismiss me or try to talk me out of my fears.

▶ When others prioritize speed over careful analysis of plans.

▶ When my coworkers don't respect processes designed to make sure we do our due diligence and take proper safety precautions.

▶ When people in positions of authority misuse their power.

▶ When people don't allow me to fully express my thoughts and opinions and play the devil's advocate as a way of testing their opinions and proposals.

▶ When people don't respect my skills in assessing risk and making sure we are prepared for every contingency and scenario.

▶ When people pressure me to make a decision when I have not fully examined all the data.

▶ When people ask me to do things, because doing things involves decisions and I don't like being the one who has to decide.

Here's What Type Sixes Can Do to Be Easier to Work With

In general, it helps people with a Type Six style to remember that not everyone needs as much time and space to test and question plans and proposals. It can be important for them to realize that others may experience their questions as a challenge or as disagreement, as opposed to an effort to support the plan's eventual success. When Sixes question people, others may believe they're trying to argue against or undermine the proposal, as opposed to trying make it better by poking holes in it to identify potential problems ahead of time. It will help Sixes to clarify their intentions when they push back or question other individuals' work.

Similarly, Sixes at all levels of an organization can be easier to work with if they maintain an awareness of the things they do and say that stem from fear—and make an effort to notice when their perceptions are based on an accurate reading of the situation vs. a projection of fear or anxiety. They can ask themselves, "Am I worrying too much?" "Is my worrying helping or hurting our efforts right now?" Do my fears accord with the evidence? With objective reality?" And they can ask for feedback, to get a "reality check" from trusted colleagues and friends.

As leaders, Sixes bring the gift of thinking deeply about their work and respecting people at all levels of the organization. Naturally suspicious of authority, Six managers may feel awkward being the authority. But they benefit from becoming aware of any discomfort they feel connected to owning and exercising their power, so that any unconscious resistance to or ambivalence about using that power can be made conscious. It will also be important for them to note any feelings or beliefs that might prevent them from being decisive and clear in their communications with employees. It helps them to have people with whom they can discuss any concerns or anxieties they have behind the scenes, so they can tackle tough issues head-on without hesitation or doubt that can confuse direct reports.

Working with Sixes

Typical Type Six Behaviors in the Workplace

You *might* be working with someone who has a Type Six Enneagram style if you see them doing several of the following behaviors on a regular basis:

▶ Every time he receives an assignment, he has what seem like a million questions for his manager.

▶ She has a difficult time making decisions and needs to go over the data numerous times before she can decide what she wants to do.

▶ In meetings, he often plays the role of "devil's advocate," testing people's viewpoints by representing the opposite perspective and pushing back on opinions that seem to dominate the discussion.

▶ She expresses a lot of doubt—even of her own proposals and work product.

▶ He frequently challenges the authority in the room.

▶ She doesn't trust people easily; it took you months to get to know her and for her to back your ideas.

▶ He pays a lot of attention to negative data he perceives in different situations and often has what seems like a dire view of what's going to happen.

▶ She thinks in terms of "worst case scenarios" and "best case scenarios"—and will take on the opposite position of the majority in meetings.

▶ He strongly supports his team, but can have an "us against them" mentality when it comes to people outside the team.

▶ She always sides with the underdog and supports underdog causes.

▶ He often focuses on assessing whatever risks are involved in a project.

▶ She sometimes displays a sense of "analysis-paralysis"—she can drive her teammates crazy because she will think and think and think about a problem and never get to the point where she feels sure enough to take action.

▶ He has a good sense of humor and often entertains the team with his dry wit.

▶ She's a good troubleshooter who often saves the team time and money by thinking ahead and pointing out the weaknesses in a plan.

What's Great About Working with Conscious Six Leaders

▶ They understand and can clearly explain complex issues and problems.

▶ They tend to be very honest, straightforward, humble, and trustworthy.

▶ They give credit to others and feel uncomfortable in the spotlight.

▶ They aren't afraid to push back and inject a note of caution when they think their colleagues are heading down the wrong track.

▶ They do all the worrying, so you don't have to!

▶ They are calm in a crisis—when something actually does go wrong, they know how to deal with it.

▶ They will call out the higher-ups if they don't agree with what they are doing—they question authorities and speak truth to power.

▶ They err on the side of safety and help the team avoid potential dangers.

▶ They are often funny and have a quick wit.

▶ They think of all the questions that need to be asked when vetting a proposal.

▶ They like to think out of the box. They are creative and enthusiastic problem-solvers.

▶ They are very good at imagining multiple scenarios and making contingency plans.

▶ They (usually) work really hard.

Typical Challenges for People Who Work with Sixes

▶ They slow down the work process when they ask so many questions.

▶ They often have a hard time making decisions.

▶ They tend to make things more complicated than they need to be—because they can look at a problem so many different ways and have so many questions about everything.

▶ They may flood people with too much information.

▶ They can get stuck in ambivalence and hesitation, and have a difficult time pulling the trigger and moving into action.

▶ It takes them a long time to develop trust—and it can be irritating to continually feel like they are testing and doubting you.

▶ Their cynical attitude can feel like criticism and resistance.

▶ They can spend a lot of time working on problems that no one else sees as a problem.

▶ They may express so much skepticism and doubt that they undermine people's or the team's confidence.

▶ They tend to talk in mixed messages—they are often highly ambivalent and so it may be hard for them to be clear and direct.

▶ They can think of 1,000 ways to look at a problem—and they will tell you about all of them.

▶ They sometimes work harder than they need to because they make things harder than they need to be.

Type Sixes and Leadership

A Type Six Leader Speaks About How Knowing Your Enneagram Type Helps You at Work

Keith Heller is Founder and Chief Strategist at Heller Consulting, a consulting firm that provides nonprofit organizations with effective CRM planning and technology strategy.

> *"The Enneagram has helped me tremendously. I identify as a Six, and it immediately helped me to recognize my anxiety—and to see that my anxiety didn't necessarily mean I was perceiving something real out there that it made sense to be anxious about. It helped me have a more balanced view of what was external and internal. It helped me to see that it was at least as likely that it was me internally perceiving things in a certain way as it was that those things actually were that way. I could at least consider the possibility that maybe it was me and not something real I was perceiving.*
>
> *"I have been very aware of my Enneagram style as I lead my company. I'm aware of my own habits so I can keep an eye on them.*

I'm a counterphobic Six. I'm scanning the territory all the time, and I'm always looking forward, looking ahead, which as a leader is not the worst thing. I tend to scan for threats. Knowing that, I also want to scan for opportunities. If I'm out there scanning anyway, I try to remember to look for opportunities too. And actually, I frame it for myself that missing an opportunity is a threat. When I'm only looking for threats, I might fail to see an opportunity.

"Being a counterphobic Six is pretty useful because when I perceive a threat, which is frequently, I immediately work on how to mediate it or avoid it—and again, that's not the worst thing. Once you construct a positive goal that you're aiming towards, you start knocking down all the things that are getting in the way and that is an effective style that's worked.

"Also, later on, when you achieve certain goals, it's important to look back and say, 'I worried a lot along the way. Was I accurate to worry?' Nine times out of ten, embarrassingly, it's no—you burned a lot of energy and wasted a lot of time and energy worrying about things you didn't have to worry about it. As a leader I tell others I work with in the firm about my style. I tell them, 'I tend to worry. I can see threats where there aren't any. Let's be aware of that together and help me balance that.'

"Our CEO, Jeffrey, and I have worked together for fifteen years. He's a Seven, and he knows his style too. He can say to me, seriously or jokingly, 'You're worrying too much.' And I can say, 'Thanks, you're probably right.' And I can say to him, 'I think you're being a little optimistic about this or that. I think you're excited about six things and we need to focus on two.'"

When You Are a Manager and You Are a Six

As a Type Six manager, you likely feel a sense of responsibility to fully explore plans and processes, unearth threats and risks, and locate and solve problems. You may feel torn when it comes to your power—you want to use it to make sure dangers are foreseen and prepared for, yet it can be hard for you to feel certain enough to make decisions and take action in a timely fashion. Also, you may be naturally suspicious of authority, and may feel ambivalent about expressing power and managing people.

You may have to get over the hurdle of your own self-doubt to lead with a measure of confidence. Depending on what subtype you are, you may doubt yourself excessively, over-rely on an outside authority or ideology, or take aggressive action to avoid feeling your fear. You likely consider yourself a good problem solver, but you may get stuck in circular thinking if you don't have the confidence to know when you've found the right approach and can move forward. At your best, however, you are able to take your tendencies into account and can balance out your habit of scanning for danger with a belief in your own competence.

When Your Manager Is a Six

The best thing about being led by a Six is that you can be fairly certain they will want to hear your ideas. They will see their role as taking the lead on solving problems, and if they trust you and know they can depend on you, you will likely get along well. Being honest and straightforward, authentic and sincere, and dependable and reliable will all help you help your Six learn to trust you, which is key. You can't fake being honest with a Six—they read people well, and they will be watching to see if your actions line up with your words. It may also be important to remember that trust takes a while to build and needs to be earned. Respect your Six manager's questions, fears, and concerns, and don't dismiss what you might see as needless negativity as "wrong." In addition to being disrespectful, it won't get you anywhere. It will be much more effective to talk through their concerns and point out any evidence or factual information that indicates their fears are misplaced.

It can be hard for Sixes to be leaders. It's a lot of pressure to have to make decisions and tell people what to do amidst all that doubt and uncertainty. You can support your Six manager by seeking to understand their fears, offering sincere reassurance, and backing up your opinions with facts and data. The more you build up a track record of performing accurate analyses they can count on and solving problems in effective ways, the more they will trust you and count on your input. At their best, Six managers have faith in their people and work to develop a sense of trust.

When Your Subordinate Is a Six

When your direct reports have a Type Six style, it will help to keep the lines of communication open so you can talk through problems as they arise and learn to work as a team. As a manager, it will be wise to develop a sense of mutual trust with Six subordinates so they will feel comfortable bringing fears, anxieties, and questions to you so they don't fester and slow down the workflow. Sixes perform well when they feel free to air their concerns and talk through any scary scenarios they create in their heads. It will help if you are someone they can trust to help them sort out fact from fantasy and tell the difference between insights and projections.

Depending on which kind of Six they are, they may be suspicious of you as the authority, seek refuge and direction in their relationship with you, or test and question you repeatedly to make sure you are trustworthy. To create a good working relationship with Sixes of all kinds, try to be transparent, spell out expectations and assignments clearly and carefully, and avoid surprises. You will create a smoother relationship with your Six direct report if your behavior is consistent and predictable, and if you avoid doing things that trigger their anxiety, like saying "you have to talk to them" and then delaying the conversation, or switching directions rapidly without explaining why.

On the plus side, if you work with healthy Sixes, and if you support them in developing their self-awareness, they may be able to own their fears and anxieties, take responsibility for their habit of asking questions and looking for problems, and work to develop trust in you and the other people on the team. If you work to engender trust and mutual respect, they will reward you with loyalty and hard work—while Sixes tend to be suspicious of authority and can be rebellious, they also want to find a good authority. So if you take steps to show your Six employee that you can be trusted to do what you say and support them, their fears will be eased and you can count on them to be a valuable member of your team.

Getting Along with Sixes: Tips for What to Do to Work Well with Sixes

▶ *Be trustworthy.* Your Six coworkers will be watching and listening to you closely to read whether you support them or not. It will help if you are honest, open, and clear about what you think and what you are going to do and why. And remember that it can take time to earn someone's trust.

▶ *Be patient with their questions.* It's important to let Sixes ask the questions they need to ask. Although they can go overboard, they often ask the tough questions that no one else will—and they can relax more when they have the information they need.

▶ *Understand and respect their fears and worries (and don't judge them for being fearful or anxious).* You will get farther faster with the Sixes in your life if you don't try to talk them out of whatever they are worried about. If you take their fearful stance as a given, and support them in doing what they need to do, they will have an easier time feeling less fear or forging ahead despite their fear.

▶ *Value their ability to assess risk and trouble-shoot.* Sixes play an important role on teams that most other types would rather not play. So, it's wise to actively appreciate them for the way they examine all scenarios, make contingency plans, and do all the checks and balances involved in a project. If they feel valued and safe, they will be easier to work with (than if they feel like no one is listening to them).

▶ *Give them time to conduct thorough analyses, but help them take action.* Everything Sixes see comes under the heading of a problem or a challenge that, if not taken care of, will end badly. You can support them by giving them the time they need to investigate and solve problems, but also help them to take action when warranted.

Actionable Growth Tasks and Suggestions: How Type Sixes Can Become More Self-Aware, Effective, and Happy at Work

All the types can learn to be less reactive and better at collaborating with others through first *observing* their habitual tendencies, thinking about the things they think, feel, and do to gain more *self-insight*, and making efforts to *manage* or *moderate* their automatic reactions to key triggers.

Sixes grow through first observing and then learning to moderate their habitual reactions to key triggers like getting alarmed at signs of danger, worrying that coworkers are untrustworthy, or perceiving danger and over-preparing for it.

When Sixes can watch what they do enough to "catch themselves in the act" of doing the things that get them in trouble, and then pause and reflect on what they are doing and why, they can gradually learn to moderate their programming and knee-jerk responses. Here are some ideas to help Sixes be more self-aware, emotionally intelligent, and satisfied at work (and at home).

Self-Observation: Things for Sixes to Watch Out For

▶ *Notice the way your perception of threats may be correct or all in your head. Learn to discern when you are detecting real danger and when you are imagining and projecting it.*

▶ *Develop an ongoing awareness of your fear and anxiety. Learn to be aware in the moment of what you are afraid of and why.*

▶ *Be aware of any tendency you have to look for problems to solve—when you identify important problems and when you potentially create them where they don't exist. Notice if your love of problem solving leads you to make things more problematic than they need to be (and not the consequences of this).*

▶ *Notice how you evaluate others' trustworthiness. Are you applying reasonable standards or asking for an impossible level of proof? Are you reading people accurately or projecting your fears out onto others?*

▶ *Observe your tendency to focus on what might go wrong in order to prepare for it. Are you really being realistic or are you focusing too much on negative data?*

▶ *Notice how you relate to your own sense of power and confidence. Do you doubt yourself? How often and why? Do you project your inner authority out onto others, and view them as more powerful? Is it difficult to own your power and goodness?*

Blind Spots: What You Don't Know Can Hurt You!

What blind spots Sixes often don't see in themselves:

▶ *Your own power and authority.* Type Sixes sometimes don't see and consciously own their inner sense of power and the authority to protect themselves and direct their own life. You may project power and authority onto others instead of recognizing, developing, and acting from a deep sense of your own confidence—which is the best way to counter fear and anxiety.

▶ *The positive data in a given situation.* Sixes tend to focus their attention on what might go wrong, so they may not pay attention to all the things that are going right. It helps to balance the tendency to find problems with an active effort to search out signs of what's working.

▶ *Your tendency to project your inner fears onto the outside world.* Sixes unconsciously use an important psychological defense mechanism to try to feel safe: projection. It tends to operate unconsciously, so it helps Sixes to work to be more aware of it. Ask yourself periodically if you are responding to a real external threat or making it up in your head and imagining it as coming from the outside. Examine the evidence. Do a "reality check." This helps you recognize and own your fear so you can manage it in conscious ways.

▶ *The effects of "splitting" the world into good and bad, scary and safe.* "Splitting" is the other primary psychological defense mechanism Sixes (unconsciously) use to feel safe. It begins in early childhood, when the Six is too young to understand that good and bad can exist in the same person, so they separate what's good and what's bad—seeing one as originating inside and one on the outside (or vice versa). This is what we do when we demonize our enemies. However, the big issue here is that splitting often has the effect of making you "bad" and others "good," or the other way around. You may feel guilty and bad, and look to others to protect you, or you may feel like the "good guy" and suspect others. Either way, it's important to learn to be aware of this defense mechanism, so you don't label yourself or others as bad when you/they aren't.

▶ *Your feelings and "gut knowing" as sources of good information.* As head types, Sixes rely on the data they generate through thinking and analyzing. And while this is a key strength, people who lead with a Type Six style may undervalue their emotions and their gut as co-equal sources of data about the world inside and outside. Accessing your emotions and your body can help you to exit from the mental loop all that thinking can sometimes lead to.

Self-Insight: Things for Sixes to Think About, Understand, and Explore

▶ *Why is it sometimes difficult to stop looking for problems and focus on addressing specific threats or fixing problems?*

▶ *What is difficult about trusting others? What kinds of things do you imagine will happen if you open up more to having more faith in people?*

▶ *What is your relationship like with your fear? What are the main sources of your main fears? Under what conditions do you create fears in your head (as opposed to responding to an objective threat in the outside world)?*

▶ *What is your relationship like with your own anger? How conscious are you of avoiding expressing it (if you are a Self-Preservation Six) or expressing it too quickly (if you are a One-to-One Six)?*

▶ *What is your experience of your own confidence and power? What kinds of things make you feel insecure? How can you develop more faith in yourself and your own abilities?*

▶ *What is happening when you take the contrarian stance and argue the devil's advocate position? Can you tell when your contrarian positions are a way of expressing fear you don't want to feel?*

▶ *Notice when you are hard on yourself and condemn yourself and look into why this happens. What is difficult about accepting yourself as who you are?*

▶ *Are you afraid of both success and failure? What is behind these fears?*

Strengths to Leverage

It helps Sixes to be aware of, actively pay attention to, fully own, and leverage:

▶ *Ability to observe, analyze, and think through problems and find solutions.* People with a Type Six style excel at noticing the flaws in a plan and generating solutions to problems. They like the process of solving problems and bring a lot of skill, competence, and energy to surfacing vital information and understanding how to act on it.

▶ *Ability to forecast problems before they happen and preparing to meet them.* A key part of business success is being able to understand the obstacles that may occur in the course of a project and prevent them from derailing things. Sixes' minds work in exactly this way—they are extremely good at mentally generating scenarios and making contingency plans. This makes them excellent project managers.

▶ *Sensitivity to power dynamics and egalitarian mind-set.* Naturally wary of authorities and their power to exploit people, Sixes have a democratic, egalitarian outlook. As leaders, they don't have a need to be significant or receive accolades. They want to be competent, but they can inspire loyalty in their people because they want to make decisions and enact policies that benefit everyone. And they want to work with others in an equal way to solve problems as a team.

▶ *Ability to be calm and competent in a crisis.* Sixes spend so much brain-power preparing for danger to hit that when it does, they handle it well—with strength and confidence. It helps them to remember this when they second-guess themselves.

▶ *Loyalty, support, dedication to people and causes.* Sixes take time to develop trust, but once they are sure of something or someone, they commit fully. They want the things they do to benefit their people, and they work hard to create security for themselves and others.

Self-Management: Challenging Tendencies for Sixes to Moderate

▶ *Welcome and respect, but manage fear.* Work to be aware of how your fear arises and what it's about. Respect and have compassion for yourself when you feel fear, but learn to manage it and counter it with courage so it doesn't run you.

▶ *Temper antiauthority and contrarian reactivity.* Notice when you communicate in contrarian ways to prove your cleverness or resist others' views out of fear you may not be fully aware of. Learn to observe your antiauthority reactions and temper them, knowing they can derail you if you allow your unacknowledged fear to surface as false strength or ego-based efforts at intimidation.

▶ *Moderate the worry.* You may not be able to stop worrying, but you can tone it down through conscious efforts to be courageous and focus on the positive.

▶ *Learn to tell the difference between intuition/insight and projection.* It's important to recognize how intuitive and insightful you are, but it's even more crucial to make sure you learn to distinguish between intuition and projection.

▶ *Develop trust more consciously.* While you may have difficulty trusting people for a good reason, you can learn to moderate your mistrust through understanding where it comes from, what it's about, and what you need to feel safe.

▶ *Notice if problem solving leads to excessive problem seeking.* When you love to solve problems, you can see them everywhere—even when they aren't there. Sometimes this can make things harder rather than easier. Reining in your tendency to solve all the problems can help you to focus on what's most important and conserve your energy.

Consciously Manifesting Your Higher Potential: Being Aware of the "Low Side" and Aiming for the "High Side"

Sixes can also grow through consciously becoming aware of the self-limiting habits and patterns associated with their personality style and learning to embody the higher aspects or more expansive capacities of the Type Six personality:

▶ Learn how fear drives you and meet your fear with confidence, faith, and courage. Allow yourself to learn to own your power, your positive qualities, and to develop courage and faith in the face of fearful fantasy.

▶ Become conscious of how you decide whether to trust someone and notice if your standards are so high that you have a hard time connecting with and collaborating with others. Allow yourself to experiment with having the courage to open up a little more earlier on, even if you aren't sure it's completely safe.

▶ Learn to recognize when you are getting over-focused on what seems threatening and get stuck in avoidance or suspicion or ambivalence or doubt. Allow yourself to open up to a wider perspective and actively index the positive data in the situation in a way that allows you to feel good and draw strength from what is working.

▶ Become aware of what you get out of overusing your intellect and realize you can find even more meaning in the things you do by accessing your emotional intelligence and "gut knowing" more often. Balance out your head-centeredness with a more active connection with your heart and your body.

▶ Learn to notice when you seek to prove your competence through being an intellectual problem-solver and broaden your vision of how you can be powerful in the work you do. Realize that you have the ability to get out of your head and into the flow of life more than you think you do.

▶ Learn to see when you are projecting out your fears and learn to tell the difference between projection and intuition. Learn to discern and call upon your intuition more. Refine your ability to open up to having more faith in others and in a broader range of your own capabilities.

Overall, Type Sixes can fulfill their higher potential by observing and working against their habit of over-focusing on threats and other problems, but appreciating their broad capability to notice subtle nuances that might have meaning. When they can consciously draw on their powerful ability to analyze what is happening and find safety through creative insights and engineering, but also develop more connection to other people as well as their emotions and their courage, they can develop the faith and trust they need to face their fears and be able to use their higher talents to greater benefit.

CHAPTER 10

The Type Seven Leadership Style

The Innovative, Optimistic Visionary,
or Focusing on the Future (and Feeling Festive)

"Creativity is just connecting things."
"Innovation distinguishes between a leader and a follower."
Steve Jobs, entrepreneur and Apple Inc. founder

"Never, ever underestimate the importance of having fun."
Randy Pausch, computer science professor

The Type Seven archetype is that prototypical person who wants, more than anything, to feel good (and not bad). Sometimes called "the Epicure" or "the Adventurer," Sevens want to stay happy, experience pleasure, and imagine all the creative possibilities connected to whatever interests them. They tend to have the unconscious belief that if they start feeling bad, they may never stop. This is why negative emotions are so threatening. As intellectual types, Sevens excel at finding unexpected connections between things and charming people with their fast-paced, flexible thinking, and their attention automatically goes to what sounds fun, exciting, or intellectually stimulating. This continual search for the best options and the best experiences is rooted in a drive to find what will make them happy. Since they don't always know what will make them happiest, they need the freedom to pursue anything and everything.

A Seven's programming tells them that the way to maintain a sense of well-being is to focus on what makes them feel good and find ways to sustain a sense of fun and excitement in all that they do and avoid negative feelings at all costs. The Seven style is fundamentally shaped by an intolerance of limitation—it's crucial for them to feel free to do what they want to do and feel how they want to feel, to choose from among options, and avoid outside constraints of any kind.

The Type Seven speaking style is "quick and spontaneous, with words released in a flurry... they tell engaging stories, shift from topic to topic, and are upbeat and charming."[20] Sevens are usually very talkative and amiable—they love to interact with people and energetically engage with them about subjects and individuals that fascinate or amuse them. Sevens naturally play with ideas and may actively express interest in a diverse range of subjects. They frequently look at "the bright side," and may and subtly avoid negative topics.

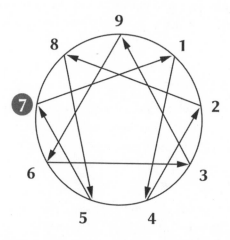

As leaders, Sevens are gifted at brainstorming and envisioning what might be possible. The Seven mind is essentially boundary-free, which is what makes them good at generating many ideas—they feel free to come up with many ideas and make connections between ideas almost without limit. As future-oriented idealists, they tend to be visionaries who have a talent for imagining new possibilities and innovations. They may be pleasure-loving networkers or service-oriented cheerleaders or optimistic dreamers, but whatever their characteristic emphasis, Seven leaders possess a freethinking entrepreneurial spirit that motivates them to lift people's spirits and expand the frontiers of our usual modes of thought.

How to Tell if You Are a Type Seven: The View from the Inside

If most or all of the following characteristics apply to you, you may have a Type Seven personality style:

▶ *Your mind emphasizes the positive data or positive elements of your work.* You enjoy envisioning future possibilities and learning about things that interest you—and you find many things intellectually compelling.

▶ *You have "bright shiny object" syndrome.* You are distracted by engaging ideas to think about and other attractive things that pop into your field of vision or your head.

▶ *You are easily fascinated by interesting people, events, and ideas.* You like learning new things, going to new places, and meeting new people— you love the thrill of new experiences and novel adventures.

▶ *You tend to be interested in many different things, but may not go very deeply into any one of them.* You enjoy the intellectual stimulation, fun and variety of a range of diverse activities, but you may skim along the surface of your experiences. The phrase "jack of all trades, master of none" may apply to you.

▶ *You enjoy enjoyment. You are happiest being happy. You actively seek happiness.* You like to feel positive emotions, and you don't like to feel negative ones. Your motto might be, "Why would you feel bad if you could feel good?"

▶ *You automatically reframe negatives into positives.* For example, when you were unemployed, you called yourself a "freelance entrepreneur." You believe it's best to always look on the bright side, and are very good at finding silver linings, the best in people, and whatever is awesome.

▶ *You rarely complain about your work. Your mind emphasizes the positive elements of your job.* When work gets boring, it's harder for you to stay engaged.

▶ *You don't like to be limited or constrained in any way.* If something or someone limits you, you will find a way around it or out of it.

▶ *You feel uncomfortable when you have to deal with unpleasant emotions.* You like to keep the mood up, so you automatically try to avoid inter-actions that feel thorny, uncomfortable, or painful. It can be really hard for you to have the dreaded "difficult conversation" with someone when things aren't going well.

▶ *You're good at winging it—you can "fake it 'til you make it" if you have to.* You can work hard and make things happen, but you are also good at looking like you know what you're doing (while you're still figuring it out).

▶ *You like to have many options.* You like to have a Plan B (and Plan C) in case Plan A doesn't pan out. This may cause people to perceive you as flaky, but you see it as flexible and spontaneous.

▶ *You don't like hierarchies.* You make friends with the people you work with—both above and below you—to flatten things out (and so no one is controlling anyone's options). You want your boss to be your friend so she won't control you. You want your direct reports to be your friends so you don't need to be strict with them and manage them too formally.

▶ *You enjoy being in leadership positions that involve generating innovative ideas and envisioning the next big thing.* You excel at brainstorming and thinking outside the box. You like to take the lead in imagining how things might be better in the future.

The Central Adaptive Strategy of the Type Seven Personality Style

Sevens often report having had a happy early life—they tend to put a positive spin on things, so even if they experience hardship, they tend to remember it in positive terms. However, whether they remember it or not, many Sevens experienced some sort of fearful or painful event or events in childhood that motivates them to take refuge in positive emotions. The Type Seven adaptive strategy grows out of a need to defend against pain or fear through thinking their way to happy feelings and focusing attention on whatever makes them feel good.

This habit of taking refuge in the imagination allows Sevens to stay upbeat and avoid difficult feelings without ever having to register pain. The Enneagram's biggest practitioners of "the power of positive thinking," Sevens are hard-wired to focus on what makes them feel good: people they like, interesting ideas to think about, good food to eat, beautiful places to go. They don't necessarily "try" to think positively, it just happens. They like to solve problems and tackle challenges, but to cope with what really feels problem-atic—unpleasant emotions and whatever stirs them up—Sevens tend to "move on," look to what's ahead, and do whatever it takes to generate happier emotions. They escape from an uncomfortable present to a rosier future.

While people with a Type Seven style are classified as "fear types," most Sevens report they don't experience much fear in their everyday life. However, their coping strategy is an unconscious response to an underlying fear of being limited and of feeling their suffering or their anxiety. Sevens often report feeling bored or anxious rather than fearful. Even Sevens who do feel fear and don't consciously run away from fear or pain are still shaped by an adaptive strategy that employs many different ways of focusing on what's pleasurable as a way of distancing themselves from any awareness of unpleasant emotions.

What Do Sevens Pay Attention To? The Type Seven "Radar Screen"

The strategy of focusing on what's positive and staying upbeat leads Sevens to pay attention to whatever feels most exciting, stimulating, and fun. If it's not awesome or interesting or delightful, it drops off the Seven's radar screen—so Sevens notoriously have trouble focusing on work tasks that are less than exciting. Sevens are not famous for their attention to detail and most Sevens I've talked to absolutely detest paperwork. It can be extremely difficult for someone who leads with the Type Seven style to not be distracted by some-thing better when they are doing something that's not very fun. They may even feel actual physical pain in their bodies when they have to focus on details they don't care about for an extended period of time.

Sevens like to relate to people, engage in enjoyable activities, and think interesting thoughts. As mental types, they live a great deal of the time in their imagination, both taking refuge there from anything sticky they might want to (unconsciously) avoid and utilizing their imaginative function to do the work they do. Their inner experience is a lively, ever-changing, creative workspace where they invent new possibilities, visualize the future, and play with new ideas. It's a mental playground where they spend much of their time entertaining themselves—in fact, some Sevens prefer living in their imagina-tions to living in reality. They can create optimistic visions of what could be in an idealized future in such a way that what they think and dream about seems more real than what is actually happening.

The View from "Planet Seven": How Sevens See the World

Generally, individuals with a Type Seven style see the world in terms of what *could* be true if everything was as great as they imagine it to be. Their view of life is so deeply colored by optimism they may have a difficult time attending to what's right in front of them in the real world if it's not so pleasant. The tendency to put a positive spin on things is so deeply ingrained, they may not know they are doing it and may believe that they are perceiving what's real.

Sevens relate to the world in terms of how great everything is. They notice all the positive things that are happening and all the reasons they have to feel good. As the saying goes, the world is their oyster, filled with exciting new experiences waiting to be had. However, they also sometimes sense forces out there that could potentially limit their freedom and their options. This is why they prefer flat organizations to hierarchies and engage in "soft rebellion" in response to authorities who might limit them by telling them what to do. They intellectually charm or manipulate people so they can keep the party going, retain their freedom, and avoid feeling trapped.

Sevens in leadership positions are often motivated by a desire to make the world a better place, especially because they are so good at imagining how the world might be improved. They generally see life as full of exciting things to try, and endeavor to have a diverse variety of experiences and taste all the wonderful things they see. They view the world from an intellectual perspective—through the mental activity of planning for fun and thinking about all the things they want to do, participate in, and accomplish. They are the most emotional of the Enneagram's three head-based styles, but, like Fives and Sixes, they may often think about feelings rather than sinking into their emotions.

The Type Seven Leader: Core Characteristics

The following character traits define the Type Seven leadership style.

- *Ability to generate imaginative visions and outcomes.* Sevens like to think about the future—they tend to be original, innovative thought leaders who solve problems in ingenious ways.

- *Good brainstormers.* Seven leaders' normal mode of thinking is very much outside the proverbial box. They love nothing more than getting together with like-minded colleagues and coming up with thrilling new angles on how to do things.

▶ *Synthesizing minds.* Sevens have a talent for finding connections between things that might seem disconnected to other people.

▶ *Positive outlook.* Sevens are masters of positively reframing things and seeing the spectacular in life.

▶ *Preference for having many options.* Sevens want to be free to take advantage of whatever opportunities may pop up, so they like to keep their noses to the wind and their options open.

▶ *Tendency to rationalize doing what feels good.* Most Sevens have never met a rationalization they couldn't get behind. Finding good reasons for doing whatever they want to do supports their ability to avoid limitation and feel okay about their choices. They may often not even realize they are rationalizing their "bad" behavior.

▶ *Enthusiastic and energetic.* Seven leaders tend to support others in powerful ways, through the sincere passion and intense positive feelings they can mobilize on behalf of a project or an idea.

Mental, Emotional, and Behavioral Patterns: Why do Sevens Think, Feel, and Behave the Way They Do?

Mental

Sevens are mental types who enjoy playing with ideas and thinking new thoughts. They live in their imaginations—as a place to think stimulating thoughts that generate positive emotions and (potentially) to escape from whatever is going on that might not be so positive. Sometimes described as having a "monkey-mind," Sevens' thinking moves from one thought to another like monkeys swinging from branch to branch. They excel at entertaining themselves and others through their mental activity, often have quick wits, and use their minds to think themselves out of uncomfortable situations, charm their way around limits or instantly recast a bad situation as a good one. By nature hedonistic and anti-conventional, their mental flexibility also acts as a defense against becoming stuck in or trapped by an unpleasant experience or a limiting authority or power structure.

Emotional

Sevens like feeling good and dislike feeling bad, and believe that people can choose one or the other at will—they can focus on "positive" emotions, like joy or excitement, and disregard, ignore, or evade "negative" ones, like fear or pain. Although they are the most emotional of the three "head types," they don't see the value in feeling difficult emotions and rationalize their avoidance of pain, automatically doing whatever it takes to feel good and ignoring any negative data that might inspire a bad mood. They sometimes express an aversion to boredom, but this may be code for not wanting to slow down enough to allow the deeper, darker emotions they avoid to bubble up.

Behavioral

Sevens move rapidly—they think fast, talk fast, and do things fast, so it can be hard for others to keep up with them. Their tendency to get distracted can mean they have a difficult time maintaining their focus on what they are supposed to be doing, especially if it threatens to be boring or dull. They may have difficulty following through on commitments and finishing tasks on time, and their preference for new ideas may lead them to put more things on their own plate—one Seven I met at a training said, "A week before a deadline I have four things to do, but two days before the deadline I will have 10 things to do." However, successful Sevens find ways to work around their tendency to lose focus, like the Seven I know who tells herself she needs to do a particular task to have the fun she wants to have later. As you might expect, Sevens are also very good at celebrating achievements and planning for next steps.

The Main Strengths and Superpowers of the Type Seven Style: What Sevens Are Really Good At

- ▶ *Maintaining an optimistic, positive attitude; keeping spirits up.* Sevens are good at keeping things light, focusing on what's working, and imagining best-case scenarios. They realize that when you believe things are going to go well, they usually do.

- ▶ *Imaginative and creative planners.* Sevens bring a spirit of play to the planning process. They enjoy using their imaginations to creatively plot out innovative visions and how to get there.

▶ *Fast-paced.* Sevens can be counted on to move things along and not get bogged down, whether they are leading a meeting, planning a project, or burning through their to-do list.

▶ *Enthusiastic supporters.* Sevens can be inspiring leaders who motivate people through their sheer enjoyment of doing the work and engaging with their colleagues.

▶ *Innovative and forward thinking; futuristic.* Sevens automatically imagine what the future is going to be like—they are very good at creating plans and mental pictures about what could or will happen.

▶ *Good at reframing negatives into positives.* Sevens automatically turn what sounds negative into something to feel good about. They easily point to the positive data or the silver lining.

▶ *Celebrating successes.* Not everyone realizes how important it is to celebrate victories as a way of reinforcing what works—but Sevens do. And they may also give themselves (and their teams) treats along the way to keep their spirits up.

When Too Much of a Good Thing Becomes a Bad Thing: How Sevens Can Go Wrong When They Try Too Hard to Make Everything Okay

▶ *Maintaining an optimistic, positive attitude; keeping spirits up.* Sevens can go too far in envisioning a rosy scenario when they overlook important information that might not be so good—just ask a Type Six! They may also avoid talking about conflicts out of a fear of being trapped in something uncomfortable.

▶ *Imaginative and creative planners.* Sevens can go so far into their imagined utopian visions that they lose touch with what's real. It's important tie a vision to reality so you can actually make it happen. And this can be a real blind spot for them—they (especially One-to-One Sevens) just think things are way more awesome than they are.

▶ *Fast-paced.* Sevens sometimes skim along the surface of things, when slowing down and going deeper into a task may be what's required to get the job done well. Their attention to detail can suffer and they can be sloppy (and not necessarily care).

▶ *Enthusiastic supporters.* At times Sevens may be *too* enthusiastic about something that's not so great as a way of avoiding facing bad news.

▶ *Innovative and forward thinking; futuristic.* Sevens sometimes miss out on experiencing what's happening in the present moment out of a fear that it might be hard to handle. And since the present moment is really all we can experience, they can end up depriving themselves of experiencing their life as intensely as they want to.

▶ *Good at reframing negatives into positives.* Sometimes it's important to understand the negatives in a situation so you can deal with them in an effective way, as opposed to just putting a positive spin on them.

▶ *Celebrating successes.* Sevens sometimes want to get to the celebratory party before the goal is actually reached. This can create problems, like when my Seven friend and I were in a canoe and he started celebrating the fact that we'd made it through some scary rapids before we actually made it *all* the way through—and tipped us over.

Fortunately, Sevens' sincere interest in doing whatever they can to be effective and get results can often motivate them to pay attention to how their relentless positive outlook can sometimes derail things. When they can balance what's great about their optimism and enthusiasm with an ability to slow down and consider different points of view and all of the data, everybody wins.

"When I'm stressed..." and "At my best...": Understanding the "Low Side" and the "High Side" of the Type Seven Personality Style

When stressed to the point of going to their "low side," Type Sevens can move so fast that they create chaos and confusion in their wake. Stressed out Sevens easily become distracted, may appear manic and ungrounded, and may have a difficult time slowing down long enough to really listen to what people are saying and face difficult facts. Some may retreat into positive fantasy such that they refuse to see the truth of what's really happening—especially if what's happening threatens to inspire bad feelings, like disappointment, anxiety, or pain.

Sevens on the low side can become more relentlessly positive and run faster and farther away from darker emotions and potential conflicts. They may speak more rapidly and their thoughts may become erratic and unfocused.

They may (unconsciously) seek to manipulate through intellectual charm, or try to force results that satisfy their personal self-interest, without regard to what's best for others. Or, they may desperately avoid getting close to anything that pushes them into what they (unconsciously) fear most, being limited by outside authorities or feeling trapped in unpleasant emotions. They may become more removed, more aggressive, or more insistent on focusing on what brings them pleasure.

On the "high side," healthy Sevens can balance their preference for positivity with an ability to slow down and take in all relevant information and points of view—including what's not so positive. They can find ways to deal with the hard stuff as a way of providing a sound foundation for making things better. More self-aware Sevens can catch themselves in the act of distracting themselves and steady their focus more and more often. They can also stick with things longer—relationships or conflicts or difficult situations—to work things out and find resolutions that bring about good feelings that go deeper and last longer.

Emotionally intelligent Sevens learn to feel their emotions all the way to their depths, even when they are painful, understanding that feeling all their emotions leads to a richer and more satisfying experience of life. When Sevens operate from their high side, their natural positivity, humor, and lightness has an even more potent effect, because it is supported and grounded in their willingness to experience all of life, even the darker parts. When Sevens learn to make their fear of pain conscious, they can be more present, more balanced, and more powerful. Instead of just skimming along the surface of their experiences, they can risk sinking down deeper into the moment and getting more of what they want the most—a more intense taste of being alive.

The Three Kinds of Seven Leaders: How the Three Instinctual Biases Shape the Three Type Seven "Sub-Type" Personalities

According to the Enneagram model, we all have three main instinctual drives that help us survive, but in each of us, one of these three impulses tends to dominate our behavior. The Type Seven style gets expressed differently depending on whether a person has a bias toward *self-preservation*, *social* relationships within groups, or *one-to-one* bonding.

The Self-Preservation (or Self-Focused) Seven Leader

Self-Preservation Sevens focus on getting what they need through taking advantage of opportunities and creating a network of friends and allies. They may experience more anxiety than the other two kinds of Sevens, and cope with this through finding creative ways to meet their needs for security and support. The most practical, materialistic, and hedonistic of the three Seven sub-personalities, Self-Preservation Sevens are very pragmatic, and good at making things happen and creating wealth to support a sense of security in the world. They tend to rely on only those they trust, and may surround themselves with a "good mafia" of friends and allies they can go to when they need something or want to feel protected. And while they can be generous in offering support, they may fail to be fully aware of the degree to which their own self-interest drives their friendly transactions.

Sevens with an instinctual bias toward self-preservation tend to always have their nose to the wind to sniff out good opportunities. They can be talkative, friendly, pleasure-seekers who enjoy the finest life has to offer—their self-preservation focus, combined with their Seven programming, leads to a love of indulgence and a search for security born of the need to have the freedom to do, go, work, eat, and drink as they choose. This Seven, more than the others, may be aware of their fear and even a bit paranoid at times—and their usually subtle antiauthoritarian streak may surface if someone tries to constrain their movements or control their actions.

As leaders, Self-Preservation Sevens tend to be practical and pragmatic—they generally evaluate the business environment more realistically than the other Sevens do and base decisions on both optimism and their own self-interest. They may employ intellectual charm and an upbeat attitude to win people over and establish connections, and will energetically implement plans and projects to get where they want to go without always considering the larger impact of their pursuit of their own self-interest. Rationalizing that what's good for them is good for everyone, they may pursue the work they want to do in the way they want to do it, and have a difficult time submitting to other authorities or being influenced by direct reports. They may try to smooth rough spots in relationships through personal appeal and humor and focus on pleasure as a way to soothe fears. At their best, Self-Preservation Seven leaders mix good business sense with careful planning and a positive outlook to get what they need, support the people they work with, and have fun doing it.

The Social (or Group-Focused) Seven Leader

Social Sevens are what is called the "counter-type" of the Sevens—while many Sevens are "self-referencing" and focus on their own inner experience, needs, and wants, Social Sevens (often subconsciously) focus their energy and attention on supporting others, giving to others, and alleviating pain in others as a way of avoiding experiencing pain themselves. They can even experience a kind of taboo on selfishness, as they sense their own desires for things, but deny or postpone them in support of an ideal of being of service to the group.

Like Type Twos, Social Sevens can put a great deal of energy and enthusiasm toward supporting and giving to others. They may feel motivated to offer more to others and take less for themselves, while at the same time expect or hope that if they support the group, the group will take care of them. Social Sevens are often drawn to jobs that involve healing, holding, or easing the pain of others, perhaps in an unconscious effort to ease their own pain without having to feel it. The "New Age" movement is in some ways a cultural reflection of the Social Seven mentality—imagining a global environment in which people are more free and more open to new experiences that free them from the constraints of the past.

As leaders, Social Sevens can be enthusiastic visionaries who imagine a better world. They may have utopian fantasies and sunny outlooks, even while they engage with people facing illness, grief, or other real-life difficulties. Social Seven leaders may work passionately in support of causes or try to improve working conditions so people can be more effective and enjoy what they do. They may demonstrate leadership through sacrificing their own needs and desires as a way of emphasizing the wisdom of making sure others get what they need to do the work they need to do and to be happy doing it. Although they may at times use enthusiasm to inspire (or manipulate) people into following their lead, and they may have a deep desire to be recognized for their dedication to being of service, they usually express a sincere commitment to the welfare of others. At their best, they combine selfless service with a clear and enlivening vision of all that can be done to improve people's lives.

The One-to-One (or Relationship-Focused) Seven Leader

One-to-One Sevens are idealistic dreamers who have a very strong focus on how things could be or how they imagine them to be. In contrast to practical Self-Preservation Sevens, One-to-One Sevens have a need to idealize reality and see the world through rose-colored glasses. They are light-hearted "enjoyers" who can be extremely idealistic, to the point of being naïve. They tend to be very enthusiastic, and their enthusiasm can be infectious. And they may be highly suggestible when it comes to being affected by other people's enthusiasm or idealism.

These Sevens look at life and work with an extreme sense of optimism—they have a tendency to be almost too happy, and are the Sevens who have the hardest time taking in negative data. Their highly positive view of life is a way to distract themselves from what they experience as a nearly intolerable sense of reality—especially when reality is dull, boring, or difficult. They imagine how things could be and then tend to act as if the positive vision they imagine is real. They may live more in the happy world they create in their heads than the actual world, with its problems and traffic jams and struggles and pain.

As leaders, One-to-One Sevens want to know that everything is okay—I'm okay, you're okay, and we're okay. And it can be hard for them to see and acknowledge when things are not okay. They can be high-minded visionaries who feel an intense commitment to manifesting the positive view of their work they create in their minds. Alternatively, they can cause problems when they don't pay attention to anything bad or difficult that might be happening—and they don't want to see that they aren't paying attention to the bad things that are happening. When they are less self-aware, they may not recognize they are living more in their imagination than the real world. But when they understand their programming, they can balance their need to idealize with a clear-eyed sense of what's really happening. When these leaders have the emotional intelligence to recognize their tendency to avoid negative data, they can counter-balance it by asking for support in evaluating all the data in a given situation. When One-to-One Sevens can see that their passion, optimism, and enthusiasm may cloud their vision in negative ways, they can learn to be more aware of their tendency to overcompensate for their fear. When they can do this, they can focus more energy more effectively on making some of the awesome things they imagine a reality.

The Type Seven at Work

Type Sevens sometime feel like working with others is hard because:

- ▶ *Not everyone sees things as positively as I do. Sometimes people rain on my parade by arguing against my perspective or dwelling on the negative data.*
- ▶ *I want to solve problems quickly and move on, but other people often want to talk about what's going wrong longer than I think we need to.*
- ▶ *I like to score quick victories I can feel good about—it bothers me when people slow me down, especially with a lot of detailed description about why something won't work.*
- ▶ *I like the idea stage of a project more than the implementation stage—when I have to spend time on boring processes, I can have trouble making myself do the work.*
- ▶ *I like to have a lot of freedom to maneuver, and sometimes I'm pressured to do things a certain way, according to certain rules and procedures.*
- ▶ *Some people don't enjoy work as much as I do.*
- ▶ *I have a hard time if I have to deal with other people's negative feelings or input.*
- ▶ *I don't like to have to operate according to what authorities tell me to do. I like to do what I want to do without feeling constrained or having to take others' opinions into account.*
- ▶ *Sometimes people don't take me seriously because I like to make work fun.*

Type Sevens' workplace pet peeves may be:

- ▶ When meetings aren't well run, are boring, or drag on and on.
- ▶ When people respond to my work with a lot of negativity.
- ▶ When people tell me their problems and expect me to fix them.
- ▶ When colleagues try to place limits on my work or control what I'm doing.
- ▶ When people shoot down my ideas instead of letting me have space to brainstorm as much as I need to.
- ▶ When the people I work with aren't friendly and pleasant.
- ▶ When people don't understand my need to have fun at work.

▶ When people are excessively serious and process-driven, so there's no room for creative thinking.

▶ When people dwell on what's not working instead of focusing on solutions.

▶ When I'm forced to do a lot of paperwork or jump through bureaucratic hoops.

▶ When people tell me what to do, especially if it seems ridiculous, meaningless, or unnecessarily difficult.

▶ When people don't appreciate the good job I did and instead nitpick about little details that they think aren't right.

▶ When someone says "no" or "we can't do that."

▶ People who go into too much detail and don't get to the point.

▶ Being micromanaged.

Here's What Type Sevens Can Do to Be Easier to Work With

As leaders, it helps Sevens to understand that not everyone moves as fast as they do. They may benefit by downshifting to allow others to catch up, or to adjust their speed so they can meet people in the middle. It also helps Seven leaders to remember that while their love of brainstorming and ability to generate creative ideas is a strength, their colleagues or team members may feel overwhelmed by the deluge of good ideas. They can make it easier on their coworkers if they clarify that while they like to play with ideas, not all of them need to be implemented.

It helps Sevens to realize that they tend to be self-referencing, meaning they pay more attention to their own inner thoughts, feelings, and needs than those of others. By understanding that this is not good or bad, just their tendency, they can (if they choose to) intentionally take others' needs into account to make sure they are aligning with the people around them. Sevens may also benefit by recognizing that others may not prioritize positivity as much as they do. Acknowledging that others may have a higher tolerance for suffering can help Sevens bow out gracefully (if appropriate) or learn to hang in there and stretch out of their comfort zone.

Finally, because Sevens are sensitive to being limited by others, it can be good for Seven leaders to be aware that they may react negatively to perceived constraints, so they can manage their reactions in a conscious way. Sevens may question authority without feeling compelled to openly oppose it—and may charm their way around potentially limiting restrictions through humor, intellectual manipulation, and seeming acceptance rather than pick a fight that leads to unpleasantness. If they can remain aware of this tendency, they can interact more intentionally within an organizational hierarchy with a clearer sense of their own motives and goals.

Working with Sevens

Typical Type Seven Behaviors in the Workplace

You *might* be working with someone who has a Type Seven Enneagram style if you see them doing several of the following behaviors on a regular basis:

- ▶ He's always very smiley and happy and upbeat.
- ▶ She talks very fast and sometimes it's hard to keep up.
- ▶ He makes friends with nearly everyone—and everyone likes him.
- ▶ She's always planning outings and happy hour gatherings for the team.
- ▶ He loves talking about new ideas and plans.
- ▶ She is very future-oriented.
- ▶ He uses humor and charm to win people over and get them on his side.
- ▶ She gets very enthusiastic and animated when she's discussing an innovative plan she's working on.
- ▶ He finds a way to make an exit when the mood gets heavy.
- ▶ When you talk to her about a problem you are having, she tells you to "look on the bright side" and reframes every reason you have for feeling bad.
- ▶ He finds good rationalizations for the things he wants to do that he really isn't supposed to do.
- ▶ She makes friends with the people above her and the people below her (so people are less likely to make demands on her).
- ▶ At his best, he brings positive energy to the team, keeping everyone focused on what's working and all the reasons they are going to be successful.

▶ At her best, she inspires people to do things they didn't think they could do because she has such a positive vision for the future.

What's Great About Working with Conscious Seven Leaders

▶ They are fun loving, they are fun to be around, and they make work fun.

▶ They focus on what's positive as a way of lifting morale and encouraging people to envision a successful result.

▶ They keep things moving.

▶ They are easy to like and they will want to like you (if they possibly can).

▶ They are sincerely interested in people and will want to get to know you.

▶ They won't want to dwell on what's not working; they like to find solutions.

▶ They tend to be diplomatic and friendly when conducting business.

▶ While they have preferred ways of doing things, they are open to listening to others and will try to adjust so team members feel heard and supported.

▶ They often see the best in people and encourage them to do their best.

▶ They are often humorous and charming.

▶ As leaders, they tend to treat direct reports more as peers than underlings.

▶ They will want to give the people they work with a great deal of freedom.

Typical Challenges for People Who Work with Sevens

▶ It can be hard to talk to them about what's not going well.

▶ They may not have the patience or the emotional fortitude to do what it takes to identify problems, talk them through, and work things out.

▶ They may have difficulty focusing on projects that don't excite them.

▶ They may overbook themselves, arrive late to meetings, and forget commitments.

▶ They may get so excited about new ideas that they don't slow down to examine potential problems and develop a workable implementation plan.

▶ Although they may know a great deal about diverse subject areas, their knowledge of specific topics may be shallower than you might expect.

▶ Their own strong desire for freedom of movement may mean they don't provide much structure or direction for their direct reports.

▶ They may move so quickly, they inadvertently leave people behind.

▶ They like to keep their options open and so may not commit to a plan of action in a timely way.

Type Sevens and Leadership

Type Seven Leaders Talk About Knowing How Your Enneagram Type Helps You at Work

Mark Kinsler is president of Trendway Corporation, an office furniture company based in Holland, Michigan.

"I tend to be attracted by new opportunities and possibilities. In my current role, I have to be very careful about what to spend the time and resources of the company on. Sometimes it's completely appropriate to shift focus from one priority to another; other times you have to be very careful about that, because you leave people wondering, 'What the heck are you doing? Why would you be interested in that? Why are you wasting time thinking about that? We've just got to get this done.' But I tend to want to look at things from multiple perspectives and explore all the options: 'This is what we could be doing differently' is maybe how I would position it.

"I enjoy examining things that aren't status quo. That doesn't mean I ultimately want to change something. But I like to explore all the options and ask the questions, 'Why?' 'Why is it we're doing it that way?' 'Is there another way?' 'Is this idea applicable to our industry?' I like to look at lots of different opportunities and potentials.

"My biggest challenge as a Seven is not messing with things that are working just fine. I think there are places where messing with things is great, and there are other places where things are working really well and until there's a problem, there are a lot of other priorities to work on. It's that balance of where to spend your time and energy, understanding and focusing my attention on the important questions, like, 'What's the strategy?' and 'Where do those opportunities fit in the prioritization

within the corporate strategy?' 'What's going to have the biggest impact?'
For me it's constantly balancing the priorities given all the options and
things to think about."

Todd Pierce is chief digital officer at the Bill and Melinda Gates Foundation. He was formerly Executive Vice President, Operations and Mobility at Salesforce.com, and Senior Vice President and Chief Information Officer at Genentech.

> *"Knowing my Enneagram type has given me a much richer development*
> *toolkit that's applicable in all areas of my life. It's not just a toolkit for*
> *leaders. It makes me a better lover, husband, friend—it helps me be more*
> *aware and mindful in all of my roles.*
>
> *"Very specifically, knowing I was a Seven (and what that meant)*
> *helped me find other ways to entertain myself that weren't disruptive to*
> *the organization.*
>
> *"In addition, seeing how even infrequent patterns affect me can be*
> *particularly helpful, like the patterns associated with the styles connected*
> *to my main Seven style by the lines of the Enneagram diagram, Types One*
> *and Four. It helps me to be aware of when I go to the real judgy, dark side*
> *of Type One or that incorporating more of the desire for authentic connec-*
> *tion of a Type Four are real development opportunities for me."*

When You Are a Manager and You Are a Seven

Sevens can feel awkward and uncomfortable being the authority—they are essentially, if not openly, antiauthoritarian, and prefer to exert influence through mental creativity and comradeship. As psychiatrist and Enneagram expert Claudio Naranjo explains, Sevens live in a "nonhierarchical psychological environment," meaning they want to be free to indulge themselves and so implicitly assume that authority is bad. Often, if you are a Seven, you simply don't pay attention to authority, whether you are technically under an authority or you *are* the authority. Sevens don't like hierarchies, so you will tend to flatten them out in your mind, making friends with the people above and below you on the organizational chart.

As a Seven, your motto might be something like "live and let live"—you don't want to be controlled or limited, so as a manager, you don't like to control or limit the people who work for you, and will want to take more of a "hands off" approach to leadership. You relish the opportunity to motivate people through inspiring them rather than directing them, and will usually choose to influence your direct reports through optimistic discussions of the fun and exciting things you want to do, or through expressions of enthusiasm about what's happening or the possibilities and options you see ahead. You may feel challenged if conditions require you to be more "hands on" and authoritarian, but at your best, you take the lead by throwing yourself into the parts of the work you really like and enjoy meeting challenges, finding creating solutions, and doing what it takes to achieve a positive result.

When Your Manager Is a Seven

The good thing about having a manager who is a Seven is he or she will likely want to make the work fun and encourage you to find the fun in it. As long as you get your work done and do it well, you will probably not be micro-managed in any way. Your Seven will encourage you to be independent and positive—and generally okay. You will likely get along with them if you don't cause problems, communicate too much negativity, or limit their movements. They may want you to be a supportive brainstorming partner and listen to their ideas.

It can be difficult for Sevens to feel comfortable in the role of the authority, so your Seven manager may want to make friends with you as a way of soft-ening the hierarchical relationship. When stressed or less self-aware, they may become unfocused or overbooked, leaving you to fend for yourself at times. They may have trouble prioritizing or switch course without notice, which can be hard on the staff, and it may be difficult for your Seven manager to address problems and conflicts, preferring to focus on something more pleasant or pretend it isn't happening. Other Seven leaders will want to face any chal-lenges head on to quickly get them out of the way so things can be fun again. At their best, however, Seven managers will be lively and enthusiastic; they will encourage and support their people, and create a positive atmosphere where people are trusted to do their best.

When Your Subordinate Is a Seven

When your direct reports have a Type Seven style, they have a strong prefer-ence for managers who are "hands off"—who give them a lot of freedom to do their job the way they want to do it, with little oversight. If they feel controlled by you, your Seven subordinate will likely 1) first try to make friends, 2) then get confrontational, and 3) if 1 and 2 didn't work and you are still their boss, they may mentally check out and start imagining future positive outcomes and events.

And if your direct reports are a Seven, don't take it personally if they don't take your authority over them too seriously. They may be breezy and casual about the organizational reality that you have power over them, and they may treat you in a familiar, friendly way, and try to make a friend out of you if you allow it. Sensitive to being constrained by outside authority, Sevens have an implicitly rebellious attitude, but won't want to openly rebel against you in a way that leads to unpleasantness or attracts negative attention. Instead, they will adopt an attitude that is diplomatic rather than oppositional.[19]

Mainly, they will want you to trust them to get the job done and not micromanage them—and that you don't infringe excessively on their ability to indulge themselves. If you need to provide them with constructive feedback, you will be more effective in delivering your message if you focus some attention on communicating what's positive first, and deliver any criticism you might have of their performance with care and gentleness. Sevens are more sensitive to criticism than they let on, and they can feel injured by critical feedback. It may also be important to remember that some Sevens can be enthusiastic and optimistic to the point of being naïve about some everyday realities, so it's a good idea to explore their perceptions of things to take into account their baseline assumptions and perspective.

Under stress, your Seven direct report may get in over his or her head and not want to tell you, so it's good to check in periodically in a light way. They may also struggle to focus on the top priorities, so it helps if you communicate your expectations and your sense of what's most important ahead of time. At their best, Sevens can be thoroughly enjoyable to work with. They will tend to be motivated to make you happy and keep things harmonious and will be forward thinking and creative.

Getting Along with Sevens: Tips for What to Do to Work Well with Sevens

▶ *Be upbeat and positive.* Sevens appreciate people who are pleasant and fun to be around. They will enjoy working with you if you endeavor to be enjoyable to work with and keep the mood light.

▶ *Work to achieve mutual respect and appreciation.* Sevens will be happy to respect your preferences and your freedom if you show respect for theirs. They want to feel appreciated and will happily appreciate you if they like you and experience you as easy to be around. Be a good team player and Sevens will enjoy being on your team.

▶ *Avoid excessive negativity and criticism.* Sevens like to focus on what's positive, so they can be bothered—and even alienated—by people who express a large amount of negativity. They are usually open to legitimate criticism, but if it doesn't have an obvious constructive purpose, they may feel hurt and resentful.

▶ *Make some allowances for them to be exceptions to the rule if the rule is unnecessarily constraining.* Although, of course, some rules need to be followed by everyone, if you can occasionally let your Seven colleague bend a rule that is particularly limiting and inconsequential, they will greatly appreciate it (and still get their work done).

▶ *Allow them to work independently as much as possible.* Sevens like to have a lot of freedom to do the work the way they want to do it. They like having a manager who trusts them to get the job done and doesn't control what they do excessively.

▶ *Give them space to generate and flesh out good ideas.* Sevens love allowing their imaginations to run wild—they enjoy envisioning different options and possibilities. They will appreciate colleagues who give them room to brainstorm and trust that they will pare the long list of good ideas later, as the next step of the work.

▶ *Understand their implicit discomfort with authority.* Sevens aren't big rebels, but, because they are friendly people who dislike being controlled by outside forces, they may engage in a kind of covert resistance to authority that gets expressed through charm and diplomacy. If you work with Sevens, it helps to understand this.

Actionable Growth Tasks and Suggestions: How Type Sevens Can Become More Self-Aware, Effective, and Happy at Work

All the types can learn to be less reactive and better at collaborating through first *observing* their habitual patterns, then thinking about the things they think, feel, and do to gain more *self-insight*, and then making efforts to *manage* or moderate their automatic reactions to key triggers.

Sevens grow through first observing, then exploring, and then learning to moderate their habitual reactions to key triggers like feeling limited or controlled by others, having to deal with others' negative emotions or moods, and having their options foreclosed.

When Sevens can watch what they do enough to "catch themselves in the act" of doing the things that get them in trouble, and then pause and reflect on what they are doing and why, they can gradually learn to moderate their programming and knee-jerk responses. Here are some ideas to help Sevens be more self-aware, more emotionally intelligent, and more satisfied at work (and at home).

Self-Observation: Things for Sevens to Watch Out For

- ▶ *Observe your desire to focus on what's positive and pleasurable. Notice if it reflects an inability or an unwillingness to look at important negative data.*

- ▶ *Notice if you move, think, and talk at a fast pace. Experiment with slowing down a little to see what happens.*

- ▶ *Notice if you feel any anxiety or fear as you go through your day. See if you can observe it and discover what it's about.*

- ▶ *Notice if you have an aversion to anything that threatens to limit you in any way.*

- ▶ *Observe what happens inside you when there is something happening that inspires discomfort and how you respond.*

- ▶ *Study yourself to see if you can note what emotions you feel more and less often. Do you spend more time feeling emotions at the positive end of the spectrum? What happens to your more painful or negative feelings?*

- ▶ *Notice what beliefs you have about feeling specific feelings. Do have any fears or beliefs about getting trapped in uncomfortable emotions?*

- ▶ *Is it important to always have a lot of options? Why or why not?*

Blind Spots: What You Don't Know Can Hurt You!

What blind spots Sevens often don't see in themselves:

▶ *How the quest for fun, positivity, and pleasure is driven by a need to avoid pain.* When I introduce Sevens to the Enneagram types and they begin to see themselves in the Type Seven archetype, they often say, "I relate to every part of the description, except for the part about avoiding pain; I don't do that." Distracting themselves from uncomfortable feelings—and the way their fast pace and desire to feel good all the time is driven by a flight from pain—can be a blind spot for Sevens.

▶ *The value of pain and discomfort as a way of connecting to deeper emotional truth.* Sevens' programming tells them that there's nothing good about feeling bad. It's hard for them to see any upside to difficult feelings and uncomfortable emotions. But our emotions represent a kind of inner guidance system, and knowing how you feel is an important part of being human and being able to access what's real for you.

▶ *The impact on others of your relentless focus on what's positive.* Sevens want very much to be taken seriously. But, if you are a Seven, you may sometimes unintentionally contribute to the perception that you are a lightweight or not very serious. And sometimes it's hard to trust someone who only wants to look at the good stuff.

▶ *Your own ability to deal with uncomfortable emotions.* Self-aware Sevens say that one reason they avoid feelings like anxiety, pain, discomfort, and boredom is they fear if they allow themselves to open up to these feelings, they will be trapped in them forever. But this is based on the automatic instinctual response that they can't handle those feelings. It helps to own your capacity for emotional strength and resilience.

The positive aspects of slowing down and being present with your experiences, no matter what you are experiencing. Sevens tend to operate at a fast pace because they are unconsciously running away from any negative emotions or hard-to-handle experiences that might happen in the present moment. But they tend to avoid being aware of the downside of moving so rapidly when they skim along the surface and focus on the future. It actually helps to slow down and allow for a deeper experience of the present moment—and to get in touch with what exactly has you moving so quickly in the first place.

Self-Insight: Things for Sevens to Think About, Understand, and Explore

▶ *Why is it so important for you to always focus on what's positive and pleasurable? What do you fear will happen if you focus on other kinds of emotions and experiences?*

▶ *Why is it so appealing to you to focus on the future? What motivates you to be so forward thinking?*

▶ *What fuels your drive to move quickly through life? What do you value about having a fast pace? What do you think would happen if you slowed down?*

▶ *What kinds of things do you fear most? How does it feel to think about that question?*

▶ *Why does it feel so intolerable to be limited? What feels threatening about others putting constraints on you?*

▶ *Why is it so important to have options? What does having multiple options do for you?*

Strengths to Leverage

It helps Sevens to be aware of, actively pay attention to, fully own, and leverage:

▶ *Ability to make work fun and enjoyable.* This gift enhances your life and the experiences of the people you work with. It doesn't even occur to a lot of people that work can (or should) be fun—they view it as a grind or a slog. Seeing work through the lens of enjoyment is a strength of the Seven style the rest of us can learn from and that can give our work lives more meaning.

▶ *Intellectual charm.* Sevens can really turn on the charm when they want to. Although you may sometimes use it to wriggle out of commitments and get around inconvenient authorities, this talent comes in handy for relating to everybody at work, whether they are clients or managers or the person whose parking space you parked in because you were running late.

▶ *The power of positive thinking.* The ability to automatically and instantaneously reframe negatives into positives has many productive uses—and much of the time probably actually makes things better. And, it just seems true that if you can envision it, it's more likely to happen.

▶ *Infectious enthusiasm.* Feeling excited about projects and plans may give you more influence and support among more people. Sevens have a way of expressing excitement and enthusiasm that makes others want to join the party.

▶ *Enjoyment of relating to people.* One of the main points of this book is that most work that gets done in the world today happens through people interacting with people. Sevens sincerely enjoy engaging with people, and this makes you good at a lot of things as leaders and in business generally: selling and promoting ideas and products, schmoozing with clients and colleagues, after-work happy hours with coworkers, and just generally chatting with people at the proverbial water cooler.

▶ *A flexible, synthesizing mind that gives you the ability to make connections.* If you are a Seven, you have a nimble mind that finds connections among things that others don't often see. You can think through problems and find innovative solutions in creative ways that make you a valuable member of any team.

Self-Management: Challenging Tendencies for Sevens to Moderate

▶ *Overdoing the preoccupation with what's positive.* Of course, you know that there are many positive aspects to being so positive—but there is also a downside, like there is with everything. If you can't rein in the need to put a positive spin on everything, you may miss something important when you avoid the negatives.

▶ *The need for speed.* Sometimes the people around you may feel like your fast pace means you are running away from something. If you can slow down and smell the proverbial roses, you may be able to take in more of what's happening and have a richer, deeper, better experience— which is usually what you are aiming for anyway.

▶ *Self-referencing and acting from self-interest.* You can be a very generous, supportive person, but your attention is first and foremost on yourself. This isn't necessarily a bad thing, but when you overdo it without knowing it, you may alienate people when you don't pay attention to their needs and desires too.

▶ *Excessive concern with avoiding limits.* It may occasionally be beneficial to meet the challenge of having fewer options or adjusting to outside constraints. Even if it just lessens your fear around limitation, that might be good for you.

▶ *Living in your imagination (as opposed to reality).* If you are a One-to-One Seven, this is your specialty. While it is a strength to be positive and enthusiastic, in some instances, bad things can happen when you believe more in the reality you create in your head than the objective reality you live in with other people.

▶ *Fear of suffering.* Chances are if you really learn to allow yourself to feel more of the bad stuff you automatically avoid feeling, it won't be as bad as you thought it would be. And if you become more conscious of your fear, you can release yourself from being so driven by fear—often fear that you don't even realize is driving you.

Consciously Manifesting Your Higher Potential: Being Aware of the "Low Side" and Aiming for the "High Side"

Sevens can also grow through consciously becoming aware of the unconscious, self-limiting habitual patterns associated with their personality style and learning to embody the "higher aspects" or more expansive and balanced capacities of the Type Seven personality:

▶ Learn to become conscious of your need to avoid discomfort and pain. Becoming aware of your fears and opening up to the full range of your emotions can give you a deeper and more engaged experience of life and relationships.

▶ Learn to notice when subconscious anxiety causes you to speed up and realize you have the power to stay safe, even if you engage your fears more consciously.

▶ Learn to notice when you use your easy charm to intellectually manipulate to get what you want, and consciously open up to the possibility that you will get more of what you want the more you share what you have with others.

▶ Learn to see when you're positively spinning out of control and find a way to open up to facing your fears and examining what's not so great, knowing seeing the bad part will only enhance your enjoyment of the good part.

▶ Learn to recognize when you are seeing things the way you want to see them or the way you wish they were and take the risk to see them as they actually are, or as others see them, knowing you can survive reality.

▶ Learn to notice when you are focusing narrowly on your own interest and pleasure, and widen your perspective to include what's good for others, or how being more sober might serve you, knowing that many pleasures can end up being less pleasing than you thought anyway.

▶ Learn to see your tendency to amp up the excitement and the enthusiasm as a sign you are avoiding something. Realize that tempering your enthusiasm doesn't mean things still won't turn out great—it just means that you will be more open to considering all of what's real in the moment.

Overall, Type Sevens can fulfill their higher potentials by observing and working against their habitual focus on forward momentum and pleasurable experiences and experiment with playing different roles on teams and widening their perspective to include more kinds of data and emotional truth. When they can combine their high energy, humor, and positive outlook with a greater openness to feeling more kinds of feelings and experiencing situations they would rather avoid, they can stop running so fast and create a more grounded approach to and internal foundation for achieving their positive visions and innovative aspirations.

CHAPTER 11

The Type Eight Leadership Style
The Powerful, Decisive Activator, or Moving Things Forward from a Position of Strength

"Nearly all men can stand adversity, but if you want to test a man's character, give him power."

Abraham Lincoln

"Power is no blessing in itself, except when it is used to protect the innocent."

Jonathan Swift

"I suppose leadership at one time meant muscles; but today it means getting along with people."

Mahatma Gandhi

The Type Eight archetype is the prototypical person who thinks big, acts decisively, and makes things happen. Sometimes called "the Challenger," or "the Boss," they're larger-than-life people with big energy who easily take on leadership roles. An Eight's attention automatically goes to the "big picture"—to what they think should happen and how to make their vision a reality. They easily sense who has the power in a given situation and look to see whether they use it fairly. Primarily motivated by the need to be strong and take action, they are assertive and sometimes aggressive, but can also be protective and generous.

Eights' programming tells them that the only way to operate in the world is through asserting strength and avoiding registering or expressing weakness of any kind. Their personality's operating system is shaped by a focus on being powerful and strong, moving things forward, overcoming obstacles, and challenging authorities (if necessary). Direct, opinionated, and relatively fearless, people with a Type Eight style naturally gravitate to positions of power and authority. They are the personality style that most closely matches the stereotypical image of a "powerful leader" and are plentiful at the highest levels of western businesses—the vast majority of CEOs in the U.S. are probably Eights.

Eights' communication style reflects their tendency to act to deploy power and authority, to get things done and assert what they think is right. Their speaking style is bold, direct, authoritative, and sometimes blunt, and they may get impatient when others are less direct.[22] They may display anger more freely than other types, and while they don't necessarily "like" conflict, they aren't afraid of it. The type most likely to use profanity (even in a business setting), Eights respect people who stand up to them and tell them the truth. They don't like it when people sugarcoat things to avoid hurt feelings—they would rather they just say it.

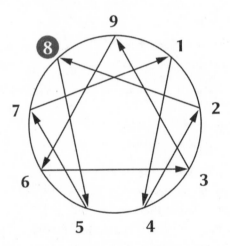

Leaders who have a Type Eight style tend to be strategic thinkers, attuned to where the power lies and how they can establish their own power base. They focus on assessing the big picture, mentoring people under them, and making significant things happen. Others may find them intimidating, though they usually find this feedback surprising as they don't intend to frighten people. But their energetic presence is large and powerful, even when they aren't saying anything or explicitly expressing power or aggression. Overall, they combine real strength with a desire to get things done decisively and quickly, whether they specialize in taking control to get what is needed, defending the weak from being oppressed by the powerful, or overpowering people with their rebellious, magnetic presence.

How to Tell if You Are a Type Eight: The View from the Inside

If most or all of the following characteristics apply to you, you may have a Type Eight personality style:

▶ *You see the work you do through the lens of how you can assert your power to get what you want done.* You naturally read what's happening in terms of who has the power and how they wield it. It's so natural for you to be powerful, you sometimes have to hold yourself back from expressing your strength so you don't overpower people or situations.

▶ *People tell you that you intimidate them, which surprises you, since you aren't doing anything to intentionally intimidate anyone.* Others sometimes perceive you as a bully, even though you are just doing what you normally do.

▶ *You don't have to be the leader, but it's easy for you to take charge.* You often get drawn into taking the lead—it feels easy and natural for you, and people often look to you for direction, even when you aren't the actual leader.

▶ *You want people to tell you the truth and be direct.* You like to be in control and know what's going on, which is why you value honesty and directness.

▶ *You make your own rules and can feel like you are above the law.* You often don't see a reason to follow rules, especially if they don't make sense or go against what you want to do. You don't readily acknowledge anyone's power as greater than your own.

▶ *You will rebel against authorities if you need or want to.* You will stand up to people with power if they don't use their power wisely or justly.

▶ *You work very hard. You may work so hard and so long that you hurt or injure yourself because you tend to deny or ignore your physical limitations.* You can "forget yourself" and overload your normal capacity, and you may not pay much attention to taking care of yourself.

▶ *You are fearless—unafraid of taking bold action and acting decisively.* You typically don't register fear—you feel like you can handle anything and never shy from a challenge.

▶ *You aren't afraid to voice your (strong) opinion or push for what you want.* You have a great deal of confidence in your views and don't hesitate to push for what you think is right. You may even confuse your truth with the objective Truth.

▶ *It's important to you to be powerful, strong, and in control.* You automatically take your own strength and power for granted.

▶ *If someone wrongs you, you can marshal a great deal of energy to right the wrong or get back at the person if you choose to.* Although you may not want to think that you like to get revenge on people who have done bad things to you, you kind of do want to get back at those who cross you.

▶ *Although you don't always need to get angry, you experience anger as energy flowing through your body, and you can feel and express it fairly easily.* Eights sometimes get stereotyped as "angry," but it's not really true. It's more that they have easier access to anger and usually don't have a problem expressing it.

▶ *You don't always know your own strength; it can be hard for you to judge your impact on people and situations.* You may sometimes apply more effort or power than is really required.

The Central Adaptive Strategy of the Type Eight Personality Style

Eights' adaptive strategy of acting powerfully grows out of an early experience of feeling powerless. Self-aware Eights tell stories of not getting their needs met in childhood, often in ways that felt traumatic and caused them to feel they must "get strong" to survive. They often have a history of having to take care of themselves (or others) when they were too young to be able to do so, or being the youngest child in a large family—a small person among bigger people—in a combative environment. From this experience of feeling vulnerable and alone, the Eight resolves to never be powerless again, and adapts by becoming super strong and capable.

Eights often see the world as divided into "the strong" and "the weak," and so decide to be strong as a way of never being weak again, to the point where they deny their vulnerability altogether. Many Eights eliminate any memory or experience of being vulnerable or weak in order to experience themselves as strong and invincible. Their central coping strategy of being powerful and strong shapes their personality style in a way that makes them truly fearless and forceful in their interactions, able to take on any challenge and do big things in the world.

At work, this makes the Eight leader a force to be reckoned with. In some ways, they are the prototypical leader, especially in the west, where we expect leaders to be tough, get things done, and handle large amounts of work and pressure. Many Eights become CEOs because they can't regulate their reliance on expressing their power, which leads to nearly always projecting an image of great confidence, strength, decisiveness, and fearlessness. Whether it's competing against worthy competitors for a top job, representing the complexities of a global company to shareholders, or making risky decisions when millions of dollars are at stake, Eights' coping strategy of automatically leaning into their strength and tuning out their vulnerability gives them the confidence and power to take on big challenges.

What Do Eights Pay Attention To? The Type Eight "Radar Screen"

The strategy of being strong and invulnerable leads Eights to focus on power and control. They don't like to be controlled or told what to do, and don't pay much attention to rules or limits, including their own physical limitations. They do pay attention to who holds power and how they express it, who is competent and who isn't, who can be trusted and who can't, and who might need their protection and support. They also attend to the big picture—what the larger goal is, what work needs to be done and the right way to it.

People who lead with a Type Eight style focus on creating a power base, extending their influence, working hard, and playing hard. They see what problems need to be solved and who can be counted on to help move things forward in effective ways. Eights take things at face value unless they have a reason not to, can see through bullshit and have no patience for bullshitters. They don't let anything stop them when they have something to accomplish, including their own physical needs or weak points, and tend to be attuned to all the ways they can fulfill their appetites for stimulating physical experiences.

Eights notice when others are being treated badly and need to be defended—they are highly tuned in to social or human injustice, and when they see someone who needs protection, they often move into action. I once heard an Eight tell an incredibly moving story of sleeping in a pen with a frightened, newly rescued pit bull all night to comfort him. Whether it's supporting those in need or achieving a difficult goal within an organization, Eights deploy a great amount of energy and power to take action, assert control, and make sure things get done.

The View from "Planet Eight": How Eights See the World

Generally, individuals with a Type Eight style view the world in terms of how power is being used or misused and how it can be drawn upon to make things happen. They believe that if you're not strong, you're weak, that it's good to be strong and bad to be weak, and that they are strong. They don't hesitate to use their strength to get what they need, take charge of situations, and protect those they care about. They unconsciously deny their own weakness and focus on how to exercise power in the world to dominate whoever might go against them or the causes they support.

Eights also see the world in terms of justice and fairness. They can be rebels or revolutionaries who want to assure that they and those they seek to protect are treated justly, and will take action to correct injustice. Type Eights are sensitive to being controlled by others and tend to believe that they are above the law, making their own rules often and disregarding or breaking rules they judge as wrong or simply decide don't apply to them. If they see a need—something important that they decide needs to be done to help someone or balance the scales of justice—they will move into action to do it, regardless of the rules.

In line with their big, energetic presence and action-oriented temperament, Type Eights have a big appetite for stimulation and typically experience a strong need to indulge in physical pleasures of all kinds. Eights are body-based types who seek to satisfy their powerful desires in the world, whether those desires are for good food, a good time, or a good challenge.

The Type Eight Leader: Core Characteristics

The following character traits help to define the Type Eight leadership style:

▶ *Big energy and presence.* Eights tend to be physically imposing, even when they are objectively small in terms of their actual physical size. They can also work long hours without getting tired.

▶ *"Can-do" mind-set.* Eights get the job done—no matter what. They have enormous confidence in themselves, and assume that they can do anything they put their minds to.

▶ *Powerful, strong, fearless.* Type Eight leaders have no problem owning their authority and "throwing their weight around" or taking on difficult tasks.

▶ *Decisive.* Even when risks are involved, Eights don't have a problem making tough decisions. They decide quickly and can become frustrated when others don't.

▶ *Unafraid of conflict.* Eights usually don't hesitate to confront people and problems that need to be managed head-on.

▶ *Honest and direct.* Eights don't see a reason to beat around the bush—they are natural straight shooters who lead with the truth and want to hear it from others.

Mental, Emotional, and Behavioral Patterns: Why Do Eights Think, Feel, and Behave the Way They Do?

Mental

Eights are "body-based" types who tend to favor action over analysis. While they can be very intellectual, they typically engage in more doing than thinking or feeling, and their thinking tends to be strategic, focusing on assessing situations in terms of the power dynamics, the strengths and weaknesses of the people involved, and the necessary actions to make something happen. An Eight's thinking also centers around control: how to establish and maintain it, how not to be controlled by others, and how to exert it to motivate people. However, the Eight outlook may be most noteworthy for what Eights avoid thinking about—their own weaknesses. The habit of denying any vulnerable feelings fuels their focus on action, which often means not pausing to think about what they are doing (and why) before they take action to do something.

Emotional

Type Eights tend to be intense, passionate people who have the capacity to feel things deeply if they let themselves. The "body-based" types (Eights, Nines, and Ones) are associated with the "core emotion" of anger, and Eights tend to overdo theirs, easily accessing the emotion when it gets triggered by a desire to correct an injustice or express displeasure. Many Eights describe anger as a sensation of energy that moves through their bodies, reflecting both the connection they feel to their physical selves and the forceful, physical way they experience the emotion. In fact, whatever emotion they feel—whether it's love or happiness or disappointment—Eights feel it strongly and deeply, although they usually don't feel emotions on the vulnerable end of the spectrum like sadness, pain, or shame.

Behavioral

Eights are people of action—they lead with their "gut knowing," often act without thinking, and tend to misjudge how much force to apply to a given action. One Eight leader described it as having a propensity for "ready, fire, aim." Because of their powerful, energetic presence and their desire to do big things in a big way, Eights often have a huge impact on the people around them, but don't always recognize exactly what their impact is or how to moderate their energy when interacting with others. They habitually take bold actions to make things happen, sometimes as a way of discharging all the energy that courses through them, or to express the passion and intense desire they feel to make an impact. Eights have big appetites for stimulating experiences and tend to work hard and play hard, resulting in a lifestyle that has been described as "too long, too loud, too late."[21] Secure in their omnipotence, they often "forget themselves" and deny their vulnerability as they take on every challenge and maintain a high level of intensity in the things they do—both at work and in their personal lives.

The Main Strengths and Superpowers of the Type Eight Style: What Eights Are Really Good At

▶ *Ability to see the "Big Picture."* Eights look at all the elements of a situation as a way of determining how to make big things happen and keep things moving in the right direction.

▶ *Confidence in tackling tough challenges.* Eights don't doubt themselves. Their default mode is to feel very self-confident (whether that's warranted or not) and enjoy demonstrating their power and abilities by taking on difficult tasks and achieving successful results.

▶ *Ability to take bold action and maintain control of whatever's happening.* Eights don't experience fear of failure or fear that people won't like them—they automatically move things forward and make things happen, even when the outcome is uncertain or movement seems risky.

▶ *Good at mentoring and empowering people.* Naturally protective of those they like, Eights easily and generously lend their strength to others as a way of helping them grow stronger and more competent.

▶ *Confident in approaching conflict.* One of the perks of not being in touch with vulnerability is the ability to do conflict with less fear and self-doubt than others do. Since leadership often involves dealing with conflicts, this is a useful superpower to have.

When Too Much of a Good Thing Becomes a Bad Thing: How Eights Can Go Wrong When They Don't Know Their Own Strength

Like all people of all types, when Type Eight leaders overuse their biggest strengths (and don't consciously develop a wider range of specialties), those strengths can also turn out to be their Achilles' heel—even though Eights' biggest strength is strength, and it may be hard to see what could be wrong with that.

▶ *Ability to see the "Big Picture."* Eights can be so preoccupied with making a big impact that they may not have the patience for dealing with small details. They prefer ambitiously aiming for the horizon to making sure every little thing goes right—sometimes to their detriment.

▶ *Confidence in tackling tough challenges.* Sometimes, a little self-doubt can be a good thing. Plus, Eights may be so used to taking on big challenges that they can't rein in the intensity of the effort they put toward everything—and they sometimes apply too much pressure.

▶ *Ability to take bold action and maintain control of whatever's happening.* Sometimes Eights forget to moderate their intensity or slow down their impulse to act. They can over-control things to the point where either they are doing everything themselves or inadvertently squelching spontaneity and creativity.

▶ *Good at mentoring and empowering people.* Eights may miss some opportunities to mentor others because they can intimidate people without knowing it—their lack of awareness of their own vulnerability can make them seem unapproachable or scary, so they may not be as connected to their direct reports as they might like to be.

▶ *Confident in approaching conflict.* Eights' ability to do conflict can lead to an over-readiness to confront points of disagreement that can actually cause or initiate a conflict, when it might be better to solve the problem through diplomacy or other methods.

Fortunately, Eights' sincere interest in furthering the work—and the best interests of their team or organization—can motivate them to learn to adjust their tendencies to exert power and control as a go-to strategy. When they focus their considerable energy on becoming more aware of the tendencies associated with their personality style, they can often temper their strength with a greater awareness of their impact on others and employ a wider range of tactics for getting things done.

"When I'm stressed..." and "At my best...": Understanding the "Low Side" and the "High Side" of the Type Eight Personality Style

When stressed to the point of going to their "low side," Type Eights can be harsh, blunt, aggressive, and controlling. They can be loudly intolerant of what they view as incompetence, express the belief that they are the only ones capable to do what needs to be done or explode at anyone who crosses them. They may have a heightened "us against them" attitude and rage at people who make mistakes. Under pressure, Eight leaders may come down on people who aren't following the rules and then break them openly themselves. They may act on impulse and make obvious mistakes, and they may take revenge on people they think have wronged them, but view their own behavior as justified as opposed to vengeful.

Less self-aware Eights can steamroll people and confuse their truth with the objective truth, believing they are always right and sometimes imposing a "my way or the highway" approach. They may say they are open to listening to others, while simultaneously acting in ways that discourage honest communication. They may be completely unable to share power or trust that anyone can do anything as well as they can. And the more vulnerable they feel deep down, the more unwilling they will be to experience it, and the worse they may act. They may abuse their power and undermine their own success by acting from unexamined anger, being excessive, and taking action impulsively without considering the consequences.

On the "high side," conscious Type Eight leaders motivate and inspire people with their confidence and dedication. They model a quiet, solid sense of strength and help people feel safe to take risks and accomplish big goals. They exercise appropriate control, but check in with people and listen to the input of team members, and are able to check themselves and slow down so that they have time to think more deeply about the actions they want to take.

Self-aware Eight leaders understand that they can intimidate people without meaning to, and they work to be more mindful of their own vulnerabilities and share them with others as a way of ensuring people feel comfortable approaching them, confiding in them, and collaborating with them.

When living more from the high side, Type Eights mindfully moderate their forcefulness and their boldness, blending their ability to express power in useful ways with an ability to stand in the background and allow others to be powerful. They balance their natural assertiveness with an ongoing aware-ness of their humanness and their weaknesses and challenges, and connect with people more easily through sharing more of their personal story and revealing more of their tender side. Healthy Eights take care of themselves more actively and don't forget themselves by working too hard without limits. They have a healthy awareness of their own limitations as well as their strengths and their natural power to lead.

The Three Kinds of Eight Leaders: How the Three Instinctual Biases Shape the Three Type Eight "Sub-Type" Personalities

According to the Enneagram model, we all have three main instinctual drives that help us survive, but in each of us, one tends to dominate our behavior. The Type Eight style is expressed differently depending on whether a person has a bias toward *self-preservation*, establishing *social* relationships and posi-tioning themselves in relation to groups, or *one-to-one* bonding.

The Self-Preservation (or Self-Focused) Eight

While they are strong, bold, and relatively fearless, Self-Preservation Eights also have a concern with material security. This can make them more focused on creating wealth and maintaining a sense of having enough resources than the other two Eights, and they may feel financially insecure, even when they have plenty of money in the bank. Self-Preservation Eights know how to get what they want—they know how to barter or bargain, and are good at getting the upper hand in negotiations or finding ways to satisfy their desires for things.

This is a more reserved, introverted, "Five-ish" Eight who doesn't need as much power over people or a large sphere of influence. They usually feel protective of others, but over a smaller group—perhaps only their immediate family and a few people they are closest to. These Eights are the most defended or "armed" Eights. They will rarely, if ever, show their emotions—especially vulnerable emotions, and tend to have a difficult time asking others for what they need, even though they can be effective in getting their needs met themselves. While they can be friendly and warm (especially female Self-Preservation Eights), they may be less communicative than the other two Eights. They will want to make things happen, but may feel no need to discuss what they are doing with others or explain themselves to anybody.

As leaders, Self-Preservation Eights will make decisions and take action quickly, without necessarily pausing to get buy-in from others. Their greater need for security will likely make them more strategic and self-interested, but they may also do what it takes to enlist support for their plans and projects— albeit in a minimalist way. They tend to possess a quiet strength, and in their need to be strong, may devalue the world of feelings as another way to avoid experiencing vulnerability. When moving forward to accomplish something or fulfill a need, they tend to avoid sharing information about themselves, and they won't show much tolerance for weakness or incompetence.

The Social (or Group-Focused) Eight

The Social Eight is the "counter-type" of the three Eights. Eights tend to be somewhat "anti-social," in that they don't always observe the norms of society and aren't afraid to go against authorities or convention. But the Social Eight is also oriented toward protecting others and establishing friendships. So this is a "social-anti-social" Eight, a person who easily rebels against established rules and authority, but also feels motivated to protect and support others. Archetypally, this is the child who stepped in to protect the mother against the father—this Eight becomes tough through going against the patriarchy out of a need to support people who may not be able to defend themselves. They take action out of solidarity.

This Eight's stronger orientation toward protecting people makes them more mellow, more friendly, and less obviously aggressive. They still tend to be direct, assertive, and strong, but they may also appear more Two-ish— more inclined toward offering support and doing for others. Interestingly, they may also take refuge in the group, or in leading groups, as a way to avoid the vulnerability they may feel in more intimate, one-to-one relationships. They may feel safer in positions of leadership, where they can control what's happening and get lost in the crowd.

As leaders, Social Eights can fiercely defend their team or colleagues, and focus a great deal of energy on mentoring people, coaching direct reports, and taking individuals under their wing. They won't always need to be the leader, but will get drawn into leadership roles if the group needs guidance. And when they see someone being oppressed or abused by someone with more power, they tend to step in quickly to offer protection. Social Eights say that they hardly ever express emotion in front of other people, though they can be compassionate with others who feel vulnerable. In this way, Social Eight leaders may take care of others as a way of addressing their own vulnerability without having to go there themselves. And while Social Eights can offer love and care to others who need their support, they don't tend to be very open to receiving that same love and care themselves.

The One-to-One (or Relationship-Focused) Eight

One-to-One Eights are the most rebellious Eights, with the strongest anti-social tendency. They like to be at the center of things—to "possess" everyone's attention—and they like the power that comes from being outspoken and going against rules and norms. These Eights express a great deal of intensity and passion and are the most emotional of the three Eight subtypes, and are more likely to feel things passionately to the point of showing their emotions. One-to-One Eights are provocative people, who may take pride in being "bad" or rebelling against traditional authorities and conventional ways of doing things.

In contrast to the other two Eights, One-to-One Eights are more colorful, more power loving, and more magnetic. They express a need for dominance and want people to surrender completely to their will, desiring to be in control of everything and everyone. They have great powers of seduction, look for pleasure in life wherever they can find it, and may indulge their appetites without limit. One-to-One Eights love feeling an adrenaline rush, which they can get from winning the game or taking over a company, and seek adventures, intense experiences, and risk.

As leaders, One-to-One Eights like the feeling of being in charge. They may fill up a room with their big energy and dominate the scene by talking louder and longer than everyone else does. They move passionately and quickly into action, usually not taking time to think things through or find out what others think. They tend to be intolerant of weak, incompetent, or slow people. And while One-to-One Eight leaders can be very clever, they may demonstrate a certain detachment of the intellect, as they have a strong preference for acting and feeling over thinking. They will focus a great deal of attention on one-to-one relationships and lead through getting people to submit to their power or their vision of what needs to happen. They may inspire people with their passion and confidence, but it may be hard for them to observe appropriate limits, understand the potential negative consequences of their actions, share power, or submit to others' leadership.

The Type Eight at Work

Type Eights sometime feel like working with others is hard because:

▶ *They aren't always as competent as I am.*

▶ *It can be hard for me to collaborate with people I regard as weak or don't fully trust.*

▶ *I can get incredibly impatient when people take a long time to make a decision.*

▶ *Sometimes people don't keep me in the loop when I want to be informed about what's happening.*

▶ *I like to take action, and sometimes people slow me down or get in my way by getting bogged down by details or trying to reach a consensus first.*

▶ *People tell me I'm intimidating, when I'm just trying to do my job (and I'm not trying to scare anyone).*

▶ *They focus a lot of time and energy on details I don't view as important.*

▶ *They don't tell me the truth.*

▶ *They aren't direct—they bury a request at the bottom of an e-mail that includes a lot of irrelevant information.*

▶ *They don't see the big picture as clearly as I do.*

Type Eights' workplace pet peeves may be:

▶ When people are weak and don't step up to the plate to just do what needs to be done.

▶ When people go behind my back or say things indirectly.

▶ When people perceive me as controlling when I'm just trying to move things forward.

▶ When people get caught up in indecision or analyzing something forever and don't take action.

- ▸ Slow people.

- ▸ People who whine about what's happening but don't do anything to solve the problem.

- ▸ People who don't say what they really think.

- ▸ When people beat around the bush instead of just telling the truth.

- ▸ When people try to limit me or get in my way.

- ▸ When people try to micromanage me.

- ▸ When people misperceive my passion and energy as hostility or intolerance.

- ▸ When people in power mistreat people.

- ▸ When other managers mess with my team.

Here's What Type Eights Can Do to Be Easier to Work With

In general, it helps people with a Type Eight style to remember that not everyone is as action-oriented as they are. People with other styles may take more time to do things, so it can help Eights to align with others by making a conscious choice (some of the time) to adjust their tempo and moderate their impulse to take action. It can also help to understand others' different decision-making processes and make an effort to meet them in the middle. Eights' decisiveness is definitely a strength, but if they can dial down their impatience and allow others to help them think before acting, they may be able to spur slow deciders to action more effectively.

It also helps Eights to remember that they have a big presence, which may intimidate some people. Others may find them more approachable and less imposing if they can moderate the force they use and share more personal information as a way of becoming more known and appearing more accessible. Actively adopting a friendly demeanor can help too. I'm not a fan of telling people to "smile" (which kind of makes me cringe for some reason), but Eights can work against their tendency to intimidate by reminding themselves to incorporate some softer, non-verbal behavior.

As leaders, Eights bring natural gifts of confidence and strength, so they tend to feel comfortable in positions of authority. Eights like to do things their way, which can be a good thing as they excel at getting the job done. But it may help Eights collaborate more proactively with others if they can temper their desire to take action in support of their ideas right away and consider other people's input more thoughtfully (even if they still want to do it their way).

Although Eights say they don't need to be the boss, many Eights may find themselves ill suited in some subordinate roles—it may be hard for them to contain their big energy and be told what to do on a regular basis. So for Eights who are not the boss, it will be important to keep some key things in mind when they need to follow someone else's directions, including their discomfort with being controlled, their impulse to react with power when feeling vulnerable, and the wisdom of consciously containing their energy.

Working with Eights

Typical Type Eight Behaviors in the Workplace

You *might* be working with someone who has a Type Eight Enneagram style if you see them doing several of the following behaviors on a regular basis:

- ▶ He automatically commands respect from everyone on the team.
- ▶ She has no patience for long explanations and will often tell someone (a bit angrily) to "just get to the point!"
- ▶ He uses profanity often, even at work, which startles people, and he has no tolerance for bull#*&%!
- ▶ She displays a "my way or the highway" attitude.
- ▶ He has no problem confronting people when he has a problem with something they did that he didn't like.
- ▶ She sometimes intimidates you, even when she's not saying anything.
- ▶ He makes quick decisions and likes to take action immediately—even though he sometimes leaves people behind.
- ▶ She gets mad sometimes, but it blows over quickly and she doesn't seem to hold a grudge.
- ▶ He likes ordering people around—and you have to admit, he's good at it.
- ▶ It's kind of a relief the way she takes charge and takes the lead sometimes.
- ▶ He seemed to respect you more after you had a fight with him.
- ▶ She's always very direct and doesn't hide how she feels.

▶ You always know where you stand with him.

▶ Some think she's aggressive and domineering, but you see her as assertive and strong.

▶ At his best, he inspires people with his confidence and ability to take bold action.

▶ At her best, she stands up for her team when outsiders criticize them.

What's Great About Working with Conscious Eight Leaders

▶ They lead with confidence and passion, inspiring their teams and colleagues.

▶ They say what they think—they don't keep you guessing about their intentions.

▶ They aren't afraid of conflict—and sometimes you need to have a productive debate to get to the best course of action.

▶ When they're on your team, they "have your back."

▶ The see the big picture, and they help you see it too—they show you where they want to go and have a plan for how you're going to get there.

▶ They don't get caught up in endless discussion—they take action.

▶ They work really hard.

▶ They delegate well—when they trust your competence, they will give you freedom to act independently.

▶ They respect competence. They don't necessarily need to do it all.

▶ They have strong opinions and aren't afraid to assert them.

▶ They have the courage of their convictions—and inspire courage in others.

▶ They are high energy and put a lot of effort into the things they do.

▶ They aren't afraid of big challenges and lofty goals—they enjoy being challenged to accomplish big things. They may even get more energized when the odds are against them.

▶ They want you to succeed—they want people to feel empowered enough to work independently and contribute in a powerful way to the team effort.

Typical Challenges for People Who Work with Eights

▶ They can be so intense that they intimidate people. And when people are intimidated, they may feel afraid to confront the Eight or tell them the whole truth (especially when there's bad news).

▶ They may confuse their sense of what's true with the objective truth—they may not consider the value of points of view that differ from their own.

▶ They may take action too quickly and not think things through or wait for colleagues to weigh in.

▶ They can be aggressive and may express anger in a way that may not be constructive.

▶ Their style may be overly authoritarian, tyrannical or dictatorial.

▶ They may be so focused on moving things forward that they "steamroll" people who get in their way.

▶ They may talk a lot, but not listen to others.

▶ If they believe they've been wronged by someone, they may get vengeful.

▶ It can be hard to know how to help them because they don't share their vulnerabilities or weak points.

▶ They may be so focused on the big picture that they miss important details.

▶ They may go too far when they break the rules—they may violate boundaries, offend people or fail to observe important processes and procedures.

▶ They may not be able to empathize with colleagues who are having a difficult emotional experience (since they don't want to go there themselves).

Type Eights and Leadership

Type Eight Leaders Speak About How Knowing Your Enneagram Type Helps You at Work

Carol Anderson is President of Child Development Inc., which manages and develops curriculum for 155 child-care centers around the State of California.

> *"I think learning about my Type Eight style through the Enneagram has been really big for me. It's been important for me to see my Eight way of being tough on the outside, of directing things, of being oriented to power and control, of loving control—all the typical Eight things.*
>
> *"I used to like to develop my own ideas and bring them 'already cooked' to my team. And then somebody said to me one time, 'Do you really want our opinion about this? Or do you just want a rubber stamp?' I thought, 'Oh, whoa!' That was a big 'aha.' So then I started to change through knowing the Enneagram, to be more collaborative. Eights don't like to collaborate; we want to work on our own. I also learned to be a better listener.*
>
> *"Now I try to understand different points of view through the Enneagram. There's a host of things I've learned I need to work on, including being more vulnerable in front of people. I'm still working on that! I talk to people now about what I'm working on. I think that's important. I think all of our senior leaders are fairly self-disclosing to their people. I want people to find that balance between self-disclosure and 'poor me, I'm failing'—whatever. I don't want that."*

Don Mather is Vice President of La-Z-Boy South.

> *"Knowing my Enneagram type has made me a better leader in that I know how I am and why I am the way that I am. Personality-wise, as Eights, our larger-than-life types gather a lot of attention. And you couple that with the fact that I'm a bigger man—I'm pretty muscular and I've been a weightlifter my whole life—and I have to temper myself somewhat so as to not be intimidating. I have at times gotten the feedback that I'm intimidating. And it's not that I'm necessarily meaning to be intimidating, but when I get passionate about something, it can come across as intimidating. I need to be careful of that at times.*

"I would say my main strengths as a leader are decisiveness, willingness to take action, and the fact that I'm not afraid of failure. I have a strong bias for action and little tolerance for talking things to death—which can be bad too.

"And, as an Eight, I'm also willing to be confrontational. A lot of people in leadership positions don't like to confront the hard stuff, don't like to confront performance issues or things like that, where I really don't mind. It's not that I like confrontation, but I believe if you're working with an individual who's having performance issues, the best help you can give that person is honesty about those issues. I've seen all too often where people are not forthright about those kinds of things, then they're ready just to get rid of them, and they never really worked with the individual to help them get better.

"Being confrontational can be a strength; however, you have to 'know when to hold them and know when to fold them'—you can't always be confrontational when you are with a group of peers or people higher up in the organization. You have to know how far you can push that and when you need to pull it back.

"In terms of my leadership challenges as an Eight, sometimes the 'ready, fire, aim'—the extreme bias for action—can make you take action too quickly. And, I guess, knowing how confrontational to be, when it's appropriate, when it's not, those kind of things—and not to let your emotions necessarily drive you. I've gotten better over the years at taking the time to keep my emotions in check."

Spence Taylor, M.D. is Vice President of Physician Engagement, Chief Academic Officer, and President of Greenville Health System Clinical University.

"In our organization, my experience of what's good about using the Enneagram has been twofold. First of all from the self-awareness and personal growth standpoint, it has exposed every blind spot that I clearly exhibit. I'm a One-to-One Eight, I'm rebellious, I make the rules. I mean, it is just totally me: here at the medical school, everybody has to do their computer-based training, but I'm not going to do it because I have the 'chair of surgery'-type attitude. It exposes blind spots. There's a lot of opportunity for personal growth in seeing those blind spots.

"We use the Enneagram as a way to share blind spots within my team; it's a way for my management team to know my defense mechanisms and how I operate. But equally, it helps me to know my direct reports better. It helps me to know what their Enneagram styles are. Eights can be incredibly intimidating; we come across as bold, honest, and with a lot of forward energy. We're different from people with other styles. But to know other people's styles and to be able to know more about how I think you're hearing me has really improved the efficiencies of our work relationships. It's just so helpful to know that I'm an Eight and I need to be careful with this person because they may be hearing it a certain way.

"Subsequent to learning Enneagram I would say to myself, 'You scare people. I scare people. I'm never going to be a great medical school leader scaring people.' It had never even remotely occurred to me. I thought I was a brilliant orator up there, talking, you know... but I was absolutely scaring people. There's a lot of emotional energy that we bring, but there's often just no awareness whatsoever. And again it's still an area I'm working on: big presence, big person, big everything. So I've got to be thinking, 'Am I scaring these people?' There's a lot of intensity. There's an awareness piece that I'd never have had, had it not been for the Enneagram.

"Here's one more example: I work with a Nine very closely. She's terrific because she's been able to come behind me, probably for years, and unscare the people that I scared. She's brilliant and terrific and I'm sure I used to shut her down. So it's this issue now of, 'Wendy, I'm going to need to hush and you need to give me your opinion. I like your vision...' Just to know she's a Nine and I need to get her to understand that she is important and her opinions are amazing and she needs to speak up and tell me what she thinks. But I wouldn't have had any insight in that if I hadn't done the Enneagram."

Jeanette Maggio is former Head of Organizational Development and Change Management for Global Technical Operations at Roche/Genentech.

"I'm pretty much a textbook Eight. But what I learned through the extra piece of learning about the three subtypes was the answer to the question of why I was so emotional. I always wondered why I was so emotional. I could be a victim, thinking, 'Why me?' and 'Why aren't they being nicer to me?' and 'Why did they say hello to my colleague before they said hi to *me?' She's wonderful, of course, but everyone gravitates toward her [as a Two] and seems to think, 'She's so nice.' I would think, 'Why don't they think I'm nice?' And then I read about the One-to-One Eight subtype, and I was able to be a little more empathetic with myself. Knowing I'm a One-to-One Eight helped me understand why I was different from some of the other Eights. I tend to be more emotional than the average Eight—and I want closer relationships, even if I'm not always able to make them happen.*

"I guess what I've learned about myself is this: I'm so focused on being strong, but that can get in the way of connection. I really want to be connected as a One-to-One Eight. I can think, 'I want you to be my best friend' (if I choose you, of course); otherwise, I don't care about you. And even in my relationship with my husband, as I told him, I don't let anyone in completely, because I might totally trust you, but then maybe you die. You can't help your own mortality. Maybe I don't think you'll divorce me or betray me, (and I don't even know that), but you might die. And then what would I do, if I'm dependent on you, to survive?

"And using Enneagram language it was a little bit easier to say to my husband, 'I can't totally be open to you, because what if I am? What would happen?' And then I had this moment of clarity as I realized, 'I have to take care of myself because no one's ever really taken care of me fully.' It's hard to trust anyone could really take care of me—even while I don't always take care of myself. But then I also tend to think (and said to my husband), 'If you aren't going to take care of me, that means you've got to get out of my way.' I think for him, hearing this from me was kind of a shock—because when you're an Eight, people don't see the weakness in you. They don't. Whenever the weakness shows up, you're like, 'F you,' you know? Seriously. That's how you respond. 'I'll be even stronger.' So there are layers, and the more you read about the Eight—and I'm getting worried about getting into the vulnerability of it because I'm so into it. I think it unmasks all of these things that you don't want to talk about. And of course, I think of myself as more than that. But I have found it a relatively easy language, in a way, to be more open and start a dialogue. How do you start a dialogue around, 'Oh, I want to learn to be really vulnerable?'—I mean, that's just awkward, you know. Especially for an Eight."

Rich Homberg is President and CEO at Detroit Public Television.

"The biggest change in my life that's occurred through learning the Enneagram has been having a more conscious sense that I have a larger-than-life presence. My wife has used the phrase 'you suck the oxygen out of the room.' With the knowledge that I'm an Eight I've had to learn to tell myself things like, 'Wait a little time. Slow it down.'

"Slowing things down' also means that I need to take the time to observe and consider. There's a woman that's pregnant that I work with; she's probably due in two or three weeks—she's a really great employee; she's a very nice person. Five years ago I would have been too busy to just send her a note that says, 'Good luck, all the best to you, I hope all goes well' or whatever.

Also, as a challenger, I need to know when I'm losing perspective or getting too invested in an idea that may be taking me in the wrong direction. However, the biggest thing for me is knowing when I need to get off stage, or when people have had enough. It's hard for me."

When You Are a Manager and You Are an Eight

As a Type Eight manager, you are likely to be very comfortable in a position of authority. You may enjoy having power to control what happens and how work is done, and you likely appreciate being able to use your abilities to help people understand your vision and take action to move the work forward. You probably want to empower people and take the lead in making sure decisions are made, the right things happen, obstacles are overcome, and the correct actions are taken.

However, you may feel more challenged when it comes to the "people" part of managing—understanding how to relate to them, how to communicate in a way that creates understanding with them, and how to navigate problem areas in constructive ways. If you think someone is incompetent or weak, you may struggle to empathize with them or help them to improve, especially if you think they may not be putting in their best effort. It may be tough for you to establish deeper connections with coworkers or to listen fully to everyone before you charge ahead with what you'd like to do. At your best, if you can hear feedback from your staff and start to understand how people experience you, you can make a conscious effort to show more of your softer side so people can get to know you on a deeper level.

When Your Manager Is an Eight

Having an Eight manager can be a very positive experience because Eights generally feel at home at higher levels of the organizational hierarchy. You can count on your Eight manager to actually manage with authority—they will probably not have a problem being direct, telling you what to do, and then letting you do it, since Eight leaders usually give people room to do their work in the hope that they will "take the ball and run with it." Unless you mess up, Eight managers are happy to learn that you are competent enough to get stuff done relatively independently.

If you are doing something wrong, your Eight manager will probably tell you directly—they likely won't hesitate to correct your mistakes and tell you to your face when you're not cutting it. And if you do your job well, you will probably hear about that too, though perhaps not through a lot of flowery language or excessive, effusive compliments. Eights usually just tell it like it is, without much fanfare.

On the downside, your Eight manager may be overly blunt, aggressive, or even scary. They may not share as much information with you as you think you need to do your job or take the time to get to know you, and they may not be open to hearing your opinions. They may get grumpy or withdrawn, or they might be impulsive and excessive. And at times, you may need to find ways to help your Eight manager slow their roll so you can think together more carefully about the action they want to take. However, at their best, Eight managers will be protective and supportive—and will usually be open to doing whatever it takes to get the job done and be successful.

When Your Subordinate Is an Eight

When your direct reports have a Type Eight style, you can count on them to work very hard and bring a great deal of energy to their work. Eights work hard and bring intensity and passion to the things they do—especially if you have a good relationship and they feel dedicated to the work. They will feel supported if you fill them in on the larger plan and motivate them by letting them know what role they can play in it. The more independence you can give them the better, and it will be important to avoid giving them the feeling you are micromanaging them.

Having a naturally powerful, confident Eight working under you can be difficult, especially if he or she decides to challenge you or rebel against your authority. Eights can tend to believe they are above the law and don't like being told what to do—even by their managers. To collaborate well with your Eight direct reports, it's essential to communicate respect for their abilities, allow them a certain degree of freedom to do their work, and be as direct and firm as possible in your interactions. It will also help to create a mutual atmosphere of respect and own your power in a confident way so they don't lose faith in your leadership and go off on their own.

Above all, try to tell your Eight subordinates the truth and let them know that you value their input and respect their opinion. When you give them feedback, be as direct as possible, keeping in mind that even though they probably won't share their vulnerable feelings, they do have them (just like we all do), even if you don't ever see them. This will help you remember to be kind, even when they seem tough or insensitive—or uncomfortable with positive feedback. At their best, Eights make loyal, committed coworkers with a great work ethic and a no-nonsense attitude.

Getting Along with Eights: Tips for What to Do to Work Well with Eights

▶ *Don't beat around the bush.* Tell the truth and don't sugarcoat it. When you send them an e-mail asking for something, put the request in simple terms up at the top—don't bury it at the end of the fourth paragraph.

▶ *Don't give them a book when they want bullet points.* Be brief, direct, and to the point.

▶ *Be competent and be able to work independently.* Your Eight coworkers will be very happy if they can trust that you will do your work and do it well and in a timely fashion—without them having to follow up with you or end up doing it for you.

▶ *Support them in taking action.* Try not to slow them down or interrupt what they are doing, unless it's really important. Understand how action-oriented they are and do what you can to support their forward momentum. If you need to ask them to pause before they act, make sure to do it in a direct way and point to good evidence

▶ *Keep them informed—don't hide things or undermine their authority.* Eights will want to know what's going on, so they can control the workflow. If you make this easy for them, everything will be easier.

▶ *Try not to be afraid of conflict with them.* It may be wise to look at working with an Eight as an opportunity to learn to manage conflict with more comfort and skill. They will trust you if you can stand up to them and not back down if you disagree.

Actionable Growth Tasks and Suggestions: How Type Eights Can Become More Self-Aware, Effective, and Happy at Work

All the types can learn to be less reactive and better at collaborating with others through first *observing* their habitual tendencies, thinking about the things they think, feel, and do to gain more *self-insight*, and making efforts to *manage* or *moderate* their automatic reactions to key triggers.

Eights grow through first observing and then learning to moderate their habitual reactions to key triggers like having their forward momentum thwarted, working with people who are dishonest or indirect, and seeing people misuse their power to oppress others.

When Eights can watch what they do enough to "catch themselves in the act" of doing the things that get them in trouble, and then pause and reflect on what they are doing and why, they can gradually learn to moderate their programming and knee-jerk responses. Here are some ideas to help Eights be more self-aware, emotionally intelligent, and satisfied at work (and at home).

Self-Observation: Things for Eights to Watch Out For

▶ *Observe your tendency to want to move into action. What is behind that? What might happen if you don't get to move forward in the way you want? How difficult is it to slow down?*

▶ *Notice your tendency to be impulsive. Notice any impatience that comes up that fuels your impulsivity. Note what causes you to be impatient and how you react.*

▶ *Observe any anger or aggression that arises. Allow yourself to learn to observe it more—what causes it, how quickly it arises, and how you deal with it.*

▶ *What is behind your desire to control everything and have a say in every-thing? What happens when things are beyond your power to control? How do you react?*

▶ *Notice your tendency to be excessive in the things you do—or feel or consume. How easy or difficult is it for you to modulate your intensity and excess?*

▶ *Can you usually judge the impact you have on others correctly? Why or why not? Do you always have the impact you intend? If not, what happens?*

▶ *Are you ever aware of feeling vulnerable? If not, what's up with that? If so, under what circumstances? Can you communicate with others about any vulnerable feelings you might have?*

Blind Spots: What You Don't Know Can Hurt You!

What blind spots Eights don't see in themselves:

▶ *Your vulnerability (and weaknesses and limitations and vulnerable emotions).* Type Eights often deny their vulnerable feelings completely and focus on being strong and powerful as a way of further keeping any vulnerable emotions at bay. It's crucial for Eights to become aware of their weaknesses, for so many reasons: 1) they're part of the truth of how you feel and who you are; 2) they balance out your strength; 3) they make you feel more approachable to others; 4) they allow you to connect more and more deeply with others.

▶ *The value of slowing down and thinking things through.* Eights can cause big trouble when they aren't able to identify instances in which it's better to take time to think about taking action before actually taking it.

▶ *Your impact on others.* Eights can improve their ability to work with people by being open to learning more about how they affect them. They often misjudge their impact because they focus their attention on doing what they want to do, as opposed to how it might affect people.

▶ *How much force is really necessary for a specific task.* Eights sometimes apply more force than matches what might need to be done. It can be good to learn when a light touch is actually more effective.

▶ *How their impulse to protect others is about projecting their vulnerability onto other people as a way of addressing it at a distance.* While the desire to protect others can be a highly positive quality in Eights, it also often serves to help them mask their own vulnerability. This happens when they project any subterranean feelings of weakness they may have (but not be aware of) onto others (instead of seeing it inside themselves) and then go into action to support others they view as needing protection. So it's good for Eights to realize that the urge to protect others can be a sign of needing to attend to their own hidden vulnerabilities.

Self-Insight: Things for Eights to Think About, Understand, and Explore

▶ *Why is it so important to be so strong and powerful? What will happen if you aren't? (Can you even imagine that?)*

▶ *What is your anger really all about? What is it really expressing, at a deeper level? What does it do for you? How might it hold you back or thwart you?*

▶ *Is your sense of being able to control things really just a defensive illusion? (In the psychology business we call this defense "omnipotent control," a form of "magical thinking" in which you tell yourself you can control everything, when the reality is, you really can't.)*

▶ *Why might it be difficult for you to show a softer side of yourself to others? What happens to your tender feelings? What might be hard about letting yourself feel them or communicate them?*

▶ *What feels hard about letting other people support and take care of you? What do you actively do to discourage people from showing you affection?*

▶ *What's going on in you when you behave in ways that other people find intimidating?*

▶ *What are the upsides and the downsides to not being in touch with your vulnerability?*

Strengths to Leverage

It helps Eights to be aware of, actively pay attention to, fully own, and leverage:

▶ *Confidence, power, and strength.* It may be more challenging for you *not* to leverage this obvious strength. Being confident and strong may be like breathing for you—and others likely count on you to be as confident as you tend to be in everyday life. And, perhaps paradoxically, if you develop your ability to be in touch with your vulnerability regularly, you can leverage the strength of your strength even more powerfully.

▶ *Fearlessness in the face of conflict and big challenges.* Your ability to tune out fear allows you to do many things without being hampered by the anxieties that can hold people back.

▶ *Ability to support and protect others.* Chances are, the people you work with count on you to lend your strength to others in different ways. This can make you a key part of any team, whether you are the leader or not.

▶ *Big-hearted and generous.* At your best, the soft side you don't always show to others shines through anyway in the way you put so much heart into work you feel passionately about—or the generosity you show to others when you care about them. The more you own this consciously, the better for everyone.

▶ *Ability to see the big picture and move big things forward decisively.* Every team and organization needs people who can develop and maintain a grand vision of what's possible. You not only hold this in mind, but it motivates you to take people there—meaning you likely play a crucial role in providing the inspiration and the fuel to help people do great things.

Self-Management: Challenging Tendencies for Eights to Moderate

▶ *Tendency to intimidate others (even though you don't mean to).* It will be easier for you to work with others if they aren't scared of you. If you can understand that this tends to happen—even though you don't try to do it—you can consciously temper the behavior some find unsettling and forge better connections with people.

▶ *Seeing your truth as The Truth.* Given your natural personal power, it makes sense that you sometimes (often) assume you are right about the way things are. But, the truth is, sometimes you're not. It will help you achieve better outcomes when working with others if you listen to their opinions and open up to the possibility that they might be right.

▶ *Not always listening to others.* Similarly, things may go better for you if you can slow down and make a point of taking in the feedback and input of others. They may have more to offer than you think they do.

▶ *Tendency to need to be invincible.* Although it may not seem like it at first, moderating your need to be invincible and softening up and sharing more will help you to relate more to others and collaborate more closely and effectively with them. Allowing yourself to be more known will probably lead to you being more liked, which could feel awkward and uncomfortable—but it will be good for you to get used to that.

▶ *Tendency to rebel against rules and limitations.* It will be good for you to acknowledge that you aren't always above the law—that some restrictions, when appropriate, do apply to you. As a leader, there may be times when it's good to model an acceptance of limitation.

▶ *Tendency to "put it all out there."* As an Eight, you have a huge amount of energy—it can help you a great deal to consciously rein it in at times, realizing you can moderate how much energy you apply when you choose to.

Consciously Manifesting your Higher Potential:
Being Aware of the "Low Side" and Aiming for the "High Side"

Eights can also grow through consciously becoming aware of the self-limiting habits and patterns associated with their personality style and learning to embody the higher aspects or more expansive capacities of the Type Eight personality:

▶ Learn how anger may run you at times, and challenge yourself to learn what's underneath it, instead of just acting it out. Allow yourself to learn to understand and regulate your aggression, balancing anger with a greater awareness of any hurt or pain or fear that might be beneath it—and learn to communicate that with strength as well.

▶ Notice how difficult it is to have an ongoing awareness of your weaknesses and this important truth: it takes a great deal of inner strength to be truly vulnerable. The best leaders are able to selectively disclose vulnerability. The more you can do this, the more you will be loved and appreciated, not just for your leadership ability, but also for who you really are under the armor.

▶ Learn how asserting yourself so strongly can merely give you the illusion of control, rather than the real thing. Learn to balance your need to take action to assert your power with a more thoughtful assessment of just how much is the right amount of oversight. (Call it "the Goldilocks principle.")

▶ Become conscious of how you may dismiss people as incompetent or weak when you haven't really given them a chance. Allow yourself to slow down, reveal more of yourself, and tune in to a deeper level with others, so you can create a more solid foundation for your working relationships. Not everyone will be competent, but some may be more skilled than you thought.

▶ Learn to recognize when you are over-focusing on the big picture and missing important details. Allow yourself to moderate any impatience you feel to move things forward and let yourself work with others to drill down into the small stuff, to make sure you ground your plans in the best ways possible.

▶ Learn to recognize when you are all about taking action and learn to balance acting with more feeling and thinking. Become more aware of how the actions you take can be wiser and more effective if you take emotions and a deeper investigation of the facts of the situation into account.

Overall, Type Eights can fulfill their higher potential by observing and working against their habit of denying their vulnerability and overcompensating through exercising power and control. When they can understand that real strength is about balancing action and force with vulnerability and softness, they can show more of who they really are to others, be even more powerful in the things they do, and draw on emotional and intellectual power rather than just their ability to take action. When they can consciously contain their energy and balance their boldness with mildness, they can create better working relationships and express their passionate nature in more fulfilling ways.

CHAPTER 12

The Type Nine Leadership Style

Leading from Consensus, Modeling Inclusion, and Defusing Conflict—or the Consensus-Building Mediator

"A leader is best when people barely know he exists, when his work is done, his aim fulfilled, they will say: we did it ourselves."

Lao Tzu

"Only the guy who isn't rowing has time to rock the boat."

Jean-Paul Sartre

The Type Nine archetype is the prototypical person who focuses on others and seeks to create harmony and avoid conflict. Primarily motivated by a need to evade discomfort and tension, they adapt (or over-adapt) to others and try to make sure everyone is heard and included. Nines focus on other people's agendas, go with the flow, and support others without drawing attention to themselves. Sometimes called "the Mediator" or "the Peacemaker," a Nine's attention automatically goes out to the environment to make sure everything is peaceful and working well. Although they don't like to be overlooked, they can proactively dismiss their views as unimportant and so not voice them, which sometimes leads to being overlooked.

Nines' programming tells them that the way to find a sense of well-being in the world is to avoid separation from or rifts with others. They feel most content when everyone is aligned and getting along, so they automatically try not to "rock the boat" in any way. This can mean that they step in to mediate conflicts among people or that they don't share their own opinion if they think it might go against what others think. Their personality style is thus shaped by a tendency to "go asleep to" their own agenda, and often their own anger, as they are motivated to tune out any of their wishes, desires, or emotions that might create friction.

Nines' communication style reflects their desire to find agreement and not make waves: They say "yes" a lot, have a hard time saying "no," and may say "yes" when they really mean "no." They may tell long stories as a way of giving a full picture, and will make sure to represent all sides in a discussion.[24] People with a Type Nine style excel at deeply understanding each person's individual perspective, which makes them great mediators. However, their desire to hear everyone and translate competing points of view so that conflict can be resolved—to play the peacemaker—also diminishes their awareness of their own perspective, such they often may not know what it is.

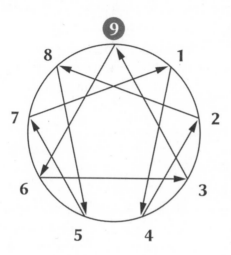

Leaders who have a Type Nine style tend to be attuned to supporting and accommodating others, often in subtle, unassuming ways. Nine leaders typically don't like being the center of attention, preferring to "lead from behind," through being likable and easy-going, gently working toward consensus, and making sure everyone feels good and work gets done in a way that benefits everyone. They may be practical and strong contributors, hard working but modest facilitators, or highly relational, sensitive partners. But whether they take a strong stand for what's best for their people, work tirelessly to support others without looking for credit, or harmonize with others to support their aspirations, they combine genuine concern for the welfare of people with a willingness to sacrifice their own interests to further their teams, organizations, or communities.

How to Tell if You Are a Type Nine: The View from the Inside

If most or all of the following characteristics apply to you, you may have a Type Nine personality style:

▶ *You see the work you do through the lens of what works best for the most people.* You genuinely want people to get along and enjoy working together, and will do everything you can to ensure they collaborate in positive ways and feel supported.

▶ *You like harmony and dislike conflict.* You feel good when your environment is free of tension. You avoid tension and conflict because you believe conflict leads to separation, and separation is painful.

▶ *You try to avoid conflict situations by helping mediate disputes and being diplomatic in the way you state your views (if you state them at all).* Often without even thinking about it, you say or do things—or avoid saying or doing things—to restore or maintain a feeling of peace in your environment.

▶ *You tend to be more attuned to the agendas of others than you are to your own.* You naturally pay more attention to what others want than what you want. What makes this particularly easy is that you often don't know what you want.

▶ *While you may have clear opinions on some things, you have trouble knowing what you want for dinner.* Nines may feel comfortable voicing views about things like politics or current events, but when it's more personal or work-related, it's harder to speak up. The answer to the question, "Where do you want to go for dinner?" is usually, "I don't know, where do you want to go?"

▶ *Emotionally, you tend to be pretty even-keeled and steady.* You don't typically experience a lot of emotional ups and downs.

▶ *Although you may work hard, you don't like being the center of attention.* When something is important to you (or important to other people who are important to you), you can dedicate a great deal of time and energy to it. But you are very uncomfortable if the focus is on you.

▶ *You often have trouble making decisions because you can readily see the value of different options and may have difficulty knowing what you really want.* Your tendency to avoid friction by going along with others means you may "go to sleep to" what you want. You will often be more aware of what you don't want than what you do want.

▶ *You rarely get angry. It's uncomfortable for you to feel and express anger.* Although Nines are an "anger type" as part of the "body-based" triad of Enneagram types, Nines unconsciously turn down the volume on their anger, so it doesn't rise up at an inconvenient moment and create disharmony with others.

▶ *You sometimes say "yes" because it feels hard to say "no," but you may not follow through on what you said "yes" to (because you didn't really want to do it).* Nines want to say "yes" so no one feels bad or displeased (or unpeaceful), even if they are aware of not wanting to actually do the thing they said "yes," to. So "yes" can sometimes mean, "I'm either not going to do it or I'm going to forget about it."

▶ *As a leader, you will want to make sure everyone is fully heard and that decisions can be made by consensus whenever possible.* Your experience of sometimes not being heard motivates you to try to make sure others don't feel that same pain. So you work to make sure everyone all people have a chance to say what they think and that they all know their contributions matter.

▶ *Your desire for harmony motivates you to "go with the flow" and avoid "rocking the boat." You are good at "going along to get along."* If maintaining harmony in your relationships means sometimes automatically erasing yourself or leaving yourself out of the picture, that's what you do.

▶ *You are good at mediating disagreements because you naturally see all points of view and want to help people hear each other and find common ground.* You enjoy the challenge of helping people understand each other such that everyone feels heard and disputes can be resolved.

The Central Adaptive Strategy of the Type Nine Personality Style

Nines often report feeling overlooked when they were young—perhaps they were a middle or younger child, or there were louder voices in their environment, leading them to adopt a strategy of blending in and going along with people who seem more powerful. Instead of fighting to be heard, the Nine child (unconsciously) gives up and decides it's easier to "merge" with others—to adopt their wishes and pay less attention to their own feelings.

This enables young Nines to ward off a scary sense of separation and find safety feeling connected to the important others in their world.

People with a Type Nine personality style experience a deep sense of discomfort if their important relationships are disturbed or threatened, so they automatically adapt in the face of any hint of potential estrangement. If they are super easygoing and "don't care" what happens, it's easier for them to harmonize with others such that tension or disconnection doesn't occur. This means Nines experience a lessening of consciousness of what they really want, who they really are, and what actions might be important for them to take to meet their own core needs and desires. While we all "fall asleep" to ourselves to some degree, Nines are the prototype of this habit of proactively separating from one's self to avoid having to experience conflict and separation from people.

At work, this makes Nines good at unselfishly working on behalf of others, their teams, or the organization. Nine leaders and individual contributors will tend to be alert to what others need them to do to be of service or achieve goals, and will defer to others' agendas instead of pushing their own. While this can be a problem if what's good for the company is, in fact, the Nine's own agenda, in many instances, Nines support the larger whole by taking into account the greater good.

What Do Nines Pay Attention To? The Type Nine "Radar Screen"

The strategy of supporting others to avoid division and maintain harmony causes Nines to pay attention to other people and their environment. They sense what's going on around them, attuned to the relative peacefulness of the atmosphere and any small signs of hostility or unease, and focus on other people's agendas while they may struggle to define their own. Going along with others' plans seems easier for Nines, both because they don't have to come up with their own and because they feel comfortable structuring their experience around doing things to help others.

People with a Type Nine leadership style pay a great deal of attention to keeping everyone happy, making people feel supported and cared about, and giving everyone a role in the work that gets done. Whenever possible, Nine leaders like to lead by consensus, and think about how to bring people together and defuse any conflicts that might arise. At work, Nines may expend large amounts of energy working to further other people's projects or putting time into programs that improve the quality of life at work for the organization as a whole.

As part of not attending very much to what's most important to themselves, Nines' attention also gets pulled toward less important tasks as opposed to more significant ones. For example, if Nines have a report due that's central to their success, they may put off working on it and instead spend time cleaning out their desk drawers. Nines habitually distract themselves with inessential work as a way of not paying attention to what's most vital to them. Just as it can be hard for them to tune in to their own personal agenda, it can be hard for them to take action on their own behalf—it can seem threatening to focus on their own well-being, both because it's unfamiliar and because it, by definition, puts more focus on them potentially being out on their own, separated from the crowd.

The View from "Planet Nine": How Nines See the World

Generally, individuals with a Type Nine style view the world as an interconnected place, where everything is happier and more peaceful when people are united in a common purpose and no one is left behind or left out. They tend to question their worth or importance in the world, and may have a default assumption that they don't matter. Because they weren't heard or their opinions were overlooked when they were young, they may (unconsciously) believe their import comes from aiding others and ensuring that no one gets overlooked the way they did.

Nines often feel called to serve the world through helping create peace and forging stronger unions among people. They tend to believe that accord comes through working toward a kind of seamless interdependence or greater connectedness, and often gravitate toward work roles in which they can work to reduce friction and increase mutual understanding within relationships or groups. Without necessarily thinking much about it, they often feel driven to help organizations and individuals think more inclusively and take practical actions that lead to more harmony in the world. They usually embrace difference, but want to help people overcome the disruptions that sometimes arise when differences aren't fully understood and accepted. Whether they're a coach, a vice president of learning and development, a CEO, or a president, Nines tend to see the world as better off when everybody's getting along and they find a sense of purpose in somehow helping that to happen.

The Type Nine Leader: Core Characteristics

The following character traits help to define the Type Nine leadership style:

- ▶ *Good mediators and facilitators.* Nine leaders excel at facilitating meetings and groups, making sure things follow a solid structure, and everyone gets heard. They naturally listen to different points of view, see the points of agreement, and hear the truth and legitimacy of different perspectives.

- ▶ *Easygoing and affable.* Accommodating and friendly, flexible and supportive, Nines specialize in being easy to be around.

- ▶ *Indecisive.* When you can easily see all sides of any issue and you have a difficult time locating your own preferences, deciding what to do can be challenging. Whether because they don't know what they want or they're motivated to avoid the conflicts that might ensue, Nines sometimes get stuck "sitting on the fence."

- ▶ *Tendency to "merge" and over-adjust.* Nines adapt to what others want as a way of staying in harmony with them, but they can overdo the adjustment to the point of erasing themselves entirely.

- ▶ *Passive resistance instead of active aggression.* Nines tune out their anger because getting angry brings the threat of separation and other unpleasantness. But when we avoid an emotion, it doesn't go away. So, Nines' anger often leaks out as passive resistance, like saying "yes," but not doing it.

- ▶ *Lovers of comfort.* Nine leaders can do great things, but one of the main things that drives them is the desire to stay comfortable. This underlies their preference for peace, their dislike of change, and their awkwardness around getting recognition.

Mental, Emotional, and Behavioral Patterns: Why Do Nines Think, Feel, and Behave the Way They Do?

Mental

Nines like routine and structure and may think about the processes involved in getting work done. However, their mental activity is primarily focused on the people around them: "Are they feeling good? Is everybody getting along? What do others want? What do they want or need me to do? How can I behave in a way that keeps them from being displeased? How can I best 'go with the program' and support people?" All that merging and supporting and blending with others' agendas can sometimes create an inner backlash, and while their first line of defense is "go along to get along," Nines may reach a point where they feel their backbone stiffen as they realize they didn't actually want to go along with that other person's agenda. They must then devote a fair amount of mental energy to resisting or thinking about how to get out of doing something they didn't want to do in the first place without raising alarms (though this may be less conscious).

Emotional

As "body types," Nines live from an energetic rootedness in their physical bodies, and are therefore more oriented toward taking or not taking action than to thinking or feeling emotions. They tend to be evenhanded and steady, and while they readily feel a range of feelings, including sadness, pain, and (more often) happiness or contentedness, their "highs" aren't that high and their "lows" aren't very low. Nines often need time to figure out how they feel, especially if they're angry and don't know it or don't want to admit it—their (unconscious) resistance to anger shapes their personality in a significant way. While they belong to the Enneagram's "anger triad" with Eights and Ones, Nines tend to under-do anger by ignoring it to avoid the conflicts it might cause. Often, Nines won't register their anger at all, and can push it down to the point where it leaks out as passive-aggressive versions of anger like stubbornness, passive resistance, and mild frustration, which may get expressed in a Nine's behavior.

Behavioral

Nines like to stay comfortable, and many of their behavior patterns relate to this central Nine need to maintain a sense of personal comfort. These include avoiding conflict and other interpersonal disruptions, resisting change, not deciding, and merging with others' agendas. Nines can become so focused on another person or agenda that normal boundaries between them disappear, and become so absorbed in an important person's attitudes and plans that they lose or forget themselves. Even a slight disruption in the relationship—including a close working relationship—can then feel highly threatening and disruptive. As mentioned, Nines may also express unacknowledged anger through behavior like passive-aggressively resisting doing what others want them to do (without saying anything). Like Eights, Nines don't like to be told what to do, but they are quieter about it, and if they feel overly controlled or disrespected by someone, they can covertly stop cooperating as a way of asserting themselves without creating open conflict.

The Main Strengths and Superpowers of the Type Nine Style: What Nines Are Really Good At

- ▶ *Unselfishly supporting others.* Nines focus on helping others succeed, making sure their ideas are considered, and working to further their goals, often without asking for anything in return.

- ▶ *Diplomacy.* Nines excel at seeing all sides of an issue or problem and communicating carefully to create alignment around shared agreements. They know just how to frame things to influence people while not offending them.

- ▶ *Being democratic.* Nines are by nature very egalitarian—they don't play favorites or think anyone is more important than anyone else is.

- ▶ *Building consensus.* Nines easily see the common truth in differing opinions, which makes them very good at finding a way to achieve consensus, even when people strongly disagree.

- ▶ *Being affable and friendly.* Nines are almost always very easy to work with because they are really nice and considerate. They go out of their way not to cause trouble, to be kind and thoughtful, and they don't need to take credit for things.

When Too Much of a Good Thing Becomes a Bad Thing: How Nines Can Go Wrong When They Try Too Hard to Stay Comfortable and Keep the Peace

Like all people of all types, when Type Nine leaders overuse their biggest strengths (and don't consciously develop a wider range of specialties), those strengths can also turn out to be their Achilles' heel.

- ▶ *Unselfishly supporting others.* Nines often pay more attention to others' agendas than they do to their own, which can cause problems for them and others when they don't attend to what they need to do.

- ▶ *Diplomacy.* Nines may frame the things they say so delicately or be so afraid of stirring up conflict that they don't communicate clearly enough about what's really true.

- ▶ *Being democratic.* In a business environment, some voices may be more important than others may. Nines may want to avoid this reality to prevent conflicts or unfairness, but they can end up causing problems when they don't take differences in status into account.

- ▶ *Building consensus.* Nines may stop the momentum of a project by taking the time to get everyone on board, even when that may not be possible or desirable.

- ▶ *Being affable and friendly.* Nines may have trouble being confrontational when they need to be to get the job done.

Fortunately, Nines' sincere interest in working harmoniously with others to get things done means they will likely be motivated to be more aware of how their desire for agreement and consensus can get taken too far. When they can focus on recognizing the limits of trying to please everyone and acknowledge that conflict can't always be avoided—and can even be useful—they can usually more effectively leverage their strengths in a way that allows for both interpersonal comfort and a thriving enterprise.

"When I'm stressed…" and "At my best…": Understanding the "Low Side" and the "High Side" of the Type Nine Personality Style

When stressed to the point of going to their "low side," Type Nines can get angry, and may act out their anger in passive-aggressive ways. They may be stubborn and resistant or get stuck in inertia and procrastinate, and may silently fume because they don't want to express their anger for fear of getting into a conflict. Nines avoid their own anger in part because they fear what they might do if they really let themselves blow up. On rare occasions, they do lose control and explode, but more often, they tend to avoid communicating their anger, which can lead them to passively resist others in different ways, including problematic behaviors like ignoring requests or taking a long time to finish a task.

Less self-aware Nines under pressure may withdraw or appear sullen or irritated. They may agree to do tasks and then not do them, put things off or avoid making decisions, thus holding up the work of others. When less conscious, Nines are extra sensitive to being overlooked or told what to do. If someone doesn't explicitly ask for their opinion, they may silently refuse to participate on work teams or impede others' forward momentum. They may avoid discussing conflicts or resentments openly while covertly and passively acting out their anger toward others they feel wronged by—usually by seeming to go along, but failing to take action.

On the "high side," when Type Nine leaders become more self-aware and conscious of their programming, they can be consummate team players. Easygoing and adaptable, they will work very hard to move projects forward, without complaining or needing to be recognized for their contributions. Emotionally intelligent Nine leaders put the team and the organization ahead of their own needs and wants. They are congenial and often funny. They don't take themselves too seriously and will surface difficult feelings or problems with sensitivity and grace (after pausing to reflect on their emotions and reactions). They will give others the benefit of the doubt, take the high road, and stay focused on what's most important for the greater good of the business.

When living from the "high side," Nines learn to sense, understand, and deal with their anger in constructive ways. They communicate about what they don't like before it festers and becomes a problem, and maintain an awareness of their tendency to avoid conflict and learn to raise issues in an open, responsive way. Healthy Nines ask for time to sort out their feelings if they need it, and they understand that it may sometimes take some time for them to get clear on what they want and share their emotions and desires with others. When Nines do the work of becoming more conscious of their habits and tendencies, they realize it's important to tolerate some discomfort, so they can engage more fully with others based on a stronger connection to themselves.

The Three Kinds of Nine Leaders: How the Three Instinctual Biases Shape the Three Type Nine "Sub-Type" Personalities

According to the Enneagram model, we all have three main instinctual drives that help us survive, but in each of us, one of the three tends to dominate our behavior. The Type Nine style is expressed differently depending on whether a person has a bias toward *self-preservation*, establishing *social* relationships and positioning themselves in relation to groups, or *one-to-one* bonding.

The Self-Preservation (or Self-Focused) Nine

All Nines suffer from a kind of "self-forgetting"—they go to sleep to their own deeper sense of "being" who they essentially are, and then distract themselves from the pain of being disconnected from themselves. Self-Preservation Nines distract themselves from their deeper desires and emotions (like anger) through focusing on physical comfort and activities. Nines tune out their agenda, their wishes, and their feelings and tune in to experiences of physical satisfaction, like eating, sleeping, reading, watching TV, or doing crossword puzzles. These activities distract them from an awareness of their own being and all that goes with it.

Self-Preservation Nines tend to be practical people with a strong presence who may seem more irritable or stubborn than the other two Nine subtypes. They often rely on familiar routines, like reading in the morning while having coffee or having a beer while watching TV at the end of the day, to structure their life and help them feel settled and peaceful. When their routines and habits get disturbed by others, they may react by getting grumpy and silently retreating to resume their activity uninterrupted. This Nine likes being alone more than the other two Nines and may display a dry or self-deprecating sense of humor.

Self-Preservation Nine leaders can be capable and forceful, but also humble and generous. When engaged and healthy, they can work very hard to move big efforts forward, and have a special talent for seeing how all the pieces fit together to make things work—they see the larger context and how the parts fit into the larger whole. If pushed or controlled by others, they may dig their heels in and refuse to move, usually without talking about it. They may also feel uncomfortable with the confrontational aspects of exercising power, and prefer inspiring people through fun, humor, and a positive focus on the goal and its connection to the well-being of others. At their best, Self-Preservation Nines know how to take practical steps to get everyone on board with a plan or project to get things done. The more they can connect with their anger in healthy ways, the more they will feel comfortable exercising power in constructive ways that benefit both themselves and others.

The Social (or Group-Focused) Nine

Social Nines distract themselves from the pain of disconnection through merging with groups. The "counter-type" of the three Nine subtypes, the

Social Nine is a very hard-working person who often takes on leadership roles. Congenial and fun loving, they are often pulled into positions of leadership to satisfy the responsibilities others want to put on them. They tend to be workaholics who put a great deal of effort into supporting their teams, groups or communities, while at the same time continually neglecting, or forgetting, their own needs. As Enneagram author Claudio Naranjo says of Social Nines, "They have full lives, full of everything but themselves."

Deep down, Social Nines often have a feeling of not belonging to the groups they are nominally in. So they work hard to gain the sense of belonging they yearn to experience, but often don't seem to feel, even when they give a group all their time and energy. While Social Nines benefit from getting in touch with their anger, they also grow through getting in touch with an underlying sense of sadness at not belonging. When they can become more conscious of their deeper feelings and focus more of their efforts on what they want and need, they can begin to take in the appreciation of others more, and finally feel more a part of things.

Social Nines make excellent leaders—they want to work in support of the team, and they don't complain or let others see the effort it takes them. Social Nines give very generously to the groups they support, but don't ask for recognition or rewards. Humble and modest, they dislike being the center of attention and often work much harder than anyone realizes behind the scenes. While Social Nines tell stories of getting "drafted" into leadership roles, they usually enjoy leading and doing whatever it takes to further the interests of the group. And although they can be indecisive or unsure, at their best, they work tirelessly to make things happen and unselfishly and unflaggingly support the larger aims of the group or team.

The One-to-One (or Relationship-Focused) Nine

One-to-One Nines are sweet, gentle, and kind—and the least assertive of the three Nine subtypes. They merge with other individuals to distract themselves from themselves, looking for a sense of purpose that they cannot locate internally and unconsciously taking on the opinions, attitudes, and feelings of the important people in their lives—whether it is a spouse, a parent, a best friend, or a manager or close colleague. They become so focused on the feelings and desires of others that they may have a difficult time knowing what they want or think, and may not know the difference between what they feel and what another person feels. And when they do know what they want or what they think, they may have a hard time expressing it, especially if it differs from what the other people they are close to think or want.

One-to-One Nines unconsciously deny the existence of boundaries among people, taking refuge in their close relationships as a way of avoiding the separation they may feel on their own. Because they rely on others for internal support, they may not have a sense of who they are and may not feel very self-confident. And when they do act to support themselves, they may do it in secret, surreptitiously rebelling against the other person, who may dominate the Nine's experience in a way neither person is fully aware of. The most emotional of the three Nines, One-to-One Nines may not realize how completely they've merged with someone until they experience some kind of physical separation, which allows them to find themselves as an independent individual. Real relationships require both people to show up fully as themselves, but One-to-One Nines may not be standing on their own two feet—and may not know they are not standing on their own two feet.

As leaders, One-to-One Nines can be both sensitive and competent. They have a special talent for understanding others' perspectives in a deep way, and blend a light touch with an ability to listen to others and empathize with their emotions. While they may at times be indecisive and insecure, when they are able to find ways to assert who they are as a unique individual, these Nines can bring great care, dedication, and personal creativity to their work. When they can work through any fear they might have of acting independently and expressing their authority, they can make thoughtful, sensitive leaders who have a great way with people. The more they do the work to discover who they are and what their particular strengths are, they more they can put their individual stamp on the work they do and the way they lead. At their best, they have a humble and gentle way of being with people.

The Type Nine at Work

Type Nines sometime feel like working with others is hard because:

- ▶ *People pressure me to produce results or take actions when the task or plan hasn't been explained in a clear way.*

- ▶ *I sometimes assume people know more than they do, so I go along with them and find out later they don't know what they're doing, and then I get taken down with them.*

▶ *The people I'm working with don't understand the larger context the way I do, which can lead to differences in the way we see what we're supposed to be doing.*

▶ *It can be hard to be the center of attention when I'm singled out for some reason.*

▶ *I worry about doing something wrong and standing out as doing a bad job.*

▶ *I worry about doing something well and standing out because I was successful.*

▶ *I don't like any kind of conflict, and working with people sometimes leads to conflict. Even receiving critical feedback can feel like conflict.*

▶ *I can feel insulted when people don't make a point of asking for my opinion or listening to what I think.*

▶ *I can have a hard time getting into the conversation when everyone is talking a lot and expressing strong opinions.*

▶ *People sometimes expect me to make quick decisions, but I need time to decide.*

▶ *People sometimes act in authoritarian ways and don't make sure everyone is on board and aligned.*

Type Nines' workplace pet peeves may be:

▶ When people go way outside of the general direction we're going in (and decided on together) and aren't considerate of the needs of the whole.

▶ When expectations aren't clear and I do something wrong that gets me in trouble (because the expectations weren't clear).

▶ When people expect me to take action, but I don't understand how the action serves the larger goals of the project.

▶ When I'm set up to fail because the strategic direction isn't clear and I'm asked to take action without knowing what we're trying to do.

▶ When people get into conflicts that could have been avoided.

▶ When people just do whatever they want to do, without even trying get buy-in from everyone on the team.

▶ When I'm overlooked and not consulted about projects and plans I'm involved in and should have a say in.

▶ When I'm not informed about important decisions that affect me that I should be a part of.

▶ When people make it hard for me to say "no" to something I don't want to do.

▶ When people autocratically tell me what to do (instead of asking nicely or finding out what I want to do).

▶ When people take my easygoing nature for granted by pushing me around or assuming I'll cooperate with whatever they want to do or neglecting to ask me what I want and need.

Here's What Type Nines Can Do to Be Easier to Work With

Nines are easy to work with just as they are—in fact, they can be *too* easy to work with, going along with others' wishes or agendas without fully deciding if they really want to. So it will help Nines to work to get clearer on how they feel, what they think, and what they want. Knowing what they want can be particularly hard for Nines, so it may take some time for them to learn to locate their desires at will, and they may need space and compassion in this process. It's important to remember that Nines' tendency to lose touch with their desires often stems from needing to go along with others who were more powerful, or an experience of being criticized or rolled over when they *did* know what they wanted.

When Nines can be more in touch with and more solid in their views, desires, and agendas, they actually become easier to work with. It can be challenging to work with someone who has trouble making decisions, doesn't know which way to go, or passively resists others' plans without voicing clear objections. So it is actually better for everyone when Nines develop the ability to access their inner knowing and feel more comfortable saying what they really think, even if it risks conflict or disagreement.

As leaders, Nines bring the gift of seeing and understanding a variety of perspectives and easily helping people develop a common vision. The dark side of this strength is that Nines often can't say what they really think—so when they can improve their ability to state their own opinions as well as clarify those of others, Nine leaders can be more powerful in their work and more effective work partners. Similarly, when they can become more tolerant and less afraid of conflict, they can be more versatile in the roles they play in the workplace. While it's great that Nines are so easygoing, it benefits everyone when they can develop the capacity to be more of a hard-ass when the situation requires it.

Working with Nines

Typical Type Nine Behaviors in the Workplace

You *might* be working with someone who has a Type Nine Enneagram style if you see them doing several of the following behaviors on a regular basis:

- ▶ She's kind of quiet in meetings, but seems to be paying attention to (and agreeing with) what everyone is saying.

- ▶ He's a nice guy. Everyone likes him. He offends no one.

- ▶ She's very agreeable, but she often turns her work in late.

- ▶ Whenever you ask him where he wants to go for lunch, he asks you where you want to go.

- ▶ She knows more what she doesn't want than what she does want.

- ▶ He works very hard to support his team, but he never wants to take credit.

- ▶ Sometimes, when she needs to make an important decision, she can sit on the fence for days.

- ▶ He seems to magically disappear whenever a conflict threatens to break out.

- ▶ She always seems to get caught in the middle when people on the team differ on which way to go. She usually helps them find a compromise.

- ▶ If you tell him to do something with a certain tone (instead of asking him politely), he often won't do it.

- ▶ She doesn't offer an opinion in meetings, but seems insulted if she's not asked what she thinks.

- ▶ He will go out of his way to help people, and then get embarrassed when they try to thank him for everything he did.

- ▶ She's great to talk to when you have a problem, because she always understands your point of view and offers support.

- ▶ He never openly challenges anyone or complains, but he will "forget" to do something you ask him to do if he gets pissed off.

- ▶ It can be hard working on projects with her when a decision needs to be made quickly—she often doesn't know when you ask what you should do.

▶ At his best, he's funny and fun loving—which makes work more pleasant.

▶ At her best, she can always be counted on for support when you need it.

What's great about working with Nines:

▶ They make people feel accepted and included.

▶ They know how to listen to people and make them feel like they were heard.

▶ They let people know that their opinions are valued.

▶ They focus more on solutions than blame when things go wrong.

▶ They blame the system and not the people if things don't go well.

▶ They look for ways to improve the system and processes (meetings, etc.) so that people can have a better experience at work.

▶ They are funny. They make jokes and bring levity to serious situations, which makes it easier to focus on tasks and work well together.

▶ They are easy to talk to.

▶ They give credit to others and model humility and generosity.

▶ They are very accepting—they focus on the best in people and rarely criticize others behind their backs.

▶ They help people find common ground when they have widely divergent ideas about how to get something done.

▶ They automatically find ways to defuse tension by being witty, gentle, and kind.

▶ They don't have big egos and easily share power with others.

▶ They work very hard—out of a sincere desire to further the aims of the team or the organization, not out of self-interest or a need for attention or power.

Typical challenges for people who work with Nines:

▶ They may be unwilling to take a stand or make a decision if there's not enough alignment or consensus.

▶ They can slow down work processes when they are slow to complete tasks and move things off their desk.

▶ They may hold back stating what they really think—they don't always share their complete perspective (as conflict avoidance strategy).

▶ They tend to procrastinate.

▶ They may say "yes" to doing something but really mean "no" (which you find out eventually when it never gets done).

▶ They can passively resist what's happening but not say what's going on for them—why they are against it or what they are mad about.

▶ They may avoid "showing up" and offering an opinion—they may defer to what others want and then (silently) not go along with it because it wasn't what they wanted to do.

▶ They may be problematically passive when they need to take action.

▶ They may not take the initiative to do things, even when they are the leader.

▶ They may seem angry, but not say anything about what's going on.

▶ They may want people to ask them questions and draw them out instead of just offering their thoughts and opinions proactively.

Type Nines and Leadership

Type Nine Leaders Speak About Knowing How Your Enneagram Type Helps You As a Leader

Andy Berkenfield is CEO and partner at Duncan/Channon, an advertising agency based in San Francisco, California.

> *"It's going to sound pretty obvious, but being effective is easier when you understand yourself. If you're in tune with who you are and how you work, you're going to be more effective. You're going to recognize, 'Hey, I need help with this thing.' As a Nine I have a tendency to avoid conflict, so I know to be on the lookout for 'Am I avoiding conflict in this moment? Am I seeking a peaceful resolution to this issue because that's my natural tendency and at this point I probably shouldn't do that?' So there's a level of awareness about the way that I'm programmed—the way I'm wired— that allows me to be more effective. I can apply my knowledge of myself to a situation as opposed to being blind to it, as opposed to being unaware of how my wiring is impacting the handling of something.*

"When you're a leader, how you handle situations—how you behave—is the majority of the job. I'm in the people business—the service business. I'm a couple of steps away from the majority of the content that is created in my business, and my job is guiding and helping to resolve problems and helping the team get to the next level. Being able to do that with some clarity about what my Type Nine biases are is really powerful.

"This may be a product of my Nine-ness, but I have a tendency to think about using the Enneagram more in terms of keeping me clear on the things I need to work on as opposed to celebrating or appreciating the things that I'm good at. But for sure, there are moments where I would look at a situation and think, 'I'm just better prepared for doing this particular peacekeeping mission.' And I can see that part of the reason why I'm particularly good at that task is that it's a good match for the way I'm wired. My 'Nine-ness' in that moment is working in my favor."

Tod Tappert is Vice President for Culture and Learning and System Chief Learning Officer, Greenville Health System, and Executive Director of the GHS Academy of Leadership and Professional Development, based in Greenville, South Carolina.

"It's really helpful knowing I'm a Social Nine. First of all, it helps me make sense of my high level of productivity and activity as I sometimes have trouble relating to the 'lazy Nine' stereotype. The other thing that has been very helpful for me is that it gives me a lens to view situations that are difficult at work. Recently, there was an incident at work in which I wasn't notified about an important change in policy. On autopilot, the thought I had was, 'Just more evidence of me not being important.' But because of the self-awareness work we've done with the Enneagram, now what I think is, 'Is there another story?' And I think about myself as a Social Nine and I think, 'You get asked to do something for the good of the larger organization and you go ahead and just do it.' So, in line with this I realize, 'I'm a leader that others know they don't have to worry about, so it sometimes doesn't even occur to them that, say, a month might go by without them mentioning to me what they were thinking or that it would matter to me that I'd been left out of the loop. Because I've been sort of off making things happen and they may unintentionally take me for granted.' So a big insight for me in using the Enneagram is when I can stop and note, 'How

am I reacting?' But it's also about looking at what's really happening in my relationships with others.

"As a Social Nine, I know it's in my DNA to work in service of something else, in service of what I believe in. It's been pretty easy for me to make personal sacrifices in regard to moving something along at work. There's a way in which I have a creative ability to picture a vision and then push towards it. And though it can be hard for me to fully take credit for things, I have had some creative ideas that have made a big difference. For example, the whole Academy of Leadership and Professional Development that we started here at our health system—it was really my idea and vision about what we were going to do and how we would make it happen that launched the Academy. I had good help from the people who work with me, but the driving force was me. It's hard for me to say and own that, but it's accurate."

When You Are a Manager and You Are a Nine

If you are a Nine manager, when you're leading well, the people you are leading will feel fully empowered to do what they think is best. Nine leaders, at their best, give their people the feeling they've done the job themselves—because you put what's good for the collective first and because you truly enjoy working as part of a team to get things done. You tend to be humble about your own efforts and abilities, and so model modesty and a real team mentality for the people you work with.

Your positive attitude inspires the people you lead—you don't hesitate to appreciate a job well done and will focus on solutions as opposed to dwelling on problems. And your talent for seeing how different people can work together and bring their individual strengths allows you to achieve great things in concert with others. It may actually help both your direct reports and your organization if you own your power and capacity for leading in ways that can be both effective and humane. When you can learn to take some credit for the good work you do and the generous way you lead others, you can provide an even stronger example of how "nice guys (and gals)" really can finish first.

When Your Manager Is a Nine

There are many benefits to having a Nine manager. Your Nine boss is likely to be very approachable—someone you can really talk to about a wide variety of things and feel supported by, who will be on your side and wants you to feel empowered to act independently and flourish in your role and your career. Nine managers are easy to get along with and easy to like, and they will want to make sure you feel heard so that you know your input will be listened to and considered. Nine managers will unselfishly promote you so you can succeed, and won't covertly compete with you or want to hold you back to lift themselves up. Especially if your Nine manager believes you are a team player, he or she will want to have a harmonious relationship with you in which you can accomplish many things.

What may be more challenging about having a Nine manager is that they may not always be a strong presence as they lead the work you do together. They may not be clear in communicating with you, especially around needed improvements in your work, as they may fear offending you. Likewise, they may not be as open as they think they are to your feedback, because they may not want to face what feels like conflict in the form of having to discuss negative information about how you experience them. If they feel uncertain about what they are doing, or they become indecisive about which direction to take, they may withdraw and be hard to reach.

The subtype of your Nine manager may also play a role—Self-Preservation Nines can be more stubborn but more strong, Social Nines can be incredibly hard working and productive, and One-to-One Nines can be very kind and sensitive to your needs. The more confident your Nine boss feels, the more powerful the leadership and decision-making will be, while if they don't learn to deal with conflict and face their anger, they may get passive or avoidant. At their best, Nine bosses will be people you can easily work with and admire, especially for their commitment to their team and their dedication to helping others through the work they do.

When Your Subordinate Is a Nine

When your direct reports have a Type Nine style, they tend to be cooperative and hard-working, especially if you develop a good relationship with them. It will be important to ask them directly to weigh in on key initiatives and decisions and to make sure they know you value their opinion and want to include their input. Nines want to feel a part of things, but they don't necessarily have to be front and center or get their way, so they usually find it comfortable to be individual contributors as long as their views are not dismissed. They tend to put others before themselves, and may work to support the people they like and feel close to, sometimes to their own detriment.

If your Nine direct reports are not very self-aware, you may have problems with them displaying passive or passive-aggressive behavior. They may turn their work in late or be lazy about attending to particular processes and procedures. One Nine I know was recently asked by a manager if she had blocked out the vacation time she was taking the following month in the "Request for Time Off" book. Her reply was, "There's a 'Request for Time Off' book?" A bit later she confided in a coworker that she didn't plan to utilize this book, even now that she knew of its existence. While Nines tend to be rule followers in the work setting, if they don't believe a rule is fair, or if they feel disgruntled about how a rule is administered, they may just not observe it and not say anything about it. However, when they don't feel insulted or pressured, Nines make excellent coworkers who tend to be easy to be around and will almost always act to support the best interests of the larger organization.

Getting Along with Nines: Tips for What to Do to Work Well with Nines

▶ *Be peaceful and kind and make an effort to make a personal connection with them.* Nines usually don't see a reason not to be nice. They lead with friendliness and warmth and will assume people are trustworthy until they prove otherwise. The Nines you work with will appreciate your efforts to get to know them on a personal level and create a positive working atmosphere where people get along.

▶ *Value everyone's opinion, including the Nine's.* When at all possible, Nines like to lead by consensus. They tend to be democratic diplomats who believe everyone's input is valuable. If you demonstrate clear respect for everyone's point of view, including theirs, the Nines in your life will probably admire you and want to work with you.

▶ *Understand their sensitivity to conflict and criticism.* Try not to stir up trouble or initiate a conflict unless it's absolutely necessary. When Nines perceive that someone is venting or indulging their anger in a way that threatens to create conflict, they may feel uncomfortable and withdraw or get angry with the angry person. They can at times express the fury of a peacemaker—they will become upset if someone is making others upset. And—if you have a conflict that's even slightly heated, make sure to circle back with them and make an effort to repair things.

▶ *Ask the Nine for input, even if it's not being offered.* Working with Nines can be tricky because they often don't proactively offer their opinion—or their full opinion—during work conversations. They can be quiet in meetings and then feel irritated that no one asked them what they think. So make sure to ask if they don't tell. And it may be especially important to solicit and support their feedback if they express an opinion that goes against the general direction of the group.

▶ *Enlist their cooperation directly to get them on board.* Coaches and leaders often ask, "How do you get a Nine to do something—especially if they have shown a resistance to doing it?" The answer is, you *don't* "get" a Nine to do anything. Nines can be tough and strong when resisting doing something someone is pressuring them to do, and in a silent power struggle, they will most probably outlast you. So instead of trying to move a Nine when you perceive them stubbornly resisting your will, talk to them openly, ask them what they think and how they feel, and be direct about wanting their buy-in and give them the freedom to say yes or no for their own reasons.

▶ *Explicitly recognize their contributions to the team.* In a way that's not too public or embarrassing, make a point of acknowledging them when they do something that helps the team or the leadership or the larger organization.

Actionable Growth Tasks and Suggestions: How Type Nines Can Become More Self-Aware, Effective, and Happy at Work

All the types can learn to be less reactive and better at collaborating with others through first *observing* their habitual tendencies, thinking about the things they think, feel, and do to gain more *self-insight*, and making efforts to *manage* or *moderate* their automatic reactions to key triggers.

Nines grow through first observing and then learning to moderate their habitual reactions to key triggers like conflict and criticism, not being heard or recognized for their contributions, or not feeling able to say "no" or make boundaries.

When Nines can watch what they do enough to "catch themselves in the act" of doing the things that get them in trouble, and then pause and reflect on what they are doing and why, they can gradually learn to moderate their programming and knee-jerk responses. Here are some ideas to help Nines be more self-aware, emotionally intelligent, and satisfied at work (and at home).

Self-Observation: Things for Nines to Watch Out For

▶ *Observe the way you tend to pay more attention to others (and their agendas) than you do to yourself (and your agenda). Notice if you put others ahead of yourself and any feelings you have about putting yourself last.*

▶ *Pay attention to your experience of anger. What kinds of things piss you off and what do you do in response? When do you not register anger (when it might be a legitimate response)? When do you express it or not express it?*

▶ *Notice any behaviors you might engage in that might be passive-aggressive. See if you can make your anger more conscious so that you can see the kinds of things you do out of anger that you don't want to express directly.*

▶ *Observe your tendency to assume your thoughts will be overlooked. Notice if you hold back from offering input because you proactively believe you won't be heard. Notice any consequences connected to this kind of holding back.*

▶ *Observe how easy or difficult it is to make a decision. What happens for you when you struggle to decide? Are some kinds of decisions easier than others are? Under what conditions might you sit on the fence?*

▶ *Under what conditions is it difficult for you to know what you want? How do you react when you don't know what you want?*

▶ *Notice if your discomfort with attracting attention leads to you not fully owning your power. Pay attention to any consequences of your potentially excessive modesty on your ability to lead.*

Blind Spots: What You Don't Know Can Hurt You!

What blind spots Nines don't see in themselves:

▶ *Your own agenda—what you want (and why that's important).* If you are a Nine, it may not occur to you that you have desires and priorities just like everyone else—and you may not register what you want and so give way to what others want on a regular basis. When this leads to you feeling resentful later, that's not good for anyone. It will help you to learn to ask yourself what you want, and keep asking with compassion even when the answer is "I don't know." You will eventually learn to connect with the desires you've gone to sleep to as a strategy for getting along with others.

▶ *Your own anger (and passive-aggressive behaviors).* Nines tend to be blind to their own anger, which often leads them to act out the anger they don't feel or acknowledge in indirect, covert ways. The more you can be aware of and welcome your anger, the less you will create problems for yourself by passively resisting others as a way of discharging your angry feelings.

▶ *Your own need for recognition and support from others.* Nines discomfort with getting attention—whether positive or negative—can mean they underappreciate their own need to be recognized for their contributions and achievements. If you don't learn to take in others' appreciation, you may get stuck in a bind in which you deflect positive feedback. Nines need to know they are valued to do their jobs well and keep their morale up.

▶ *How the desire for harmony actually leads to conflict.* When you don't take a firm stand or express a clear opinion, you can actually create disharmony because you can't work through the natural disagreements that occur when people work together in a conscious, direct way. When people don't know what you think, it's hard for others to get the clarity you all need to move forward.

▶ *Your lack of clarity in communicating with others.* Your desire to keep the peace and stay positive may lead you to hold back important information or not be clear when giving instructions or feedback. Your desire to avoid conflict and tension may lead you to think it's better to stay positive, even when you need to be clear about constructive criticism to improve things.

▶ *Your own stress.* If you are a Nine, you may tell yourself, "I'm okay," when you aren't. You may believe you need to be "okay" for others. But not acknowledging when you are not okay doesn't help you or others—and can lead to big problems at work.

Self-Insight: Things for Nines to Think About, Understand, and Explore

▶ *Why is it difficult for you to know what you want? What problems would it create for you to know what you want more of the time?*

▶ *What might be hard about focusing on your own priorities, as opposed to the priorities of others? In what way do you actively avoid attending to what's most important to you and why?*

▶ *Why do you turn down the volume on your anger? What fears might be connected to feeling your anger more fully?*

▶ *Why is it important that everyone be heard? What feelings do you have about being overlooked or unheard? Where do they come from?*

▶ *What feels hard or uncomfortable about being the center of attention?*

▶ *What feels difficult or scary about conflict? What kinds of things feel like conflict? What kinds of things do you do to avoid conflict of any kind? What are the consequences?*

▶ *How might you hold yourself back from being as powerful as you are capable of being? What kinds of habits are you in that detract from owning and expressing your power?*

Strengths to Leverage

It helps Nines to be aware of, actively pay attention to, fully own, and leverage:

▶ *Ability to see the big picture and how all the pieces fit together.* If you are a Nine it will be important for you to give yourself credit for your capacity to understand the larger context of the work you do and see how the different parts fit into the whole. The more you own this strength, the more power you may own around being able to direct the work to make things happen.

▶ *Ability to work with others to move big projects forward.* You have many ways of motivating people to work harmoniously to get significant things done. The fact that you value everyone's contribution and want to hear everyone's input empowers people and allows your teams to achieve solutions to important social and work problems without worrying about who gets the credit.

▶ *Ability to mediate disputes and handle difficult situations diplomatically.* The upside of your discomfort with conflict is that you have an easy way of seeing the way forward when people are far apart. When difficulties arise, you rise to the occasion, with the great strength of being able to know exactly how to frame things such that people can increase their understanding of people they initially disagreed with.

▶ *Sensitivity to inclusion and ability to create alignment amidst diversity.* Your sincere desire to make sure all are listened to and decisions are made by consensus when possible helps you to appreciate and accept differences, but also unify people.

▶ *Tendency to unselfishly put greater good ahead of self-interest.* You gravitate toward goals that will benefit others, you inspire people with your selfless approach to leadership, and you model a way of being that shows how people working together are more than the sum of their parts. It will help if you remember this.

Self-Management: Challenging Tendencies for Nines to Moderate

▶ *Avoidance of conflict.* Sometimes conflict is healthy and necessary. So it's important to understand why you dislike conflict and moderate your desire to avoid it so you can incorporate it in conscious and productive ways.

▶ *Avoidance of anger.* Because you avoid conflict, you (often unconsciously) tend to go to sleep to your own anger. But your anger can be an important signal that something needs your attention. Anger is also connected to power—so you can more effectively show up in the world as a leader and own your power in conscious ways if you can moderate your habit of turning the volume down on your anger.

▶ *Tendency to act in passive-aggressive ways.* When you are more able to feel, own, and express your anger, you will naturally channel it less into passive-aggressive behaviors, like slowing the pace of your work, "forgetting" about things, and quietly avoiding adhering to rules and procedures. Becoming more active and more proactive in the things you do will make you more direct and more powerful.

▶ *Putting others first.* It will be important for you to notice how you pay more attention to others than you do to yourself. If you can right the balance by taking care of yourself more and prioritizing others less, you can take stronger action in support of what you really need. Taking care of yourself is one of the best ways to serve others—they will get the best of you when you make yourself more of a priority in your own life.

▶ *Sensitivity to not being heard and included.* Often the way you react to your sensitivity to being unheard or excluded or overlooked is to further overlook or exclude yourself. This can lead to a vicious cycle in which you forget to include yourself, making it easier for others to regard you as unimportant, and so on. When you put yourself in the mix, you increase the likelihood that you will not be taken lightly or forgotten.

Consciously Manifesting your Higher Potential:
Being Aware of the "Low Side" and Aiming for the "High Side"

Nines can also grow through consciously becoming aware of the self-limiting habits and patterns associated with their personality style and learning to embody the higher aspects or more expansive capacities of the Type Nine personality:

▶ Learn how you go to sleep to yourself and your priorities and challenge yourself to be present to yourself more and more often. Allow yourself to enjoy putting yourself out there in the world more, enjoying the challenge of any discomfort that entails as part of the process of being alive and awake.

▶ Learn more about what happens to your anger and why and experiment with turning the volume up and expressing it more. Allow yourself to experience exactly how your anger is connected to your power—and how good it can feel to be more powerful in the world, even if it means getting mad.

▶ Learn to notice how you often know more about what you don't want than what you do want, and how that can lead to getting trapped in passive resistance. Allow yourself to become more conscious of how your anger leaks out in passive forms and channel it into finding your purpose and taking action, even if it creates some healthy tension with others.

▶ Learn about why it's so hard for you to know what you want and allow yourself to gradually get more in touch with your desires. Trust that communicating your desires more benefits everyone. Your clarity and ability to include yourself leads to you feeling a deeper sense of belonging.

▶ Become more aware of how you effectively erase yourself when you don't say what you think or proactively assert your opinion. Figure out what it takes to speak up without having to be asked or invited.

▶ Learn that sometimes achieving consensus isn't possible or desirable and try going more for alignment—or being okay if some people don't like what the majority decides. In achieving alignment, you acknowledge the limitations that come with consensus but still use your talent for finding commonalities to create balance and get people on board.

Overall, Type Nines can fulfill their higher potential by observing and working against their habit of diminishing their awareness of their own desires and priorities and emotions—especially their anger. When they can become more conscious of their tendency to fall asleep to themselves and wake up to their own experience, they can learn to value and support themselves as much as they value and support others. When they can consciously overcome their own inner barriers to expressing their anger and their power and their opinions—no matter what the consequence to their relationships—they may find that putting themselves in the picture actually improves their own life and work and that of others.

CHAPTER 13

What Next? The Enneagram as a Business Tool

How to Put It into Action in Your Organization

"What got you here won't get you there."
Marshall Goldsmith, author and executive coach

"I just use the Enneagram. I'm not interested in other tools. There's something simple and elegant about it. I haven't seen anything as good, mainly because it's a growth model. The Enneagram has the energy of wanting me to grow and evolve while other tools don't have that purpose. It's easier to trust the Enneagram because it's about initiating evolution."
Andrew Greenberg, CEO, Greenberg Strategy

We've almost reached the end of the book, and having read this far, you may be asking some important questions:

1. How can the Enneagram help my organization—what's the business impact of applying this tool? How exactly will using the Enneagram positively impact my organization?

2. If I decide to use the Enneagram, what do I do? How do I proceed? How do I use the Enneagram to ensure the best return on my investment?

This final chapter will provide the answers to those questions, along with real-life examples from a variety of high-level leaders who have used the Enneagram to help their organizations become even more successful. I'm grateful to them for generously sharing their stories.

The Enneagram has become more and more popular over the last two decades. People who spend the time to get to know it usually find that its personality type descriptions immediately generate personal insights that are powerful and often life changing. And, after dipping a toe in the Enneagram pool, many individuals ask the crucial question, "What do I do now that I know my type?" I also hear leaders in organizations say, "Now that we've had one introductory Enneagram training, how can we put it to use in ways that create a lasting impact?"

In what follows, I discuss how the Enneagram can, when used well, positively impact leadership and professional development, working relationships, team development, and the growth and health of organizations as a whole. As you will see, an important theme that emerges throughout the examples I cite in this chapter is that, in varied ways, the Enneagram model powers lasting growth and development. It's not a framework designed merely to describe a static list of traits. As I believe the following illustrations reveal, when you use the Enneagram to create positive change in your people or your business, you set the stage for personal, professional, and organizational transformation. This is why some of the leaders here talk about how they deployed the system during high-growth periods of time. It's also why the Enneagram has the potential to help leaders lead at this interesting and challenging moment in history in such a profound and lasting way.

Enneagram Impact: Leadership and Professional Development

"Simply put, leaders need to understand themselves before they can understand others. Self-awareness requires seeing one's self in an objective way. Research has shown that those leaders who know themselves better are more successful than those that do not. Highly effective leaders encourage development by openly developing themselves."

> Teresa Roche, former Vice President and Chief Learning Officer, Agilent Technologies

"The single most important thing about the Enneagram is the power to be able to reflect on your personality as if in the third-person—not being so in it."

> Jean Halloran, former Senior Vice President of Human Resources, Agilent Technologies

All forms of collective growth within an organization, whether it's two business partners discussing their working relationship, a senior leadership team engaging in a team-building exercise, or a large organization launching a new training program, rest on the foundation of individual development. When leaders, in particular, make efforts to know themselves and understand their motivations, habits, and reactions, they model what it means to take responsibility for one's own behavior and set a tone of openness and compassion that inspires their people to engage in their own self-reflection.

The professional growth the following leaders experienced through working with the Enneagram has enabled them to serve their organizations much more effectively and successfully.

Dave Aitken is CEO at FNB Tanzania, a bank in Africa. He leads with the Type Eight style, but also says he relates a lot to Type Seven. In this excerpt from my interview with him, he talks about the way his development as a leader took off after he took a coaching course that incorporated the Enneagram as a key tool.

> *"When I first learned my type, it was astonishing how real it was. I've never visited a psychiatrist or spoken to a therapist, but so much of me started making sense when I understood what shapes me and what makes me who I am. And once you have that awareness, you have such a powerful tool to work with. Then you can actively start managing your own life and fixing things and improving things.*
>
> *"What has also been important to me is understanding that there is no single story. There are multiple stories that are as valid as your story. To acknowledge that mine is not the only story has been good for me. It puts a completely different perspective on how you deal with situations.*
>
> *"My wife keeps saying to me she can't believe how different I am now and how much more accommodating I am. The biggest shift in my leadership style after being through a coaching course using the Enneagram is that I'm more receptive to constructive criticism. I ask my staff now: 'What should I do to be a more effective leader?'"*

Chris Houlder is Chief Information Security Officer at Autodesk. He was introduced to the Enneagram when he was associate director of communications, storage and security infrastructure at Genentech and continues to use it with his current team of direct reports at Autodesk. Here, he describes the way in which he was able to grow as a leader through increasing his empathy for the diversity of types of people as highlighted by the Enneagram's nine types.

> *"The biggest benefit of the Enneagram to me as a leader is actually being able to develop more empathy for others. I keep going back to it and expanding my understanding of myself. However, the most valuable thing*

about it is getting exposed to an understanding of the diversity of person-
ality types. It's helped me to not use myself as a reference point by which
everybody should be judged. It's helped me to see that I'm operating based
on what I see as 'the norms,' when the fact of the matter is that one set
of norms doesn't exist. To understand that there are eight other types—
that's even before getting into the understanding of development levels and
subtypes—but there are eight other types and their truth is as strong for
them as mine is for me has been huge. For me, it opened up a whole world.
I could start to see how I could understand and empathize with the other
lenses. Empathy came almost immediately for me knowing that. It was a
real 'wow' moment of, 'We actually see things differently.' "

Spence Taylor, M.D. is Vice President of Physician Engagement, Chief
Academic Officer, and President of Greenville Health System Clinical
University in Greenville, South Carolina. He is a vascular surgeon and the
former Chair of Surgery at Greenville Health System (and a former Enneagram skeptic). In this excerpt from my interview with him, he tells a story
about how another senior leader was able to coach him on his leadership style.
Spence says that this experience of having a leader he respected point out the
ways he needed to develop, combined with learning he was a Type Eight on
the Enneagram, changed his life and revolutionized his ability to be a good
leader—and to successfully lead the establishment of a new medical school.
Although Spence was once skeptical about the Enneagram, he now serves
on the Greenville Health System's internal Enneagram faculty, charged with
helping people throughout the health system learn about the Enneagram and
use it for their professional development.

"Several years ago I was asked to start this four-year medical school. As
an Eight, I went full-bore, I went right after it. They told me I'd be able to
lead it. Sort of like, if you can build this you can have it. Later on they said,
'Spence, you continue to do the work, but we're not sure you can lead it,'
which didn't seem fair to me. They told me I needed some more political
polish, and they were going to have me work with Andrew Sorenson, the
former president of the University of South Carolina. They said he would
lead it and I could work with him.
*   "Andrew was a master at politics and very self-aware. And they had*
me work with him so he could coach me. I was pissed as hell. I thought,

'This is nuts. I've done all the work and now this guy's coming in and he wants me to continue to do the work while he takes all the credit.'

"We were about halfway through the process of setting up the medical school and we were figuring out the answer to all these questions: 'How many students shall we take? What are our admission criteria?' Answering these questions was a stakeholder engagement process. So about halfway through this, Andrew pulls me aside and says, 'Spence, listen. Can I coach you for a second?' I said, 'Yes, sir, what do you want to coach me on?' He said, 'It's your style.' I said, 'What are you talking about?' He said, 'You lead like a bandleader.' I said, 'Yep.' And he said, 'You need to learn to lead. You're out in front doing all the talking—do you realize you're doing all the talking? You're not listening. You shut people off. You need to learn to lead more like a shepherd. You need to be further back.' I said, 'Andrew, we do not have time to push these sheep along.' And he said, 'You're scaring people. Do you feel your emotional energy? You're scaring these people.' It was an epiphany. He said, 'Let me show you how to do it.' I'll never forget. At the next meeting he said, 'I want you to sit in the back and keep your mouth shut. Can you keep your mouth shut for an hour, Spence?'

"Andrew was a master at guiding people in a process of answering the questions we needed to address. He would say, 'What do you all think about this?' I was rolling my eyes in the back. But people would come up with answers and Andrew would say, very skillfully, 'That's interesting. Let's talk about it...' He was just a master. Afterward he said, 'Son, that's how you lead. Everybody left thinking they made meaningful contributions to the medical school. That's how you lead like a shepherd. And you've got to get better or this thing is going to fail.' That was the epiphany. At that point I thought, maybe all this Enneagram stuff is real. We had been working with an Enneagram consultant, and I had thought he was a complete kook. But at that point I said to myself, 'Maybe he's not a kook. Maybe I'm the kook.' That was the epiphany and it was all about my Eight energy."

Enneagram Impact: Developing Better Working Relationships

"The Enneagram's such a good tool because it gives you some indication about how people are likely to respond to a really bad day and a really hot situation. And as a leader, it helps you help them through that situation."

Dave Aitkin, CEO of FNB Tanzania

One of the most significant ways working with the Enneagram contributes to a more harmonious and productive workplace is through improving relationships. As I pointed out earlier in this book, business happens through people interacting with people. Despite the fact that work today is becoming more global and more defined by new technologies, it's increasingly obvious that the more people know, understand, and accept each other, the easier time they have working together. And in a modern business environment that requires more and more collaboration, the need to increase efficiencies and minimize interpersonal tensions that can sap energy and resources has never been more clear.

As the following instances of people using the Enneagram to enhance their work relationships show, the personality descriptors provide a powerful way to quickly and compassionately establish mutual understanding and trust and clarify points of disagreement so they can be overcome.

Andy Berkenfield is CEO and Partner at Duncan/Channon, a leading advertising agency based in San Francisco. Andy discusses the ways in which he uses the Enneagram framework to improve his ability to serve his clients and understand his direct reports so he can more effectively relate to them. He is also part of a CEO group that uses the Enneagram to deepen their conversations about how to deal with leadership challenges and opportunities.

"A colleague and I were working with a client together when I first learned about the Enneagram. Once we understood that our client was a Six, it actually became easier for us to orchestrate the way that we were going to do the work for them. We had a sense of their type that was useful in knowing how best to work with them.

"Having such a clear framework with which to evaluate people, understand them, and work with them proved instantaneously useful for me. I understood, all of a sudden, much more about our interactions; it's like having a personality reference sheet that I could go to in moments of

being stuck or in conflict or unable to resolve something successfully—I could literally go to the Enneagram and look at it and use it as a reference point to understand, 'Oh, I get it, she's feeling threatened and doesn't trust the people around her.'

"I think there are two sides of it that help me with my relationships. Knowing what my tendencies are, so as a lens into myself—that obviously helps me with everybody, my whole job, my whole world. But being able to look at them and understand where they're coming from is also invaluable. Understanding what a Two's tendencies are—that they are going to say 'yes' to too much stuff, they're going to overload themselves in their desire to say yes to everybody who's asking them to do stuff. They need to learn how to say no. That's a real example of somebody who works for me who's a Two, who I know gets herself in trouble by saying yes to too much stuff. As a result, she can't put enough time into the things that matter. So it's helped me manage her, and I'm not doing it without her knowing it— we can talk about it. They're aware, so it's helped me help them."

Steve Jurvetson is Partner at Draper Fisher Jurvetson, a venture capital and growth equity firm. Steve first learned the Enneagram through a course he took when he attended Stanford University's Graduate School of Business. Steve leads with the Type Three style. He has used the system in his own personal and professional development as well as with his senior team to increase mutual understanding and enhance working relationships to support the overall health and success of the firm.

"One of the biggest benefits in knowing the Enneagram is learning about others and my relationships with the people I work with. In addition to appreciating diversity in groups, I have also been able, in at least two cases, to really understand someone who I thought—prior to understanding our Enneagram types—I couldn't get along with. There was one instance in which I realized everything I was doing to get work done efficiently and quickly was actually making my colleague less and less comfortable. He was a Six, and he was very nervous at the cavalier comfort with which I got things done. And the more that I would try to convince him that everything's fine—even if I was doing things at the last minute—and telling him he has nothing to worry about, the more what I was saying made him even more worried.

"And then more recently, there's someone I work with, one my part-ners—he and I are about as different as it gets, and there were many cases where I just didn't understand him. I thought he was getting on his high-horse or being very moralizing—like thinking there's a right way or a wrong way to do everything. Now [that I know he's a Type One] I totally understand where he's coming from, and we've been able to partition the work that we do to play to each other's strengths.

"For example, he's wonderful at interacting with our investors. When we want to make sure our investors are speaking to someone who is on top of the details and has everything just perfect and really engages with them around the details, we have them talk to him. I'm much more looking toward, 'How high is up? What is the next great achievement we can do at the firm?' So I'm more involved in the marketing and positioning and future fortune-telling of our business. And he's much more the nuts and bolts guy who asks, 'What is real? What is not? What's the proper way to run the business?'—and sets up structures and processes that will make the business run well."

Don Mather is Vice President of La-Z-Boy South. Don is a Type Eight, and he's used the Enneagram to improve his relationships with his colleagues and get a more objective understanding of the dynamics of his team. He told me his team's work with an Enneagram consultant to better comprehend the make-up of his leadership team was incredibly helpful in allowing them to see what they needed to do to be more successful. Here he gives an example of how he has seen the power of the Enneagram to clarify working relationships.

"I recently witnessed one example in which two people using a knowledge of the Enneagram types made a big difference. One of my colleagues is a very driven Three. And I had another colleague who had a hard time relating to him to the point that they were not going to be able to work together. Fortunately, our Enneagram consultant knew both of their personality types, and was able to help my colleague understand the char-acteristics and motivators of the Type Three. And he took that to heart and changed his communication style with him and absolutely turned their relationship around 180 degrees. They're close today. It was just amazing. It was thanks to our leadership consultant sharing the characteristics of the Three and some communication strategies for working with a Three.

That to me was one of the best examples of the use of the Enneagram to really turn a situation around that I've ever witnessed."

Art Blum is Vice President of Regulatory Affairs at BioMarin Pharmaceutical Inc., a biotechnology company based in San Rafael, California. Art first learned about the Enneagram working with a coach, who encouraged him to look into it as a way to both develop as a leader and support his team. In keeping with his Type Five tendency to gather knowledge, Art particularly enjoys reading different books about the Enneagram and having it as a lens through which to deepen his interest in people. In this short excerpt from my interview with him, he describes the ways in which the personality model has helped him to better understand and relate to the people he works with.

"The Enneagram tells me, for example, that when one of my colleagues, who's a Type One, is sitting there not saying anything, he hasn't tuned us out. He is absorbing information and at some point, when he speaks, he's going to say something that's worth listening to. Whereas we'll hear from our Eight colleague and he'll tell us exactly what he's thinking without a whole lot of coaxing. Those are the kinds of insights that I think are really helpful, getting to where we're going with everyone's participation, and understanding how each enneagram type is most effective in the process.

"For me personally, the biggest benefit has been the interest I take in different individuals now. I'm learning about how they think and how they operate and this extends to my personal life. I use it routinely with my wife. It's really helpful to me. My type investigates things, is inquisitive, and this is a system of understanding that is right up my alley. I'm trying to leverage it on the business side and also on the personal side, to enhance relationships."

Enneagram Impact:
Understanding Team Dynamics and Development

"I think a lot about team composition. I think [the Enneagram] helps you understand why certain teams are functioning a certain way, how certain leadership styles may be working or not working, and things like that... I think what's probably most interesting is having the teams themselves understand their types to understand where people are coming from. Then you can see where

people are in terms of different levels of awareness and what some of the classic conflicts are that develop between people of different types."

Arash Ferdowsi, Co-founder and CTO of Dropbox, Inc.

One of the most vital and often challenging aspects of establishing a productive and successful enterprise in the modern business environment is to create and maintain well-functioning teams. Managing not only individuals, but also multiple one-on-one relationships and the systemic complexity of interdependent teams, can make the job of leading and guiding your organization and its people incredibly difficult, even for the best of leaders. When it comes to the care and feeding of teams and intra-team relationships, the Enneagram's value as a leadership tool becomes even more evident.

Chris Houlder, Autodesk. Here Chris talks about different ways the Enneagram helps him foster better communication and manage interdependence within his team, including explicitly welcoming diverse perspectives and using the Enneagram as a nonjudgmental language to talk more openly about what's happening.

> *"Understanding types through the Enneagram becomes the process that helps guide you, which is about saying, 'I want to understand this person so that we can communicate effectively, manage conflict, and get results together.' The Enneagram gives us a whole framework for being able to more consciously direct the interactions you have with the individuals on your team—to discover what you need to know about the people you work with. It becomes a toolset to experiment with, to try to have more productive relationships while still being open-minded. I don't want people to think they're being assessed or that I've got this secret codebook. It's more about trying to experience the relationship in an authentic way and knowing the types helps as a kind of guidebook to understanding people better.*
>
> *"To me the biggest benefit for the team is everyone developing an understanding of each other. An important thing for me with the Enneagram is that you keep it as everyday language—and there's a balancing act with that. You don't say as soon as they start speaking, 'That's the Four in you,' because then people are going to feel dismissed and like you're not understanding them authentically. But if you can integrate it into everyday language, it opens the door for people to understand that*

being different is okay, not everyone has to be a certain way—and differ-
ences can actually be exploited by the team as a benefit. I can say, 'We
really need some diverse thinking here. How are our types coming into
play? How can we leverage that? Have we heard from different perspec-
tives?' It keeps the sting out of people taking action.

"*Someone just approached me the other day who would not have*
approached me before and we used 'straight talk' as an example. I've
seen this exact thing happen with the Enneagram. He came up to me and
said, 'You know, I kind of feel like what you said in the e-mail you sent
was punitive. I'm bringing this up because we agreed that we want to do
'straight talk.' He's expressing his need to be responsible to what we've
all agreed to do. We had a great conversation because he misunderstood
something I said and we were able to understand each other.

"*To me It's the same thing with the Enneagram: it opens the door for*
people to discuss diversity in personality. It then opens the door for people
to be able to more safely have conversations about differences with regard
to things like communication and conflict management. When those situ-
ations come up, it opens the door for people to say, 'Well, regardless of
rank, I hear your opinion and I have this one.' It keeps EQ and develop-
ment as a common language within the team."

Don Mather, La-Z-Boy South. Here's how Don was able to understand
an important dynamic that was occurring within his team. Getting clear
on what was happening allowed him to understand and leverage his team's
strengths with more awareness.

"*We had an off-site in New Orleans with a consultant, and I had my*
senior leadership team of eight people take an Enneagram assessment. We
then talked about our types, and, interestingly enough, out of eight of us,
there were six Eights and two Ones. And the Enneagram helped us to
understand the differences between the two Ones and the Eights and how
we could leverage those differences. This was important because six of us
were far too much alike and had a propensity for 'ready, fire, aim.' One
of the Ones was very much a planner, perfectionist type, and we learned
how we could help him not have to feel overly responsible and search
for ways to make things perfect all the time. And he could help us back
up and put a little more sauce in the planning and have more successful

outcomes because of it. It really is about learning how to use and leverage one another's strengths."

Morey Gladden is Director of New Product Operations and Facility Operations and Maintenance at Herman Miller Inc., a major manufacturer of office furniture, equipment, and home furnishings based in Michigan. Morey uses the Enneagram extensively with all the teams he works with, beginning with their introductory training when they join the company.

"I first encountered the Enneagram maybe ten years ago when I was looking for some way to have my team communicate better and understand each other better. At that time, I was the director of new product operations with ten people on my team. We included two other groups of engineering teams that were interested and had our first Enneagram session.

"Very quickly I saw that this was an interesting approach to understanding other people. I had already had training in other approaches. I've been in management for a long time and so I've been around a little bit. But when I learned the Enneagram, I thought, 'This is so much easier and so much more relatable than some of the other tools that are out there that we've used in the past.' Then people started talking using the language. I think language is really, really important. Being in product development, the most important thing—the thing that gives you the most power—is everybody having the same language.

"Shortly after we learned our types you saw people saying, 'Why does that person act that way? I know why—they are an Enneagram One, so they are very process-driven.' When they understand that about themselves and each other, I can help them work together better, I can understand where they're coming from, and I can tailor my message and how I work with them in a different way to be successful. (I'm an Enneagram Three, so I just like to get stuff done.)

"In essence, using the Enneagram as a regular part of working on teams here is just about being more productive. From my Three standpoint, I just wanted people to get stuff done. My learning has been, you can get stuff done when there's a process that helps you improve, to reach a certain standard. So, using the Enneagram has been the way I've set a standard for how the people on my teams understand each other."

Jean Halloran is principal at Halloran Consulting LLC and former Senior Vice President of Human Resources at Agilent Technologies. Jean used the Enneagram at Agilent as part of a self-insight process facilitated by a consultant, in which people would use knowledge of their Enneagram types and in a coordinated development effort, combining individual work, relationship conversations, and work within teams.

"We used the Enneagram with our teams at Agilent in three ways through a process called 'self-insight coaching.' It encompassed three pieces: individual coaching using the Enneagram, relationship conversations or sharing (called 'relationship syncs') and team work. The relationship sync conversations always included the leader. It was not done in the division unless the general manager was doing it.

"As part of this process, people would discuss their individual Enneagram styles and the way they interacted as a larger group, as a whole. And they would talk about what types they didn't have enough of and which types they needed to make more use of. Somebody might say, for instance, 'I've really become aware that I can be too rigid, I can become too black and white, too right and wrong. And I'm really trying to work on this. When I ask questions, I don't mean to come across as unkind or so critical.'

"I think we took something like eighty people through an Enneagram training at that point. So you have this language that people are using to describe themselves. The Eights never said their numbers. And Fours rarely admitted theirs. But it sure helped us. And there were some general managers that then started using it as a way to do group work. And they realized things such as having only one Five on their team who they were in the habit of overlooking because the person was so inclined to solo work. Then these teams began to behave differently, in that they would more purposefully take into account the skills and the inclinations of the whole group. It was very interesting.

"Some people who were disruptive in their 'asleep versions' of their type began to realize they were being disruptive, that they were endlessly talking things over when things were ready to be drawn to a close, or they were in the habit of interrupting people all the time. Some of it inspired self-management. The other piece was taking account of the team dynamic. For example, my colleague Teresa's group realized they needed

to understand the power of the Eights on their team as three of the people on her team self-identified as Eights and their gifts for driving things to a close and making a plan for what was next was invaluable. Particularly when the team figured out that they collectively were lacking in an inclination to get things to actionable momentum, they start looking at their Eights differently."

Enneagram Impact: Creating a Culture of Conscious Professionalism

"We use the Enneagram in support of a bigger idea we promote in our organization: conscious leadership and conscious professionalism. Because this is a central focus of the organization, we invite people to build the muscle of self-awareness and emotional intelligence.

We build an organizational culture around the idea of consciousness and we believe that because of this, we are more highly aligned, we get more done, and we figure out how to not get overly caught up—how to deal with issues when they show up."

Tod Tappert, Vice President for Culture and Learning and System Chief Learning Officer, Greenville Health System

When you use the Enneagram to help leaders become more self-aware, the benefits of approaching work with more consciousness and emotional intelligence inevitably filter throughout the organization. Top executives become happier and more productive, which impacts their direct reports, and ultimately moves deeper into all levels of the organization. When this happens, the whole enterprise becomes a positive force—potentially inspiring everyone connected to the business to wake up and ensure that their actions are more conscious, sustainable, effective, and supportive of the greater good.

In this section, you will find examples of how successful leaders have used the Enneagram in innovative ways to make their organizations more flexible, more creative, more healthy, and more productive. The conscious leaders who shared their experiences with me tell stories about how working with the Enneagram to increase awareness, improve communication, and strengthen team work had even more far-reaching effects—these individuals describe business impacts including lowering a troublesome turnover rate, increased success in recruiting top talent, and real financial savings in the areas of hiring, retention, and product development. While I'm not saying this is hard proof that the Enneagram causes every wonderful thing that happens to these organizations, as Teresa Roche explains below, there seems to be a strong connection between cultivating an organizational culture of conscious development and open communication that, over and over again, contributes to business success of different kinds.

Arash Ferdowsi is cofounder and CTO at Dropbox, Inc., a San Francisco-based file sharing and storage company. Arash first discovered the Enneagram when he was taking a month off work because he was feeling burnt out. In taking some time to focus on his health and wellness, he explored things like yoga and mindfulness in an effort to do some introspection and better understand himself and what was causing him stress. He became increasingly interested in self-awareness and psychology and found his way to the Enneagram.

In one of the first Enneagram books he read, Arash found a paragraph description of the Type Four personality. He says it was the best description he had ever read about himself, addressing parts of himself that he knew existed, but hadn't been "fully called out on." Arash has used the Enneagram to further his own growth, brought it to his senior team to facilitate better working relationships, and has advocated the use of it throughout his organization. He shared his enthusiasm for the system when he returned to Dropbox through an e-mail he sent to the whole company, which he's allowed me to quote from below. Now, a significant percentage of Dropbox employees know their Enneagram type and use it in the work they do as a way to be more self-aware.

> *"Several groups at Dropbox... have done Enneagram workshops. We had an expert join us to give an overview of the system and help us figure out our types. It was a fun way for us to learn about ourselves and how we can better work with one another. It can be a pretty great offsite/team-bonding exercise that has the added bonus of helping leads get insight into team dynamics.*
>
> *"... As we continue to grow rapidly, figuring out how to collaborate effectively is going to become both increasingly complicated and increasingly important. It's going to be a never-ending job to protect the collaborative culture we've carefully built. Delight at scale is hard! While there are more traditional ways we'll go about keeping Dropbox healthy, I think that promoting a culture of self-awareness and empathy will take us far."*

(From an e-mail from Arash Ferdowsi to the employees of Dropbox, Inc.)

"Earlier on, before I fully understood myself through the lens of the Enneagram, I don't think I fully realized how some of the ways the company is being built is a consequence of me feeling like the culture, our brand, our values, the way the product looks and feels is related to me trying to communicate my personal values. But learning about my Enneagram type has been good because it's helped me understand some of the emotional reactions I've had defending certain things that are important to me—it's helped me understand why I care about these things so much.

"It also helps explain my almost irrationally emotional reactions to certain things. I think if it can help me try to not be so emotional about the things that I care strongly about, I can be more objective and strategic about making sure I'm clear about explaining why certain things are important. To me, it's obvious why something should be a certain way. Realizing that's because it's tied to my value system and I need to get better at articulating that value system—and tying it to why it's strategic to the company and why it's important for us to be able to realize our mission.

"Knowing I'm a Type Four helps me to realize that everyone is not going to have those same instincts. If they don't, it's not their fault. It's just that the burden is on me to articulate those things clearly. What are our brand values? Why does it matter to have specific values reflected in our brand? It has helped me articulate these things that are very intuitive to me. I need to provide the translation layer to help people who don't see the world in as nuanced a way to help them understand the kinds of decisions I want to make.

"Our mission is very much about collaboration and simplifying how people work together, allowing people to create great things through working together as a team. To do that, you need a culture that is really team-oriented and has people of different personality types that ultimately figure out how to work together and appreciate each other's gifts. I think that sending that e-mail about the Enneagram was actually quite powerful, because I think it kick-started this interest in the Enneagram and set the tone for greater openness by saying, 'Hey, we want this to be a culture of empathy where empathy and collaboration are valued... And here's a tool to understand yourself better and the people you work with.' I think it is really cool that a lot of people here know their type. It's cool to have the opportunity to do that, and it was well-received across *the company. It's hard to know, if I hadn't done that, how different the company would be."*

Tod Tappert is Vice President for Culture and Learning and System Chief Learning Officer, Greenville Health System (GHS). Tod has made the Enneagram a core piece of the Academy of Leadership and Professional Development he created at the Greenville Health System to help leaders and employees develop a culture of conscious professionalism.

After deciding to incorporate the Enneagram as a key element in GHS's conscious leadership program, Tod did extensive training in the Enneagram system, taking several courses to become his organization's top Enneagram expert. He then worked to establish an internal "Enneagram faculty," his "Enneagram Organizational/Business Applications team," who have also received in-depth training in the Enneagram system. This team of 25 in-house Enneagram specialists is made up of individuals from all over the health system and includes organization development professionals, doctors, nurses, chaplains, and administrators. What they have in common is a deep commitment to supporting the development of conscious professionalism within the larger organization—and they teach the Enneagram to leaders and employees throughout the system. They offer classes, events featuring panels of people of the same type discussing their personalities, and opportunities to talk about how they see the Enneagram at play in their working relationships. The Enneagram has become one of the ways Tod and his colleagues communicate their commitment to creating a conscious culture.

"At work, I apply my knowledge of the Enneagram types with our executive team. When meeting with the team, I look for 'teachable moments.' In meetings that I'd normally be in, if there were exchanges that exemplified the personality types interacting, I'd ask them to take a timeout and talk about what was happening in Enneagram terms. I'd insert a kind of Enneagram lesson to highlight what might be going on in the interaction. As a Nine, one of my strengths is to be gentle and name what's happening in a way that lands, so people were almost always receptive.

"Here's another example of the kind of thing I might do to use the Enneagram to create awareness about what's happening in the team: We were in a CEO meeting and we were looking at some data that showed a

downward trend in one area of the organization. Several people started reframing what we were seeing in positive terms. I was able to point out that every person who was doing this was a type Seven. Since this is their type bias, we were able to acknowledge that maybe we had to deal with the issue rather than make the mistake of seeing it in positive terms, as Sevens tend to do.

"Now more people in the organization have been doing deeper learning and taking the more intensive training programs. We now have over 700 leaders that know their Enneagram type. Most of the time the way it lands with people is they have an experience of a light bulb going on. We have tried to create a culture that allows for people to talk about their personality without feeling exposed.

"I would say one piece of evidence of the positive effects of our use of the Enneagram and our focus on conscious awareness is that when we recruit senior leaders to our organization—new physicians, department heads, etc.—to a person, when they come in they observe the effects of what we're doing and they comment on it. I often get to meet with the candidate and the search committee near the end of the interview process, and I like to ask candidates, 'Is there anything you've observed about our organization and how it works?' They often say something like, 'I can't exactly put my finger on it, but this organization seems to be aligned around goals and culture in a way I haven't seen anywhere else.' Always, whether they can name this or not, to a person they say, 'I don't know what it is, but this is something I want to be a part of.'

"Using the Enneagram to focus on being aware and emotionally intelligent means that we don't let the extraneous stuff get in the way. For the past 10 years I have been involved in many significant projects—engaging our board, leaders, and staff in redoing our health system's mission and vision, starting a medical school, and more. For most people in my position, any one of these things would have been a high point, but I've had seven or eight of these big high points just in the nearly ten years I've worked at Greenville Health System. And there's a harmonic convergence between embarking on these major initiatives and the work we do with conscious leadership. It makes us more nimble, more aligned, and as a result, we get more done."

Todd Pierce is chief digital officer at the Bill and Melinda Gates Foundation. He was formerly executive vice president, operations and mobility at Salesforce.com and senior vice president and chief information officer at Genentech. Todd pioneered the use of the Enneagram to help develop leaders and individuals when he was at Genentech. He first discovered the Enneagram through working with an executive coach. He later brought it in in a bigger way, introducing the Enneagram to more than 400 individual contributors in his section of the company. He continued to apply the Enneagram while at Salesforce.com, and he now uses it in his current position at the Gates Foundation. Todd has found creative ways to apply the Enneagram, using it as part of innovative development programs such as a structured, year-long coaching process, ongoing development conversations, and the creation of a "social intelligence hiring" process, developed by veteran organization development consultant Ginger Lapid-Bogda.

> *"The way I've applied the Enneagram in my teams and organizations has evolved over time. That's one of the things that I've really enjoyed about it. When I first used it with my leadership team we had more progress in an afternoon than we had for multiple other interventions—so how quickly that moved got us really interested. And so then we thought, 'Hey, we have a quarterly off-site meeting with all of our managers. Let's offer it there.' And that was such a huge hit that we were like, 'Let's make it available to all managers for them to do with their groups, and let's just make it open to everyone.' It was always voluntary—I think it's important in work to try to make things as much voluntary, or pull as opposed to push—and we got high-nineties participation rate and sustained that over multiple years. Now I've been using the Enneagram since about 2004.*
>
> *"I think the biggest benefit of using the Enneagram is that it really lets people become a better version of themselves, as opposed to just typecasting themselves. I think it allows people to do a 'you are here' with whatever is arriving for them, and it gives them a map so they can go on a journey to get wherever they want to go. It's not overly prescriptive—there's no score that you need to have, or type that you should get. It's more nuanced—it doesn't just describe you and say, 'Well, you're an INTJ, good luck,' or, 'You're an orange,' or you're a this or a that. It lets you discover layers of yourself, whatever they are, and then asks you to go on a journey at your own pace. It's very interesting.*

"*The superpower of things like mindfulness and the Enneagram is giving you increased capacity to access the team 'consciousness' or 'observing self'—this ability to see yourself in real-time and see many more options in front of yourself than your reactive pattern. One of the things that makes it hard to change is having the awareness of both 'What piece of software—what rule set am I running, what reactionary frame am I in?' and 'What's the context that I find myself in?' Starting to observe patterns or what things don't work, and then giving you a way of noticing that, slowing down and making different choices.*

"*In terms of bringing about business results, there's been a suite of interventions that I think have been important. The Enneagram has been very complementary to the mindfulness work, to the personal excellence program that I developed, to the idea of multi-centers of intelligence in our body, and how to integrate those. It has a pretty open platform, I think, that works well with some of the other consciousness work I'm interested in.*

"*If I were to narrow-in and say, 'What are unique attributes of the Enneagram relative to this holistic kind of work?' it's incredibly accessible. I've yet to meet somebody who couldn't get value out of it. And that's not true of everything. Meditation takes a little bit of practice and commitment to get into. You can't just drop right in and get benefit out of it. People find the Enneagram energizing, for the most part; some people have some reactivity through comparing it to other experiences that they've had, but if you can get them past that, then it's very engaging. It's very enduring.*

"*How many tools have you known that you would stick with over 11 years across multiple organizations, in multiple contexts? There just aren't many. You get bored with them or they don't seem to work as well, or you feel like—my God, how many Enneagram classes have I been in? I couldn't even keep count. And I still find it interesting.*"

Carol Anderson is president of Child Development Inc., which runs 155 child care centers throughout California and develops early education materials. Several years ago, they realized they had a turnover rate of 35% and looked for ways to lower it. They conducted a survey of all their staff and found, among other things, that 50% of people didn't like their supervisors. So they developed a set of values and a training program for all of their managers called "Foundational Supervisory Skills." Carol and her team then created a leadership institute, which included Enneagram training. In five years, they cut their turnover rate in half, from 35% to 18%. Although several things went into lowering this rate, Carol believes their goal of developing better leaders was a major factor—and the Enneagram was a large part of that. She told me about the unique way her organization has thoroughly integrated the use of Enneagram training and discussion groups into their successful efforts to retain high-quality teachers and staff through focusing on leadership.

> "So we're trying to build a better leader. A lot of that content dovetails with the Enneagram. There's a lot of focus on, 'What's your story?' 'How can you be self-reflective about what's going on with you, and not necessarily put that on other people?' 'How can you be a good listener?'—those kinds of things.
>
> "We ended up developing three goals for our Enneagram training. The first goal is self-reflection and self-awareness. We wanted personal growth for people. The second goal was the groups working together collaboratively so they could get synergy. Understanding each other's strengths and challenges and what they brought to the group and also identifying their weaknesses or things that they didn't like doing—somebody else might like it. And then the third thing was that they would become better supervisors, with the people they work with who are their supervisees.
>
> "I supervise our supervisors using the Enneagram. In our one-on-one meetings, we strategize about a problem they might have with an employee, somebody they're supervising. I go through with different people: 'How's it going with so-and-so?' One of our goals was to give people a good supervisor, so I strategize with them. One supervisor works with a Type One whom she's had some challenges with, and so we discuss strategy: 'What do you think she needs as a One? How do you think she's thinking about this? What's important to her?' We look at what she's needing.
>
> "Personally, I think one reason the Enneagram's been so effective for us is that the Enneagram isn't a canned program that can be implemented in a step-by-step process, and after you get to step ten it's in place. It's not like that. I tell people it's a sophisticated, complex, deep tool to use, and that you can study it all your life and not ever know everything there is to know about it. But the real sense of learning and growing, from your heart and with the individuals in the groups, comes from your willingness to be open, to be self-reflective, to create your inner observer."

Teresa Roche is CEO of Roche Consulting, LLC, and is the former vice president and chief learning officer at Agilent Technologies. Of all the leaders I spoke to, Teresa has been studying the Enneagram for the longest time, since the late 1980s. During her long career as a human relations executive, she has used the Enneagram for her own personal and professional development and has employed it in her work in many different ways.

"I'll never forget when the CEO of Agilent was having a conversation with all of these emerging leaders and alums, and somebody asked him a question, and he said one of the most powerful things he had learned is understanding that not everybody is like him.

"It's not like I've done evidence-based tracking to be able to say the self-insight process we used with our leaders (which included learning their Enneagram types) led to a higher-customer loyalty score or higher revenue. I do believe, however, if you looked at Agilent's success, I do believe that one of the underpinnings is the level of consciousness that so many executives had.

"On one of my Performance Feedback Forms I would talk about Total Shareholder Return, which had grown higher than the S&P 500. Our customer loyalty scores had gone up. And we captured more market share. You can't say this one thing did it, but I do think there's a line of sight. My team stayed together for twelve years because we just kept growing and learning. I kind of felt like we were the Navy Seals—we were asked to go in to tackle different challenges and we had a wonderful reputation.

"There's an article I read recently where they talk about how much time is wasted in business by people trying to hide who they are. We lose a lot of time defending and worrying about how we're presenting ourselves. One of the things I said to my CEO is, this is not just about heart-based 'woo woo' space. This is about speed to opportunity. This is about speed, because when you understand yourself, you can have a five-minute meeting instead of a 20-minute one where you walk out thinking, 'what did they mean?' I think there's real evidence that the Enneagram saves time and creates better solutions when people who know their types work together."

How to Use Your Newfound Knowledge of Personality to Improve the Way You Work

A Guide to Applying the Insights of the Enneagram

"I think using [the Enneagram] as a way to drive creativity and insight, along with a lot of other things that leaders do, is incredibly useful. It can give you insight and ways of working with any business process."

Todd Pierce, the Gates Foundation

While this book has detailed the benefits of using the Enneagram in leadership development and workplace relationships, it's important to remember, it's not necessarily the right tool for everyone, or for every business. I think the Enneagram works best when there is a real, felt business need—a burning platform or a strong motive—for people to know themselves and understand the people they're working with. The Enneagram system of personality is an ideal approach when people have the desire and the capacity to self-reflect and allow for a degree of vulnerability in talking about themselves with their coworkers to improve working relationships. With that in mind, here are some suggestions about how to apply it in your leadership development program or organization.

Because the Enneagram addresses growth and development, you can use it to develop a wider repertoire of strengths and manifest your higher potentials. If the leadership of an organization does not prioritize the growth of its people as a value—if they do not consider greater awareness to be relevant to their business practices, processes, or products—bringing in the Enneagram may not be the right investment. However, if you do want to find ways to increase business success through actively supporting greater self-awareness and emotional intelligence, as many of the leaders quoted here attest, there is probably not a better way to do it than the Enneagram.

Here are some suggestions about how to apply it in your leadership development program or organization.

Individuals and Leaders

Working with a Coach

One of the easiest ways to use the Enneagram for individual or leadership development is to work with a psychotherapist or a coach who knows and works with the system. A coach who specializes in the Enneagram can help you learn about your type, structure a plan for continuing to deepen your self-knowledge using the system, and help you to leverage your strengths and expand your capacities.

The major caveat to keep in mind is to choose your coach carefully. There are a lot of "instant experts" in the world of "Enneagram professionals"— people who say they work with the Enneagram who don't know it well enough or have a broad enough base of expertise to support the work. So make sure to get referrals from people you trust when possible, check out your coach's credentials, and don't be shy about asking them about how long they've studied the Enneagram and what qualifications they have to use it in their practice.

Enneagram Trainings and Leadership Development Programs Focusing On Individual Growth, Self-Awareness, and the Development of Emotional Intelligence

Bringing an Enneagram trainer or consultant in to teach the individuals in your organization can be another way to introduce the system to your people. A day-long or a half-day introductory session with a qualified Enneagram expert can be a great way to give leaders and individual contributors a taste of what the Enneagram can do and how it works, familiarizing people with the Enneagram as a tool for self-awareness, and allowing you to kick-start other kinds of individual coaching or development initiatives. Many leadership development programs have the Enneagram as a key element in that it helps guide a process of self-awareness and professional growth.

Self-Work

Enneagram author Helen Palmer points out that the Enneagram types are "self-verifying." One of the nice things about the Enneagram is that, through books, videos, web content, and trainings, people who are interested in exploring the Enneagram or discovering their personality type can do quite a bit on their own to enhance their self-understanding. This book is designed as a reference for people to consult on their own or with a coach as a guide to expanding self-awareness.

One-To-One Professional Relationships

Individual Work in Support of Relationship Development

Working with a coach, an Enneagram consultant, or on your own, you can utilize Enneagram courses and materials to understand your communication style, relationship tendencies, responses to conflict situations, and your general impact on others. Often combining Enneagram work with 360 feedback can be an excellent way to identify areas of strength and challenge. In these ways, individuals can work on understanding their communication tendencies and the perceptual filters of other styles and how to work well with them as a precursor to having developmental conversations with colleagues.

Facilitated Conversations Mediated by a Coach or Enneagram Consultant

Once individuals understand their Enneagram styles and their preferred ways of relating, communicating, giving feedback, and other specific elements of interacting with others, it can be a good idea to engage in a facilitated conversation. By having a coach or consultant mediate conversations with important colleagues, you can proactively discuss different aspects of your work and your relationship to improve the way you work with each other.

Teams

Enneagram Training and Applications to Business Challenges and to Understanding Team Dynamics

An Enneagram consultant who specializes in working with teams can be an ideal way to introduce the system to your work group. There is a variety of ways to use the Enneagram as the basis of a team-building activity or daylong event. By presenting the system and the types and then showing how they can be applied to explain team relationships and dynamics, you can get a large amount of learning and insight into how well your team is functioning, as well as how it could improve to be even high performing.

Teams often benefit from first learning the Enneagram, and then applying it to specific business functions and scenarios, like communication, giving and receiving feedback, managing conflict, and negotiating change. Depending on the particular needs of your team, you can bring the Enneagram into a discussion of how to manage or address a range of business topics.

Integrating the Enneagram with Business Tasks and Initiatives

More and more, when I work with teams, I'm integrating the different Enneagram perspectives and type patterns with different business concepts or issues that specific teams need to wrestle with. For instance, I've combined the nine Enneagram styles with business tasks like decision-making, achieving excellence, and assessing and coping with risk. Through understanding that people with different personality styles will tend to see the same business issue through different lenses, and then being able to highlight what those differences might be around a specific subject area, you can focus, enliven, and clarify your team discussions, making your team interactions more effective, more successful, and more enjoyable.

Organizations

Enneagram Trainings

Just as you can have an experienced Enneagram consultant design introductory and follow-up trainings aimed at individual leadership development or understanding and improving team dynamics and cohesion, you can also offer Enneagram trainings focused on larger groups and the whole organization. Again, depending on the specific business challenges or needs of the organization, you can hire an Enneagram savvy organization development consultant to design trainings, interventions, or ongoing programs to leverage the insights of the Enneagram types to clarify, work through, and resolve different kinds of organizational problems, or take advantage of particular business opportunities.

It's usually wise to begin with an introductory Enneagram training in which people can become acquainted with the system, learn their types, and then start applying it to different aspects of working relationships, like communication, giving feedback, and team dynamics. After an initial training, you can do follow-up trainings to build on your learning, potentially integrating the personality types with whatever subjects are important and timely for the organization and teams within the organization.

Ongoing Enneagram Events

One issue that leaders express after doing an introductory Enneagram training is, how do we make it stick? How do we continue to apply and make the Enneagram actionable for our leaders, teams, and organizations?

There are many ways to help the Enneagram and its insights and uses take root in an organization. Here are some ideas about ongoing offerings that can help make the Enneagram more actively useful and help integrate it into your organizational culture:

- ▶ Scheduled, recurring Enneagram conversations about different business or developmental topics.

- ▶ Enneagram "panels" of people of the same type—people deepen their learning about specific types (and their coworkers) through having groups of people of one type speak together about how their type operates. I do this when I have a mixed group, including some people who already know the Enneagram and others who are new.

- ▶ "Lunch 'n' learns"—people gather at lunchtime to discuss specific Enneagram types or topics.

- ▶ Ongoing developmental programs—leadership programs or coaching programs that integrate the Enneagram.

- ▶ Enneagram social gatherings or happy hours—for instance, a hosted gathering once a month on a Thursday or Friday afternoon at 5 p.m. where there is a speaker talking about a topic or facilitating a group discussion.

Integrating the Enneagram with Business Trainings, Tasks, and Opportunities

The Enneagram is a flexible tool that can be used in conjunction with different organizational business tasks and opportunities. For instance, if the organization is going through a period of change or facing a particular challenge, like going global or shifting priorities, the Enneagram can be used as a common language to help facilitate a clearer understanding of how different people are coping with what's happening. Targeted discussions about specific topics could be followed by an open discussion about how each person's Enneagram style is affecting their view of the situation. A qualified consultant can often help design and implement this kind of an organizational intervention.

Creating a Conscious Culture

As Arash Ferdowsi and Tod Tappert describe earlier in this chapter, the Enneagram is an excellent tool to inspire or build in to formal efforts to build a more conscious organizational culture. Companies in different industries are prioritizing awareness and emotional intelligence more and more, and the Enneagram is an ideal element to catalyze and help implement practices, developmental opportunities, and programs that can support the purposeful evolution of a culture that is more conscious, flexible, and aligned.

I hope this book has enabled you to see all the positive ways the Enneagram can be used to support the development of more emotionally intelligent leaders, teams, and organizations. And how more conscious leaders paves the way for a more alive, productive, and successful workplace. As the personality style descriptions and the leaders' stories of using the Enneagram system hopefully demonstrate, the Enneagram is a powerful, time-tested map that can help you chart a course of conscious development throughout your life. Whether you are a CEO, a manager, an individual contributor, or just an individual, I believe the Enneagram can support you on your adventure of accessing a deeper level of personal awareness so you can liberate yourself from the limiting constraints of your habitual patterns and work to manifest your highest potential. And when leaders and the people they lead are all working together to become all they can be, we can truly change the world.

Thank you for joining me on this journey introducing you to what I believe is an incredible growth tool. In the last 20 years, it has been my honor to witness my clients use it to become happier, healthier, and more effective and successful in their lives and their work. I hope it helps you as much as it has helped me and so many of my friends, clients, and colleagues.

Endnotes

Chapter 1

1. Daniel Goleman has written extensively on the subject of emotional intelligence and how it can help people be more effective at work. He is the author of the seminal book on EQ, *Emotional Intelligence: Why It Can Matter More Than IQ* as well as the books *Working with Emotional Intelligence, Social Intelligence: The New Science of Human Relationships* and *Primal Leadership: Unleashing the Power of Emotional Intelligence,* as well as the *Harvard Business Review* articles "What Makes a Leader" and "Teams at Work: Emotional Intelligence."
2. *Good to Great,* Jim Collins, pp. 12–13
3. *The 15 Commitments of Conscious Leadership,* Dethmer, Chapman, and Klemp, p. 14.
4. *The 15 Commitments of Conscious Leadership,* Dethmer, Chapman, and Klemp, p. 15.
5. Daniel Siegel, *Mindsight,* pp. xi–xii
6. Rick Hanson, *Buddha's Brain: The Practical Neuroscience of Happiness, Love & Wisdom,* p. 42.
7. Ibid.

Chapter 2

8. In his book *Travels with Odysseus* Michael Goldberg outlined in simple terms the themes and lessons of each of the nine mythic lands Odysseus visits. Although he does not mention the Enneagram, these themes can be seen to match up to the Enneagram personality types.
9. The descriptions of the 27 subtype personalities described throughout this book are derived and adapted from the work (books and trainings) of Claudio Naranjo.

Chapter 3

10. Tony Schwartz article, "Seeing Through Your Blind Spots," *Harvard Business Review,* August 15, 2012.
11. Ibid.
12. Ibid.
13. Ibid.

Chapter 4 (Type One)

14. Ginger Lapid-Bogda, *Bringing Out the Best of Yourself at Work,* 2004, p. 32.

Chapter 5 (Type Two)

15. Ginger Lapid-Bogda, *Bringing Out the Best of Yourself at Work,* 2004, pp. 33–34.

Chapter 7 (Type Four)

16. Ginger Lapid-Bogda, *Bringing Out the Best of Yourself at Work*, 2004, pp. 38–39.
17. Claudio Naranjo often uses this phrase in his workshops to highlight the nature of the Social Four habit of believing in their own inadequacy—when the only thing "wrong with them" is believing there is something wrong with them.

Chapter 10 (Type Seven)

18. Ginger Lapid-Bogda, *Bringing Out the Best of Yourself at Work*, 2004, p. 45.
19. Claudio Naranjo, as cited in Beatrice Chestnut, *The Complete Enneagram*, 2013, p. 151.

Chapter 11 (Type Eight)

20. Ginger Lapid-Bogda, *Bringing Out the Best of Yourself at Work*, 2004, p. 48.
21. This is a phrase that Helen Palmer uses to describe the Type Eight personality in, *The Enneagram: Understanding Yourself and the Others in Your Life*, 1988.

Chapter 12 (Type Nine)

22. Ginger Lapid-Bogda, *Bringing Out the Best of Yourself at Work*, 2004, p. 52.

Bibliography

Collins, Jim. *Good to Great: Why Some Companies Make the Leap... and Others Don't*. New York: Harper Collins, 2001.

Dethmer, Jim; Chapman, Diana; and Klemp, Kasey Warner. *The 15 Commitments of Conscious Leadership*. Conscious Leadership Group, 2014.

Goldberg, Michael. *Travels with Odysseus: Uncommon Wisdom From Homer's Odyssey*. Tempe, AZ: Circe's Island Press, 2006.

Goleman, Daniel. *Emotional Intelligence: Why It Can Matter More Than IQ*. New York: Bantam Books, 1994.

Goleman, Daniel. Working with Emotional Intelligence. New York: Bantam Books, 1998.

Goleman, Daniel; Boyatzis, Richard; and McKee, Annie. *Primal Leadership: Unleashing the Power of Emotional Intelligence*. Boston: Harvard Business Review Press, 2013.

Hanson, Rick. *Buddha's Brain: The Practical Neuroscience of Happiness, Love, and Wisdom*, p. 42 Oakland, CA: New Harbinger Publications Inc., 2009.

Lapid-Bogda, Ginger. *Bringing Out the Best in Yourself at Work: How to Use the Enneagram System for Success*. McGraw-Hill: New York, 2004.

Palmer, Helen. *The Enneagram: Understanding Yourself and the Others in Your Life*. San Francisco: Harper Collins, 1988.

Schwartz, Tony. "Seeing Through Your Blind Spots," *Harvard Business Review*, August 15, 2012.

Siegel, Dan. *Mindsight: The New Science of Personal Transformation*. New York: Bantam Books, 2011.

Recommended Resources

Introductory Enneagram Books

The Complete Enneagram by Beatrice Chestnut

The Enneagram Made Easy: Discover the Nine Types of People by Elizabeth Wagele and Renee Baron

Principles of the Enneagram: What it is, how it works, and what it can do for you (2nd Edition) by Karen Webb

The Essential Enneagram: The Definitive Personality Test and Self-Discovery Guide (Revised and Updated) (2009) by David Daniels and Virginia Price

Enneagram Business Books

InsideOut Enneagram: The Game-Changing Guide for Leaders by Wendy Appel

The How and Why: Taking Care of Business with the Enneagram by Karl Hebenstreit

Bringing Out the Best in Yourself at Work: How to Use the Enneagram System for Success by Ginger Lapid-Bogda

The Enneagram Development Guide by Ginger Lapid-Bogda

What Type of Leader Are You? Using the Enneagram System to Identify and Grow Your Leadership Strengths and Achieve Maximum Success by Ginger Lapid-Bogda

The Enneagram in Love and Work: Understanding Your Intimate and Business Relationships by Helen Palmer

To find a list of recommended coaches, trainers, and business consultants with Enneagram expertise, visit my website: www.beatricechestnut.com.

About the Author

Beatrice Chestnut, MA, PhD, is a licensed psychotherapist, coach, and business consultant based in San Francisco, California. She has a PhD in communication studies and an MA in clinical psychology. She is also author of the book *The Complete Enneagram: 27 Paths to Greater Self-Knowledge*. She served as President of the International Enneagram Association (IEA) from 2006 to 2007, and in 2008 and 2009 Chestnut was a founding co-editor of the IEA's *Enneagram Journal*. Chestnut offers trainings on the Enneagram internationally, focusing on using it as a tool for personal transformation.